THE MODERN SPANISH NOVEL

Comparative Essays

THE

MODERN SPANISH NOVEL

Comparative Essays Examining the

Philosophical Impact of Science on Fiction

by Sherman H. Eoff

NEW YORK UNIVERSITY PRESS

PREFACE

THE PRESENT STUDY takes for granted the necessity of reducing broad areas of thought to a few fundamental ideas in order to appreciate the deepest motives underlying literary works. The Spanish novel occupies the greater part of a discussion in which special attention is given to the philosophical influence of science on fiction, but an effort is made to observe Spanish works in company with other European works as reflecting important phases of modern thought. Too often, perhaps, the followers of Spanish literature are called upon to view their subject in a purely national context. If the similarity between the novels grouped together seems more obvious in some cases than in others, let it be remembered that our objective is not specifically to examine one work in terms of another but to see all of them in the light of their common intellectual background. The coverage of Spanish works and authors may seem small, but the restriction in number is based on the belief that concentration on a few representative novels is more revealing than a rapid glance at many.

I wish to express my gratitude to the John Simon Guggenheim Memorial Foundation, with whose aid part of the present investigation was made possible.

S. H. E.

CONTENTS

vii

I

Introduction

THE MODERN NOVEL is a philosophical novel. In this century, especially, it has shown its affiliation with metaphysics and dealt with metaphysical subjects in manners that vary from subtle and tantalizing suggestiveness to an open, and sometimes excessive, reflection on man's origin and destiny. Since the most notable works are sober intellectual endeavors, they throw upon the reader the heavy responsibility of thinking and make it necessary to seek after their philosophical meaning in order to enjoy them fully. Serious gropings for new assurances, these novels plainly manifest the suffering attendant upon the accumulation of knowledge that man knows not how to integrate. Perhaps in no other age has the tree of knowledge seemed to be so devastating in implications and yet so much a challenge to the artist. The challenge to think as well as depict no doubt accounts in some degree for the noticeable decrease in twentieth-century fiction in the everyday kind of social and psychological subject matter so characteristic of the nineteenth century.

The fact, however, that the nineteenth-century novel was not so openly involved in the necessity of philosophical reflection as is the later novel does not mean that it was lacking in philosophical motivation. The difference is to be explained primarily as a difference in degree of directness. For the outstanding novelists of the preceding century, while directly engaged in the presentation of social, moral, psychological experiences as something visual and concrete, were indirectly preoccupied with broader problems pertaining to man's cosmic position. Apparently concentrating on man's place in society, they were sometimes more interested in his place in the universe; and even when not consciously expressing a specific ontological or metaphysical viewpoint, they exhibited definite marks of philosophical orientation. It may seem farfetched to speak of philosophy in discussing Charles Dickens, and certainly his novels do not induce rationalistic reflection in the same way as a novel of Jean-Paul Sartre, for example, but they nevertheless express a philosophical outlook just as faithfully as any novel written since Dickens' day.

The term "philosophical" as it is being used in the present connection has reference above all to the general goal of synthesis toward which philosophy strives — specifically, to the synthesis between the implications of scientific developments and man's irrepressible religious sentiment. The divorce that has arisen in modern thought between science and religion has not kept the philosopher from trying to bring them together. The literary artist, also, insists on merging the two; for he finds it difficult to separate himself into compartments that will accommodate in unrelated channels two distinct views of the world, one having to do with tangible phenomena and one with abstract values. Through the medium of art he is preoccupied with the problems that the philosopher tries to solve through systematic reasoning. In the modern age, especially in the past one hundred years, science has undermined a number of cherished religious beliefs. Poets and philosophers alike have been deeply affected and have striven, sometimes desperately, to make an adjustment to new viewpoints. The fact that religious skepticism, that is, the abandonment of certain traditional beliefs (such as the belief in a personal God), runs through most modern literature does not mean that the literary mind has forsaken its desire for religious orientation. Whatever the concept of God, or whatever the substitute raised in His place, the literary artist is continually asking: Who am I, what is my relation to whatever it is that explains my being, and what is my destiny? The novel of the nineteenth and twentieth centuries is an eloquent mouthpiece for this kind of thinking, and it is from this particular viewpoint that the present study proposes to examine a number of representative works.

One can hardly overemphasize the fact that science has had

a tremendous influence on man's conception of himself as an individual, and we should not underestimate the literary significance of the subject. The gloomy aspects of this influence have been most in evidence since the mid-nineteenth century, which may be considered a dividing line between an old world and a new one. To visualize the general course of development embracing both sides of this line, we may say that in the past two centuries man's outlook has undergone a gradual change from faith in a world order under divine control to a world order under human control, with man's consequent loneliness — not to say hopelessness — in a role that he did not ask for. The eighteenth-century outlook inherited from Descartes and Newton was mechanistic but orderly, meaningful, and optimistic. There was, of course, a trend toward materialistic monism, associated particularly with the sensation psychologists, but the dominant view was dualistic. A dichotomy of mind and matter, soul and body, God and nature, was characteristic of the age and acceptable to scientists and theologians alike. Within a grand perspective of separateness man and all other species were beheld as separate creations having specially assigned places in the total scheme, being systematically classifiable once and for all, and conforming always to the established pattern of their kind. Since God was believed to be apart from His creation and in complete control, it was easy to be a materialist in science and a spiritualist in religion at the same time; to believe in determinism and free will; to assign the world of evil to the devil or some yet unaccounted-for source, and to God the more powerful domain of good; and to be for the most part happy. For, where all is according to plan in the world of a benevolent God, merely being alive is sufficient reason for contentment.

This world view, which is fundamentally a combination of Newtonian and Cartesian ideas, was probably more dominant in England than elsewhere in Europe and carries over well into the nineteenth century, far enough at least to include the "Age of Dickens." In this era of neighborly separateness, of fundamental types, of systematic arrangement under a benevolent ruler, of dualism of body and soul, we can logically locate Dickens and José María de Pereda, who comes chronologically almost a generation later than Dickens but belongs philosophically to the same epoch. These writers stand on the dividing line between two radically different world outlooks; and though it will not be appropriate to read as much philosophy into their novels as in the case of other writers, they are of special interest to us. For by contrast they make developments of the past one hundred years stand out in bold relief as they take us back to what now seems almost like an ancient world, in some ways more desirable than our own.

The basis on which a distinction is being made between the old and the new is the shift on the part of Western thought from a dualistic view of the world to a unitary concept of being in which God and nature are brought together. What this change amounts to, from a general, philosophical standpoint, is the forsaking of Descartes for Spinoza. The statement is a deliberate oversimplification for the purpose of underscoring fundamental trends. The transition from one world view to another was of course gradual and can hardly be assigned to specific dates or identified with only one or two thinkers, however influential they may be. But there is probably some advantage in thinking of the eighteenth century as dominated philosophically by Descartes and the nineteenth century by Spinoza. The latter, or to be more exact a monistic view that leans on him for support, ushers in the age of naturalism, which for the novel proves to be in large degree an extension of the pantheism of the Romantic age, but with the addition of a heavy coloring from the biological sciences.

The first stage of naturalism is marked by a more or less static reflection upon the idea of fusion of mind and matter. In the background are the rise of evolutionary theories and the abandonment of belief in the separate creation and the fixity of species. There were, moreover, in scientific circles a predominance of materialistic psychology and a belief in the spontaneous generation of life from inorganic matter. Small wonder, then, that the literary imagination could combine with the material aspect of Spinoza's One Substance a rank pantheistic vision of God's breath moving in the earth itself, rising out of the soil, and assuming forms of life. On the other hand, when thought was given to the rational aspect of the One Substance, the concept of God lost its emotional appeal and left the poet pondering the futility of loyalty to personal sentiments. It would be unjust to attribute to Spinoza some of the extremes to which his idea of Oneness led; for the popular imagination and that of philosophers, also, added in their own way to his provocative thought. But there is no denying the fact that his influence contributed toward driving from the concept of God man's favorite divine attribute: the attribute of love as it is humanly known. His influence can be properly appreciated only in conjunction with the increase of respect for the sciences. The inevitable skepticism that grew up with scientific rationalism cast aside the belief in a soul independent of the body belonging with a God independent of the world; but the literary mind found it difficult to adjust to the alternative provided by Spinoza because it could not be content with the concept of a God who, in the cold mathematical necessity of His very nature, knows not human passions and errors. This notion of divine impersonality, which chilled the religious impulse, was laden further with the dryness of positivism, which in effect called the ideal unreal and hence unworthy of serious thought.

In an intellectual environment of this kind, where imagination was scorned by positivism and where sentiment was denied eternality by metaphysics, in a mood of vain seeking after a God capable of bestowing love, Gustave Flaubert composed *Madame Bovary*. The Spaniard Leopoldo Alas in several respects was similarly motivated when he wrote *La Regenta*. Both novelists were oppressed by what they considered the mediocrity of a positivistic age, but perhaps more significant was their preoccupation with the possibility that human love is incompatible with the concept of God.

This particular attitude toward the subject of love may be considered an effect of the wide cult of impersonality that overshadows a good part of the nineteenth century and urges man to surrender private sentiments in favor of an awesome World Spirit that withholds reality from the individual. As replacement for a personal God who exists apart from nature and intervenes incessantly in its activity, an indeterminate God is enthroned who is more or less identified with a synthesis of all matter and all life and from whom individual forms arise only to be reabsorbed at death into the total mass of material and

mental energy. It is as though the theory of the conservation of
energy were wed with certain Oriental doctrines that behold the
return of individual souls to the mundane Soul or cosmic intelligent principle. Life thus visualized belongs not to man singly
but to nature and hence to man only as he exists en masse. Combine this image of mass fusion with the dynamic historical view
climaxed by Darwinian evolutionary theory, and one has a
good idea of the kind of visions that might besiege the literary
imagination in Europe around 1870-1880. The One Substance
by this time has become a biological force working through an
evolutionary process. Spinoza's God is thus endowed with
earthiness and clothed in physiological dress. A divine impersonal kind of intelligence, rational and eternal, is converted into
an eternal unconsciousness, which effectuates itself in human
beings at the subrational level but not at the higher level of
consciousness where the sense of personality arises. The eternal
thus assumes an animalistic aspect, which sometimes becomes
monstrous, because the individual, far from being unrecognized
by the distant perfection of the Spinozist God, is delivered in
bodily sacrifice to the species, which in turn serves the almighty
Life Force.

The philosophical outlook most thoroughly in tune with the
one just described is that of Schopenhauer, who, long before
the naturalistic movement established itself in literature, had
already set its dominant mood. Schopenhauer is truly the philosophical spokesman for the age of naturalism; for he sees the
species completely overshadowing the individual in significance and places all things in obedience to an endless irrational
Force — which he chooses to call Will. Among the novelists,
Emile Zola is perhaps the one who most sharply portrays a
fusion of God and nature in earthy biological form. Awed by
scientific developments, Zola was a would-be materialist who
could not be content with materialism and a would-be positivist
whose imagination and emotions far outweighed his desire to
abide by the positivistic method. Possessing a great measure
of literary talent, he underlaid his scenes of contemporary
society with a vivid view of primordial nature, combining Darwin and Schopenhauer in a kind of witch's brew. A comparatively minor outcropping of this kind of naturalism appears

in Spain and can best be observed in the novelists Emilia Pardo Bazán and Vicente Blasco Ibáñez.

The grim world view here indicated undoubtedly represents a major phase of modern thought, and when we consider that it is still very much in evidence today we are probably correct in pronouncing it the predominant modern outlook. At the same time, we must remember that there was an irrepressible optimism in the nineteenth century, now sometimes referred to as a naïve belief in progress, and that it was just as easily associated with Darwinian evolutionism as were darker thoughts about man's animal origin. A good number of Darwin's contemporaries, including at least a few churchmen, granted as he did that nature seen through evolutionary theory supported a noble conception of Deity. Thomas Henry Huxley, one of Darwin's most prominent defenders, exemplifies the bold optimistic attitude that takes the advances of science in stride and adjusts accordingly. He concluded that the law of natural selection had dealt a death blow to the argument from design (since it put chance mutation and hence a nonteleological cause in the place of change through purposeful adaptation,[1] but he did not for this reason feel disturbed about man's place nor did he lose faith in the meaningfulness of the total system of nature.

It is simply a matter of shifting the emphasis from the past to the future to behold in evolution a plan that glorifies spiritual attainment, and it is easy to go a step further and suppose that the Supreme Mind is at work realizing itself in the natural process. Contributing to this view, a strong current of Hegelian thought becomes manifest rather late in the nineteenth century, after having been overshadowed by the upsurge of positivism. Just as Schopenhauer appealed to the mood that results from a vision of nature as the futile striving of warring elements having no destiny other than to satisfy the blind urge to live, so Hegel lent support to the contrary inclination to believe in a divine spirit engaged in meaningful activity. It is quite common now to attribute to Hegelian influence the evils of Marxist socialism and the excesses of German nationalism. But Hegel is, above all, the outstanding philosopher of spiritual evolution and a

---

1. "Criticism on *The Origin of Species*" (1864), in *Lay Sermons* (New York: D. Appleton & Co., 1903), p. 301.

brilliant spokesman for the idea that the world is Mind at work in evolutionary process. However abstract his theory may be, there is no denying its solidity and its modernity when it is translated into everyday social and psychological relationships, where the interdependence of personalities, competition and co-operation, challenge and response, and growth through triumph over paradoxical situations are granted fundamental significance in human experience. To those, therefore, who looked for divine design in the theory of biological evolution and at the same time believed that God and nature are somehow to be identified, the spiritual evolutionism of Hegel had a definite meaning and can be discerned in the last quarter of the century especially, when psychology as a science begins to counterbalance physiology.

There was, in short, another kind of naturalism, a "spiritual naturalism," which visualizes nature's organic constitution from a psychological or, more exactly, socio-psychological viewpoint and which presents a picture of man achieving, singly and on his own responsibility but always in the association with others, his oneness with the divine Mind. The outstanding Spanish representative of this phase of nineteenth-century thought is Benito Pérez Galdós, a personality of greater European stature than his comparatively small international recognition would indicate. Since he exemplifies one of the two major aspects of naturalistic outlook, comparable to but essentially different from Zola's world view, he is accorded a separate chapter in this study.

The swell of optimism, of which Galdós was a worthy spokesman, could not brook the predominant current of thought that grew out of the identification of man with nature; and as the nineteenth century draws to a close, the collective mood sinks into the throes of pained reflection upon man's tragic entrapment in the bonds of matter. Evolution turns out to be a remorseless succession of events toward no meaningful goal. Individuals and even communities and nations continuously come into existence only to cease and disappear forever as entities in their own right. The specter of death thus looms larger than ever in man's imagination because of the overpowering thought that it is terminal. The flux philosophers, as William Ernest

Hocking has remarked, "have been unintentional worshipers of death — for when change is ultimate, death becomes permanent." [2]

The twentieth century, deriving little satisfaction from the heritage handed down by its predecessor, began with signs of rebellion, which does not mean, however, that a new orientation was quickly forthcoming. The rebellious spirit was manifest, for one thing, in a literary reaction against the heavy sociological and psychological content of nineteenth-century realism; but from a philosophical viewpoint, the shift in style and techniques can just as rightly be called a quiet adjustment to the inevitable as liberation from an old bondage. There were Nietzschean cries of spirited revolt against the God of mass consciousness and mass energy bequeathed by Schopenhauer, and thus in a way there was a declaration of independence on the part of individuality striving to transcend its incidental role in the total world order. The well-known Spanish philosophical essayist and littérateur, Miguel de Unamuno, is a striking example of heroic efforts on the part of subjectivity to free itself from the world "that tries to make me its own." But despite a sharp preoccupation with the ego, which makes itself felt in the first generation of the twentieth century with all the force of a new Romanticism, the dominant mood is one of passivity. Schopenhauer's heavy shadow is still unmistakable, although the passivity in evidence is not so much his voluntary anesthetization of self in an attempt to avoid suffering as it is a hapless paralysis of will, which may be considered the climactic aftermath of nineteenth-century naturalism and the trough of modern gloom.

In so far as the novel is concerned, it is probably safe to say that the writers belonging to the early years of the twentieth century (Unamuno must be considered an exception) have less to offer in the way of ideas than any other group included in our survey.[3] Possibly the reason is to be found in their pre-

2. *Thoughts on Death and Life* (New York: Harper & Brothers, 1937), p. 83.
3. Cf. Alfred North Whitehead's comment on the late years of the nineteenth century: "the century closed with one of the dullest stages of thought since the time of the First Crusade.... The period was efficient, dull, and half-hearted. It celebrated the triumph of the professional man." *Science and the Modern World* (New York: The Macmillan Co., 1926), p. 148.

dominantly passive attitude. Yet there is no overlooking the fact that the inclination toward abstract art in this period is also the manifestation of a serious intent to establish new viewpoints revelatory of a positive conception of man's place. Noteworthy in this probing for newness is the artist's preoccupation with the concept of time. The evolutionary view had enthroned time as a relentless one-way succession of historical stages in the organic world; and even at the turn of the century, when interest shifts from concrete biological and social phenomena to more abstract images, the stream of time remains an inexorable force that envelops all in its irreversible flow. But the early twentieth century is a period of transition as well as a trough of quietude, and the contemplation of time as a stream carries with it the thought that both past and future are held together in fusion, such as belongs to consciousness, and that each moment is in eternal company with the whole. The individual may find it just as difficult to bolster his desire for immortality from this Bergsonian concept as from any other, but at least an effort is made to escape the bondage of time by converting it into timelessness.

Of the novelists chosen to represent the early twentieth century in the present study, Maxim Gorky exemplifies a mood appropriate to the fag end of nineteenth-century naturalism, which finds thoughts of death and the meaninglessness of life especially debilitating. Pío Baroja is oppressed for reasons very similar to those motivating Gorky and in similar fashion reacts with a predominant passivity. Baroja, however, is a writer of wider intellectual perspective than Gorky; and although he makes no pretense of offering us philosophical consolation, there is about him an intense wistfulness that turns us to profitable reflection upon philosophical subject matter, including the concept of time.

If it can truthfully be said that we are now living in a new age and that our world view has undergone a fundamental change, the second quarter of this century can be designated as the most decisive period of change. One can never establish precise boundary lines in the history of thought, but somewhere around 1920 the contours of a new world begin to take form and new viewpoints begin to appear whose significance can now be felt even though they are still difficult to appraise. Some of the most important aspects of newness are evident long before 1920 in the thinking of Miguel de Unamuno, a personality who stands almost in a class by himself and who, like Galdós, is discussed in a chapter devoted to him alone.

In the shifting of perspectives which has taken place in the twentieth century, literature has shared the spotlight with philosophy and science, although the latter has attracted the most attention, and perhaps rightly so since it constitutes for the philosophically minded a necessary component if not the unescapable starting point of any comprehensive system of thought. Scientifically, physics has been dominant in this century, just as in the nineteenth century the life sciences reached into all areas of thought and cast their shadows over all literary endeavor; and, in general terms, probably the two most significant developments have been the break with Newtonian mechanism and the "retreat" of matter in the role of a concrete irreducible substance. It is very much a debatable question whether or not the mechanistic view of nature has been replaced by an essentially less deterministic view. For although a certain unpredictability seems undeniable in the subatomic realm and the world of particulars at large, the broader, macroscopic view still places emphasis on stable laws. Statistical mechanics, or the principle of large numbers, has simply taken the place of a mechanics of strict causation. Nevertheless, modern physics encourages the imagination to construct new concepts of reality. With the undermining of time and space as absolutes in themselves, it is no longer necessary to look upon things and persons as lumps of reality inhabiting concrete, localized areas. Instead, time, space, and things are merged into one, and we are obliged to depend heavily upon abstract mental constructions in our search for new meanings. To the layman the abstractness can seem formidable if not altogether obscure. Indeed, the physicist himself is rather mystified; for before his very eyes he observes that matter fades into something else, apparently following pathways comparable to those of mind. The physicist has, in fact, found himself unintentionally drifting into the realm of metaphysics, and in individual cases the consequent surprise has undoubtedly been a pleasant one. For there is something exciting about the thought of translating matter into mind, even though the latter be of a mathematical kind only and capable of being captured only in mathematical formulas.

The impact that science has had on philosophy and literature in the second generation of the present century is not so easily defined as that of the nineteenth century, possibly because of our proximity to the major scientific events. Moreover, it is quite probable that the full impact of quantum physics and Relativity has not yet been realized. Still, one can perceive clearly enough a general relationship; and, as in the nineteenth century, the influence appears to be more a disturbance than a comfort. On the optimistic side, the implications of modern scientific developments are perhaps most appropriately associated with the term "freedom." The new science, it may be argued, "has given us not merely a more imaginatively open universe in which to breathe, but also a more emotional and released man to do the breathing." [4] However inexorable cosmic law may be when viewed in its totality, one can hardly ignore the great margin of "choice" or undetermined action that falls to the individual particles of nature. The physicist has been obliged to admit "that *the contingency of being . . . is perpetual, and not an affair of a single and initial event.*" [5] That is, each particular being faces an indefinite future, depending on this or that combination of factors with a limitless number of possibilities. The word "chance" seems an appropriate synonym for this kind of freedom; but if we take into account the vast evidence of consistency in nature, and not in the field of physics alone (organismic biology, for example, argues for the presence of a regulatory principle aiming at systematic wholeness), we can also think of an orderly advance into an unpredictable future and call it a promising adventure. Modern science allows for such a viewpoint, and certain philosopher-scientists adopt it. As Alfred North Whitehead's philosophy of organism bears testimony, nature can be regarded in the light of contemporary science as a creative and meaningful advance into novelty. Life thus viewed is a per-

4. F. S. C. Northrop, "Literature and Science," *Saturday Review of Literature,* Aug. 5, 1944, p. 33.
5. Bernhard Bavink, *Science and God,* trans. H. Stafford Hatfield (New York: Reynal and Hitchcock, 1934), p. 117.

petually indeterminate, adventurous activity, and God Himself
is in the very midst of the adventure.

The mystery, however, that is necessarily a part of adventure
is two-faced. It can frighten as well as beckon invitingly. When
matter fades into something intangible and unknown and when
electrons behave spontaneously as though possessing free will,
the disturbing thought quite naturally arises that perhaps caprice
reigns supreme.[6] Reason is severely jolted and put on the defensive in its collision with the irrational; and twentieth-century
thought clearly reflects the effects of the collision. Existentialism, the dominant philosophical attitude of our day, while taking
its stand on the assumption of a radical freedom (undetermined
essence) for man, exhibits the pain that accompanies the exercise of reason in a world order where reason seems incidental
rather than supreme.[7] A person, we may assert from an existentialist viewpoint, is assumed to be facing existence completely
detached from any established essence, possessing not being but
only the potentiality of being, toward whose attainment he follows a path marked out by his own intending. While declaring
his independence of the naturalistic mechanism of environment
and heredity as well as his disbelief in an initial essence established by divine decree, existentialist man finds himself loaded
with the responsibility of determining his values and making
his decisions on the basis of his own temporality. Emphasis thus
falls on reason, almost to the point of deification. But it is difficult to enthrone reason on high when contingency runs rampant.
It is not strange, then, that contemporary man inclines toward
the suspicion that a sinister unreason is dominant. He has tried
to escape naturalism by breaking out of mechanism, attempting
to maintain himself as pure self-consciousness. But if he can
rely on no ultimate reality of rational consciousness with which
to find a permanent home, he must exist in an isolated rational
loneliness that has the prospect of becoming an eventual nothingness, or he must fall back to a natural world of the unconscious
— a subrational and possibly irrational world.

6. C. E. M. Joad, *Guide to Modern Thought* (New York: Frederick A.
Stokes Co., 1933), p. 82.
7. I do not mean to imply that Existentialism rises out of modern physics.
The two intellectual developments are contemporaneous, but there may be
a closer kinship between them than has yet been observed.

The region of the unconscious, overhung with the shadow of irrationality, has swayed the imagination of twentieth-century writers as much as anything else perhaps, accounting for a rank pantheism in which man is sometimes seen looking for his divine identity in the very bowels of the earth. Naturalism thus still asserts its powerful hold, but more violently than ever before man shows his resentment to the thought of being left to fend for himself in his natural state. In the eighteenth century, reason or reason and science together took the terror out of nature.[8] The loss of faith in reason and religion, which in the nineteenth century left the Unknown colored with direful tones, has resulted in even sharper notes of direfulness in our day. The increased sharpness may be explained in part by the scientific support given to the suggestion that caprice is a major factor in nature, but more important no doubt are man's unwillingness to give up his allegiance to reason and his consequent discontent with remaining in the dark — a discontent long nourished by the scientific attitude. As though responding to his frustration, he has converted the Unknown into a fearful *Mysterium Tremendum*.[9]

In Spain during the past twenty years a literary manner has arisen called *tremendismo*, which places a stamp of violence and absurdity on the mystery of human life and death. The term *tremendismo* has been used in reference to literature appearing since the Spanish civil war (1936-1939) but it could also apply to works of an earlier date; for it seems to be only an extension and accentuation of a general tendency to place the concept of God — or the substitute for God — in the context of a grim, mysterious, and capricious Will. The novelist Ramón J. Sender, now living in the United States, exemplifies this philosophical-literary manner in what is probably the major aspect of his writing, though he plainly shows in some of his works a milder kind of forlornness in quest of a God of reason and justice. The association of an impression of absurdity with the concept of Divinity is also evident in the French existentialist

8. Cf. Basil Willey, *The Eighteenth Century Background* (New York: Columbia University Press, 1953), pp. 3 ff.
9. The term is taken from Rudolph Otto's *The Idea of the Holy* (1917), (London: Oxford University Press, 1931); see below, pp. 236-37.

Jean-Paul Sartre, who, however, is more inclined to create an effect of dull repugnance than of violence. Harboring within himself a conflict between reason and nature, he lifts rational subjectivity almost to a Cartesian plane of separate reality, only to realize that in its ungrounded and unattached state it is probably unreal. He consequently falls back on a "practical" reason as a guide for moral orientation. One might say that he embraces Kant's practical reason without the God whom Kant beheld therein.

How much there is of an affirmative and constructive character in the contemporary novel is a debatable question. Anyone must admit that contemporary literature is heavily colored with the disillusionment natural to a breakdown of faith in old, especially absolute, values. But the gloomy aspects and the *tremendismo* are probably more indicative of a determination to discover a new and wholesome outlook than was the quiet passivity at the turn of the century. The writers of the past two or three decades force us to think of eternity as being incorporated in our own unavoidable presentness. They leave us with tantalizing and unanswered questions and, above all, they present us with the overwhelming necessity of reacquiring God. They do not direct our sight toward a personal Deity, such as the Newtonian God, designer and creator of a perfect mechanism and independent of His creation. But God in some other guise is a powerful reality in the background of the writers' imagination, even when His existence seems most doubtful. He stands like something "which is real" — to use Whitehead's words referring to religion — "and yet waiting to be realized; something which is a remote possibility, and yet the greatest of present facts... something which is the ultimate ideal, and the hopeless quest." [10] The quest goes on unabated in the modern novel and produces occasional flashes of brilliant insight.

The résumé presented in the foregoing pages is offered as an introductory sketch of general trends having special relevancy to the novels later to be discussed. It should by no means be regarded as the promise of a comprehensive history. Nevertheless, it must claim comprehensive validity in the sense of designating

10. *Science and the Modern World*, p. 275.

fundamental moods and currents of thought in man's shifting interpretation of his position as this is viewed in the light of his scientific pronouncements and his metaphysical inclinations. The intention has been to emphasize the major shift in perspective from a dualistic concept of the universe as divided into God and nature, mind and matter, to a vision of the world as a fusion of the two seemingly contradictory realities. In this fusion the God of old has disappeared, leaving man by himself cogitating the mysterious Abstraction that has taken His place; and since man's desire to commune with a Being higher than himself is as fervent as ever, he shows the effects of frustration at being unable to place faith in a personal relationship. Preoccupation with his own importance as a person is unmistakably a basic source of his uneasiness. And his concern arises not merely from contemplating the ominous meaninglessness of materialism. It is just as strong within the context of spiritualistic monism; for here too the question haunts him with respect to the validity of individual personality in the sense of a continuing self-consciousness after death. This is one of the basic subjects discernible in the modern novel. It will be kept in mind throughout our discussion of specific works and will be given still further attention in a final chapter. For the present, it is sufficient to remind ourselves that in an age when individual human dignity is exalted more than ever before man experiences a severe jolt when he faces what seems to be, on the plane of intellectualism, a nullification of the principle of individuality.

The part that science has had in coloring the uneasiness of modern man is no doubt large and has brought opprobrium upon it from some quarters. To blame science, however, seems on the very face of the matter unjustified. If man cannot adjust to new discoveries and new views of himself and nature, he has no one to blame but himself. The adjustment, of course, is easier to recommend than to achieve, and literature is a vivid reminder of the fact. The difficulty lies not in the acceptance of facts but in the assessment of meaning. The problem, therefore, is philosophical; and the poet, like the philosopher, acts under the urge to embrace knowledge and feeling in a perspective of wholeness. Scientists, on the other hand, can stay within the boundaries of their method, unwilling to indulge in philosophic interpretation and unmoved by the responsibility of reshaping the world outlook. The very nature of their professional activity requires this kind of self-limitation. But since the influence of science reaches into all areas of human experience, the scientific posture of objectivity can have and undoubtedly has had a deplorable effect on the human mind. The elimination as far as possible of personal factors colored by sentiment and traditional beliefs tends indirectly to glorify "facts" and to set human life in "a series of total frames which are essentially meaningless." [11]

The scientific attitude, while thus producing indelible effects on collective consciousness, is easily detached from the person of the scientist, as it is from other individuals, in response to private demands of freedom from limitation. For when scientists step outside their professional roles they sometimes feel at liberty to adopt a compartmentalized view of the world and to profess beliefs that do not necessarily follow from their scientific activity. So it was that Newton beheld in the cosmos the handiwork of God. So, too, Darwin refused to see in his theory of evolution the working of blind chance and declared that "there is grandeur in this view of life, with its several powers, having been originally breathed by the Creator into a few forms or into one; and that, whilst this planet has gone cycling on according to the fixed law of gravity, from so simple a beginning endless forms most beautiful and most wonderful have been, and are being evolved"; [12] and in this century Robert A. Millikan heads a group of scientists, religious leaders, and others in proclaiming: "It is a sublime conception of God which is furnished by science, and one wholly consonant with the highest ideals of religion, when it represents Him as revealing Himself through countless ages in the development of the earth as an abode for man and in the age-long inbreathing of life into its constituent matter, culminating in man with his spiritual nature and all his God-like powers." [13]

In referring to these statements one can allege a certain bifur-

11. William Ernest Hocking, p. 161.
12. *The Origin of Species and The Descent of Man* (New York: Modern Library, 1936), p. 374.
13. "Notes and Correspondence," *Isis*, VI (1924-1925), 43.

cation as between the laboratory and the religious sanctuary — an ability to live in two different worlds at the same time without feeling the necessity of bringing them together. The statements indicate the kind of compartmentalization that the literary imagination has found increasingly difficult to accept. But it is only just to say that the attitude revealed by the quotations above, more than anything else perhaps, is a refusal to fall victim to the limitations inherent in the scientific method, at least in so far as the method is positivistic. For, however much the scientist may rely on imagination and speculation, and however much theoretical science may underscore belief in an ideal world, the effect of emphasis on verifiable data acts hypnotically on the collective mind and tends to encourage the notion that the ideal is unreal. The hypnotic effect is especially likely if simply because of not being "scientifically" provable God be left out of the picture. It is one thing to search for the truth of God's world and quite another simply to search for truth.

This positivistic hypnosis, however, probably should be attributed to human nature rather than to science. It is, paradoxically, a result of the irrepressible human inclination to go beyond "facts" while accepting them, to generalize and jump at conclusions on the basis of any tangible evidence. Strictly speaking, therefore, our aim in the present discussion turns not so much to what science has done as to what people in general (including scientists) think it has revealed. Hence our task is to assemble as background for an understanding of the modern novel a compendium of interpretive comments on scientific developments. To this end our attention will turn especially to sources contemporary with or previous to the novels chosen for discussion; and, although a sampling technique is resorted to, it is believed that the ideas and attitudes presented are major and representative. The *Revue des Deux Mondes* alone is literally an index of current scientific and philosophic thought pertinent particularly to a study of the French and Spanish novel of the nineteenth and twentieth centuries. In a word, our intention will be to look upon the novel as the expression of an age. The pairing of a Spanish work with one from another country, in epochs representing major phases of modern thought, is in itself a means of visualizing epochal perspectives. An acquaintance with the non-Spanish works and their thought background, at the same time, throws important light on the Spanish novels chosen for comparison. A further word of explanation seems appropriate regarding the method used in examining the novels included in this study. Since our interest will have to do especially with themes centering on man's preoccupation with his place in the cosmic order, particularly as pertains to his status as an individual, an effort will be made to show how this concern operates in the various stories as a basic stimulus. The subject was not decided upon in advance of novelistic analysis. On the contrary, it has appeared as the result of analyzing a number of novels with the intent of determining their underlying motivation as this is judged on the basis of the central narrative development. The analysis may be called a thematic appraisal in terms of narrative structure. The essential story (and meaning) depends upon the central narrative development. It should be understood, of course, that the "story" necessarily encompasses the character and plot relationship, and even style and technique. If these last two elements enter rather incidentally into our discussion, it does not mean that they are being ignored. They can, in any case, be expected to harmonize with the broad narrative sweep, which constitutes the very essence of a novelistic composition and probably should be the first and foremost novelistic feature to comprehend. If there is one thing that we expect of a novel above all else it is a *story*, and our responsibility will be to determine for each composition what the story is. For this reason it will be necessary to remind the reader of the narrative framework and to recount the most important happenings. It is to be hoped that this method will in each case result in an interpretive retelling rather than a matter-of-fact summary.

What is produced by this combination of scientific-philosophical background with narrative analysis may be called both a commentary on the modern age and a commentary on the modern novel. In one sense, we are using the novel as an expression of man's philosophical mood, and hence as a source book for the history of ideas. But should we not also think of ideational background as part of a work of art's essential character? A novel's aesthetic quality and its lasting appeal may sometimes appear to be independent of the milieu from which it springs — though it is very doubtful that such an aesthetic separation is possible — but one can hardly deny that an understanding of an author's intellectual environment contributes to an understanding of his works, and hence to their appreciation.

2

A Fatherly World According to Design

Charles Dickens   José María de Pereda

CHARLES DICKENS
1812-1870

WHEN WE SPEAK of the "Age of Dickens" we think nostalgically of a world that can never return. It is an old-fashioned world of stagecoaches, village inns — and poorhouses — but, in a much profounder sense, it is the expression of a world outlook which, from an intellectual viewpoint at least, seems to be receding further and further from our grasp. Dickens' understanding of emotions, ideals, and human peculiarities will not pass out of fashion, we may be sure; but even as his portraits were being drawn the general perspective in which they were framed bore the marks of a heroic last stand. For Dickens was a spokesman, and undoubtedly the most effective in all Europe, for an intellectual viewpoint already being placed on the defensive by scientific and philosophical ideas that would not be denied. It is not that he was out of touch with contemporary thought, but simply that in a transitional period he spoke for that phase which reaches back into the past. His literary affiliation with an earlier age, particularly with the English novel of the eighteenth century, is everywhere taken for granted and perhaps adequately understood; but there is still something to be gained by inquiring into the scientific, philosophical, and religious ideas that form the background for his fictional world.

As we survey this background and then examine *David Copperfield*, it will be well to keep in mind for later comparison that José María de Pereda also looked back nostalgically to his boyhood days, and beyond these, for his major inspiration. Although his writings plainly exhibit the marks of a later and stronger realism than that of the English novelist, his understanding of man's place in the world leaves us with little doubt regarding his similar orientation to the past. To those already acquainted with Pereda, the similarity will perhaps be apparent before we come to the discussion of *Sotileza*, at least in so far as our attention rests upon Dickens' attitude of awe and wonder as an inhabitant of a systematical universe under divine direction and upon his special interest in the colorful specimens of nature that can be found in almost any locale.

One can best understand the significance of the view here referred to by observing certain broad trends in the early nineteenth century that harmonize with the spirit of Dickens' writings, rather than by seeking his own pronouncements. Neither in his role as novelist nor in his capacity as a private citizen was Dickens ostensibly attracted to specific theories or inclined to philosophical reflection. A survey of his correspondence will convince anyone that he was much more interested in personal affairs — friendships, writing commitments, and his own activities as an amateur actor, for example — than he was in current intellectual topics. Notwithstanding the novelist's interest in social conditions and the wide discussion of social welfare in England during the time that he grew to maturity, he apparently read little from the works of economists and social theorists, being motivated by a general ideal of charity and benevolence rather than by any particular doctrine.[1] One can be certain, however, that he absorbed a great deal from his intellectual environment and professed allegiance to broad philosophical principles. It is his peculiar greatness that without being what we would call an intellectual he embodied the fundamental philo-

---

1. See Humphrey House, *The Dickens World* (London: Oxford University Press, 1941), pp. 50, 73, *et passim*. Cf. also George Orwell's assertion that Dickens' social criticism pointed to a "change of spirit rather than a change of structure": *Dickens, Dali and Others* (New York: Reynal and Hitchcock, 1946), p. 22.

sophical outlook of a historical epoch, so much so that the mere mention of his name evokes the fullness of an entire "age."

The philosophical view that Dickens represents may be said to reflect a peaceful coexistence of science and religion, in which an enthusiasm for the classification of natural specimens combines with a willingness to believe in the systematic arrangement of a divinely ordered universe. Newton had set the pattern for such an outlook, and his influence contributed for a century or more after his death to the predominantly peaceful vision of a statical world order whose compartments of matter and spirit pertain respectively to nature and to God.[2] Buffon followed his lead, thinking of man as separate from the animal kingdom, accepting in fact the Cartesian dualism of body and soul,[3] while setting for himself the grandiose task of studying all things in the universe. Buffon, it is now recognized, anticipated the evolutionists, but his interest centered primarily on classifying the different species in all their colorful variety; and the reading public of his day knew him only for his picturesque description of animals.[4] A later comparable enthusiasm is seen in the work of Alexander von Humboldt, whose love for traveling and exploring the marvelous things of the earth would have made him a suitable scientist companion for a novelist like Dickens. For in his own particular field, as Dickens did in his, he sought out the unity and harmony of the earth and hoped to give a grand and general view of the universe;[5] and his viewpoint was "contemporaneous," as one reviewer comments,[6] rather than historical.[7]

2. Cf. John Herman Randall, Jr., "Introduction" to *Newton's Philosophy of Nature. Selections from His Writings,* ed. H. S. Thayer (New York: Hafner, 1953), pp. xi-xiii.

3. "L'homme intérieur est double; il est composé de deux principes différents par leur nature et contraires par leur action. L'âme, ce principe spirituel, ce principe de toute connaissance, est toujours en opposition avec cet autre principe animal et purement matériel...": *Œuvres complètes de Buffon,* ed. J.-L. de Lannessan (Paris, 1884), IV, 446. Cf. the following from *A Natural History...from the Writings of Buffon, Cuvier, Lacépède, and Other Eminent Naturalists* (New York, 1831), I, 114: "Man is a being compounded of two distinct natures, body and soul. The soul exists independently of the senses, but receives all its information by their means."

4. J.-L. de Lannessan, "Préface" to *Œuvres complètes de Buffon.*

5. *Cosmos: a Sketch of a Physical Description of the Universe,* trans. E. C. Otté (New York, 1851), p. 24, and author's preface (1844), p. vii.

6. *Westminster Review,* September, 1845, p. 77.

7. Even in works like Charles Lyell's *Principles of Geology* (1830-1834) and R. Chambers' *Vestiges of the Natural History of Creation* (1844),

During the time of Dickens' rise to fame, of course, scientific
thought was in the process of a gradual shift in emphasis from
an observational and descriptive to a historical and analytical
method. Belief in the fixity of separately created species was giving way to belief in one continuous natural development that involves within it a creative world Intelligence or Spirit. In this
transitional period a halfway stand was taken by some of the influential scientists, who were inclined to reject an outright dualism setting Deity apart from nature and yet were unwilling to
abandon the comforts of older views. A prominent example is R.
Chambers, who in his *Vestiges of the Natural History of Creation* partially identifies the Creator with His creation. Chambers
thinks of God not as a Person apart who continually intervenes
in the natural world but as a Deity who creates by having established in the beginning a natural evolutionary law which of its
own necessity entails all future development: "The Eternal One
has arranged for everything beforehand, and trusted all to the
operation of the laws of his appointment, himself being ever
present in all things." [8] The similarity to Leibniz is unmistakable
in regard to the principle of plenitude and a pre-established system of regulation,[9] by which the necessity of a constantly repeated miraculous intervention is avoided. But Chambers could
not (nor could Leibniz) go so far as to identify Deity with nature completely. God's creativity operates in the world and He
at the same time retains His independent ability to support the
whole world system by His providence and to use created things
as instruments of His will.[10] The fundamental viewpoint is not
far removed from Descartes's concept of God's relationship
with nature, which in a general sense is considered "the order
and disposition established by God . . . in created things." [11]

---

two widely read examples of the evolutionary approach, there is much
attention to the information supplied by the traveling, descriptive naturalists.

8. P. 138.
9. Cf. Leibniz, *Selections*, ed. Philip P. Wiener (New York: Charles
Scribner's Sons, 1951), pp. 114-16.
10. Chambers, pp. 118-19. Cf. Leibniz, *Selections*, p. 109: "God governs
minds as a Prince governs his subjects, and even as a father cares for his
children, whereas he disposes of other substances as an engineer manipu-
lates his machines."
11. *Meditations and Selections from the Principles of Philosophy*, trans.
John Veitch (Chicago: The Open Court, 1925), p. 94.

Many scientists, however, as well as theologians, clung stubbornly to traditional views. Lamarck's theory of evolution, set forth in 1809, was more than counterbalanced for some three decades by the immense popularity and influence of Cuvier; and for years after the appearance of Darwin's *The Origin of Species* in 1859 not only his but the general theory of evolution was contested by biologists of the old school. As late as 1867 Louis Agassiz expressed opposition to "the new scientific doctrines which are flourishing now in England," [12] and apparently maintained to the end of his career that metamorphosis of all things is explainable only by supernatural intervention.[13] The compromise position adopted by Chambers, therefore, was sharply challenged by some of his contemporaries as being sheer heresy and a false philosophical stand because it pointed the way to a virtual elimination of God in favor of natural force.[14] Undoubtedly a more popular view was that held by William Paley, whose *Natural Theology* (1802) makes use of the argument of design in the universe to support belief in "the *personality* of the Deity, as distinguished from what is sometimes called nature, sometimes called principle." [15] Paley takes for granted the mechanistic structure of the universe and hence concludes that there must be a Maker, since a machine is incapable of self-creation or self-regulation. More than a century earlier Newton had argued in similar fashion and with similar faith: "This most beautiful system of the sun, planets and comets," he says, "could only proceed from the council and dominion of an intelligent and powerful Being"; and in opposition to the trend toward the identification of God and nature, which was following Spinoza, he declares that "This Being governs all things, not as the soul

12. *Louis Agassiz, His Life and Correspondence*, ed. Elizabeth Cary Agassiz (Boston, 1886), p. 647.
13. See E. Jourdy, "Darwin et Agassiz," *La Philosophie Positive*, VIII (1872), 67-68.
14. An example of the opposition is found in a review of Chambers' book included in the edition cited above. The reviewer decries what he thinks is a materialistic view that conceives of God as being little more than an electric spark, and he states his own desire for a personal Creator who can take part in the ordinary proceedings of mankind.
15. *Natural Theology or Evidences of the Existence and Attributes of the Deity, Collected from the Appearances of Nature* (New York, 1875), p. 229. According to the publisher's notice, some forty editions of Paley's work had appeared before 1854.

of the world, but as Lord over all." [16] It is not surprising that a novelist of Dickens' generation should reflect a full-fledged pre-evolutionary viewpoint.

One can easily understand, also, that the influence of Descartes and Newton should harmonize and produce an attitude of placid contentment. If one can affirm, with Descartes, that "it is certain that I, that is, my mind, by which I am what I am, is entirely and truly distinct from my body, and may exist without it"; [17] and if one can believe with Newton that final causes are not inherent in matter but are originated and controlled by a God who personally exercises dominion over his "servants," there is no reason to be depressed by fatalism or doubts of immortality. Such a Newtonian-Cartesian perspective could optimistically embrace determinism and freedom at the same time, because it bespeaks a willingness to believe that the paradox exists only because we cannot fully understand God's plan. [18]

This harmonious combination of scientific, religious, and philosophic views was undoubtedly more suited to the intellectual climate in England than in France, [19] and held sway longer there. The "cosmic Toryism" which settled over the eighteenth century actually extended far into the nineteenth. Despite the Romantic revolt against mechanism and the accompanying trend toward pantheism, the Newtonian outlook persisted. For that period known as the Age of Dickens, the world remained essentially a divine machine, whose operation conformed to a regulated system of checks and balances. Evil for some inscrutable reason was present, possibly because one's freedom outruns one's understanding, as Descartes says. [20] But evil could be overcome in individual lives by the assertion of man's innate goodness and his ability to bring his rational understanding into the control of impulses and thus elevate himself toward his Maker. As the naturalist Lesson said, "Man differs from all other beings. . . . By the power of thinking he raises himself to the di-

---

16. *Newton's Philosophy of Nature . . .*, p. 42.
17. *Meditations and Selections . . .*, p. 91.
18. Descartes says as much in *The Principles of Philosophy* (*Meditations and Selections . . .*, p. 150).
19. Cf. Basil Willey, *The Eighteenth Century Background*, p. 155.
20. *Meditations and Selections . . .*, p. 69.

vinity from whom he emanates ... happy were he, did not war, and its scourges, and death, and sickness, perpetually remind him that the great work of nature must be accomplished." [21] The accomplishment of "the great work of nature" caused no tragic disturbance in man's mind, because it was under the vigilance of a Supreme Being, whose patience could allow that the human race go through "a career of impulsive acting for a few thousand years," and whose tolerance, in view of an inevitable progress, could abide "the cruelties of ungoverned anger, the tyrannies of the rude and proud over the humble and good ..." [22]

In brief, the first half of the nineteenth century witnessed a growth of the "controversy respecting the mode of government of the world, whether it be by incessant divine intervention, or by the operation of primordial and unchangeable law," [23] an emotionally charged subject that became more and more consequential as the century advanced. Dickens must be placed in the company of those who looked to a benevolent Ruler separate from His creation; and his religious outlook constitutes a fundamental quality of his stories, no matter how indifferent he may have been to the formalities of worship. Of particular relevancy in a discussion of his novels from the standpoint of science and philosophic background is, first, the attitude of enthusiasm toward all created things, exemplified by the descriptive naturalists who set out to explore on a grand scale the systematic and static categories of nature. Of still greater significance is the optimism inherent in the argument from design, by which nature is said to evidence God's existence and His intelligent rule. *David Copperfield*, Dickens' favorite and probably most representative novel, may logically be viewed as an enthusiastic, and in a way exemplary, journey into a vast world of classifiable beings created by a wise God who looks down on His children's struggles and supplies enough strength for the triumph of good over evil.

21. *A Natural History ... from the Writings of Buffon ...*, p. 171.
22. R. Chambers, pp. 256-57.
23. John William Draper, *History of the Conflict between Religion and Science* (New York, 1875), p. xv.

David Copperfield (1850)

The nostalgic, autobiographical retracing of David Copperfield's personal history is both the account of an exploration and the record of an education acquired through reflection upon what has been explored. The narrator thus occupies a dual role, shifting his attention back and forth between the vantage point of a spectator who surveys a broad expanse and the purely subjective position of one who reflects on the problem of finding his place in the world. A number of the chapter headings themselves indicate the dual viewpoint. The spectator's position, for example, is illustrated by the following: "I observe" (chapter 2), "I enlarge my circle of acquaintances" (chapter 6), "Some old scenes and some new people" (chapter 21), "The emigrants" (chapter 57); and the personal focus is seen in: "I fall into disgrace" (chapter 4), "I become neglected" (chapter 10), "I make another beginning" (chapter 15), "Depression" (chapter 35). The two fields of vision constantly interweave throughout the narrative, but the emphasis rests at first on the subjective element as it pertains to the emotions of childhood. The focus on self gradually gives way to a larger interest in other people's affairs, and finally attention to self and others is combined in approximately equal proportions within a common perspective, which includes the two major intellectual aspects indicated in the foregoing introductory sketch of Dickens' thought background: the classificatory view of nature described by an enthusiastic observer and reflection upon a divinely regulated order in which balance is fundamental. Disturbance of the balance constitutes the dramatic action.

With a sensitivity deriving in some degree from his own childhood memories, the author divides the child's world into the sharp opposites of love and neglect, friends (the Peggottys) and enemies (the Murdstones). The balancing of joy and sorrow, which is a basic feature of the novel, goes hand in hand with a strong sense of curiosity and an attendant love of adventure. These prominent features are quickly blended and point to the story of a youth's good and bad fortunes in combination with travel and a widening acquaintance with the wondrous things to be seen along the way. The tale of vicissitudes begins with major attention given to the hero's hard knocks; for Davy is soon compelled to leave home and experience cruelties of the world: the rough reception at Mr. Creakle's school, the news of his mother's death (after a brief period of gaiety and friendship at school), his unhappy employment in London, where he finds some relief from his misery in the acquisition of his new friends, the Micawbers.

In this early part of the personal history there is an unmistakable resemblance in narrative form to the picaresque novel; for we have not only the general plan that recounts the fortunes of an orphan boy sent forth by dint of circumstances into a cruel world, but also the review of youthful experiences in melancholy retrospect. Within this framework there are a number of typically picaresque adventures. While on his way to Mr. Creakle's school, for example, Davy is duped out of a meal by the waiter at an inn (chapter 5).[24] Similarly, when he leaves London to seek shelter with his aunt Betsy in Dover, he loses his possessions to a strapping youth whom he had hired to carry his baggage (chapter 12); and later, on another trip, he is talked out of his box seat by a coachman (chapter 19). The mischief, rowdiness, and cruelty of school life at Mr. Creakle's also is in the spirit of the old picaresque tale, which was undoubtedly in the author's mind as he wrote, since he has Davy read to the other boys at night from *Peregrine Pickle* and *Gil Blas*. Even Davy's attachment to Steerforth recalls the picaresque situation in which a boy in an unfavorable position attaches himself to a person of power and influence.[25] The essential similarity, however, lies

24. Dickens is said to have admitted borrowing this episode from Holcroft's autobiography: Earle Davis, "The Creation of Dickens's *David Copperfield*," *University Studies Bulletin* No. 9 (Municipal University of Wichita), XVI (1941), 11. The incident, nevertheless, has a remarkable similarity to a scene in Lesage's *Gil Blas* (I, chapter 2), which was borrowed from the seventeenth-century Spanish novel *Marcos de Obregón* (I, chapter 9) by Vicente Espinel.

25. In general appearance, though not in detail, the picaresque novel most specifically brought to mind by this school episode is *El Buscón* (1626) by Francisco de Quevedo, which contains all the elements mentioned above: pranks, stern schoolmaster, rowdyism, and the pairing of a boy of humble circumstances with one of strong social position. The school episode in *Roderick Random* (chapters 2 and 5) might possibly have served as Dickens' model (cf. Earle Davis, p. 12), though the resemblance is rather remote. In tone and realistic detail, of course, Dickens is like a gentle

not in specific episodes but in the broad narrative objective of tracing the ups and downs in the life of a youth who sets out from an unfortunate background, travels along the world's highway, and looks back philosophically and moralistically on his mistakes. As the author tells of Davy's going to work in London, later seeking out his aunt Betsy in Dover, then going to school in Canterbury, traveling here and there, meeting people of curious stripe, and eventually deciding on a career and marrying Dora, he is recording the hardships and humorous adventures of a simple, gullible youth who grows up in the broad world, a victim now and then of the deceits of society and occasionally the dupe of his own folly. The retrospective view of fleeting joys and sorrows, which constitutes a central tonal refrain in the novel, rounds out the picaresque form.

In so far as the character of the hero and the general outlook of the author are concerned, of course, *David Copperfield* is actually antipicaresque. Dickens, in fact, seemed determined to reverse the typical situation, in which the *pícaro* is contaminated by evil company, and to make the goodness of human nature triumph by having his hero associate with good and friendly people.[26] Because of the predominance of sympathy and sentiment the picaresque resemblance diminishes as the story of David Copperfield progresses; and it should be observed that the change is gradual and perfectly consonant with a gradual change in perspective that takes place in the hero himself as he turns more and more from his own problems to the problems of his friends. The sympathetic involvement of self in the welfare of other people goes counter to the typical picaresque pattern, which keeps the protagonist always entangled in his own difficulties and weaknesses.

The projection of self into the world outside of self, which

morning breeze compared with the harshness of the seventeenth-century Spanish novelists — or with their eighteenth-century English followers, for that matter.

26. Similarly, *Oliver Twist* is converted into an antipicaresque novel after having followed a picaresque pattern at first. Some of the details in *Oliver Twist* indicate a direct connection with *Lazarillo de Tormes* and *El Buscón*, a relationship all the more plausible in view of the fact that English translations of these and other Spanish novels were in Dickens' library at the time of his death. See my article "*Oliver Twist* and the Spanish Picaresque Novel," *Studies in Philology*, LIX (1957), 440-47.

with Dickens is a psychological necessity, naturally causes the author to place great weight upon the role of spectator, and the reader at times forgets the protagonist and thinks only of the spectacle described. When Davy heads for a new and more favorable start in life, the horizon rapidly expands and the world seems to pass by on parade. The reader is asked to enter into the spirit of a day at the circus, or that of a journey with Alice in Wonderland, where belong such characters as the funny Charley to whom Davy sells his jacket on the way to Dover, the dwarf Miss Mowcher, the addled Mr. Dick; and it would not be improper to include in the same group the resilient Mr. Micawber and the bugbear Uriah Heep. The amusement of the spectator is tempered with an ample portion of sentiment, which is created on behalf of the variegated coterie of acquaintances who are involved in different kinds of difficulties. Davy's personal vicissitudes, including his marriage with Dora, his career as writer, and his sorrow at Dora's death, are all overshadowed by the experiences of others, among them the plight of Mr. Wickfield and Agnes hounded by Uriah Heep, the uncertainty of Dr. Strong's domestic situation, and especially the tragedy in Mr. Peggotty's family caused by Steerforth's elopement with and eventual abandonment of Little Emily. The main body of the narrative, therefore, weaves together a grand assemblage of human specimens and human experiences seen through friendly eyes; and the narrator, having shouldered his friends' burdens, complies with his responsibility of seeing their problems through to a plausible solution, which is at the same time a peaceful adjustment to the rules that govern human existence. So it is that Mr. Peggotty recovers Little Emily and takes her to Australia, where she can re-establish herself; Mr. Wickfield and Agnes are saved from the clutches of Uriah Heep, who ends up in jail, as all villains should; Ham and Steerforth lose their lives in a storm at sea, the one as a hero in an attempted rescue, and the other in dignified payment for his treatment of Little Emily; Aunt Betsy is finally relieved of the nuisance caused by her worthless husband, when he conveniently dies; and Mr. Micawber, who has gained the stature of hero by detecting the thievery of Uriah, emerges from debt at last and begins life anew.

With the burdens of his friends satisfactorily disposed of,

Davy's attention turns once more to himself, and in the last few chapters of the novel the personal note seems to regain ascendancy. As Davy attains tranquillity in happy marriage with Agnes and indulges sentimentally in one "last retrospect," the autobiography ends as it had begun, with reminiscent reflection on personal fortunes, thus giving the novel its subjective unity. The melancholy subjective refrain, moreover, has a certain moralistic color, with respect to the vagaries of impulsive youth, which remains true to the picaresque pattern so evident in the early part of the story and which bespeaks the necessity of corrective action. The "softened regrets" (chapter 60) of an "undisciplined heart" (chapter 58), bearing principally on the sentiment of love, can in fact be considered a unifying theme. Even so, the mistakes, the pains, and the pleasures of love belong not to Davy's experiences alone but to almost all the other prominent characters.[27] We must not fail to see, therefore, that the hero's personal interests are merely reincorporated in the group picture and not restored to a dominant position. The conclusion of the novel, which thus blends on more or less equal terms individual and group experiences, as it does soft reflection and gay observation, makes plain that the "essential story," after appearing at first to be a record of ups and downs in an individual's life, has carried forward a collective adventure embracing ups and downs in the lives of a group of friends. The protagonist, who starts out on a journey through life, becomes inseparably attached to his traveling companions, forming with them a veritable family and sharing their activities with amusement and sentiment. The journey has its exciting moments and its mishaps, but the coach pulls into its haven at last with most of its occupants intact, and with fond memories more than offsetting the misfortunes of the trip.

In a narrative structure of this kind there is little point in looking for a compact "plot" centering on a single personage. Each character's experience is necessary to the whole as long as it shares in the group picture of ups and downs. The broad

27. Cf. Gwendolyn B. Needham ("The Undisciplined Heart of David Copperfield," *Nineteenth Century Fiction*, IX [1954], 81-107), who recognizes that this theme embraces various characters in addition to Davy.

world of human nature, as seen in a multitude of characters, is as central as Davy's personal history. "The Copperfield Survey of the World as It Rolled," which is a title that Dickens thought of using,[28] would have been very appropriate. Some of the chapters are very plainly medleys of diverse subjects, but the novel's "unity" is not for this reason any less certain. The termination within a single focus of numerous plot ramifications requires a great deal of dexterity — more perhaps than the pursuit of a single personal theme — in order to avoid the appearance of formlessness and improbability. But it must be said to Dickens' credit that he achieves a broad synthesis, bringing together the fortunes of his many personages and combining chance and necessity, the usual and the unusual, the tragic and the comic, with enough balance and decisiveness to satisfy our demands for authenticity. He is, after all, depicting life on a grand scale, and his method demands that we contemplate a comprehensive pattern that reflects the grandiose rhythm of a world order.

Dickens' character portrayal, for which he has frequently been criticized, should also be viewed in relation to the broad perspective that controls his narrative method. His major characterizations are neither local social types nor particular individuals but generic representations of the human species and are therefore just as authentic as the human traits that they most prominently illustrate. It would not only be an injustice to Dickens to judge his personages as though they were meant to be particular people, but it would also detract from the reading pleasure by causing the reader to pull in a direction contrary to the author's aim. The latter's portraits, simply drawn with a few bold strokes, are perhaps more abstract than those of most nineteenth-century novelists. In a general way, therefore, they conform to the practice of a long line of novelists of the two preceding centuries. But it is also interesting to observe how well they fit into the abstract pattern of the classification stage in which the biological sciences found themselves during the latter part of the eighteenth and the early part of the nineteenth centuries. Dickens' aim, on a human level, could very aptly be com-

28. Hesketh Pearson, *Dickens. His Character, Comedy, and Career* (New York: Harper & Brothers, 1949), p. 166.

pared to that of Humboldt on an animal level, in that each looks beyond the individual organism to the "fundamental type." [29] The following statement by the naturalist could just as truthfully have been made by the novelist, if allowance be made for the difference in areas surveyed: "Travels, undertaken in districts such as these [South America and Northern Asia] could not fail to encourage the natural tendency of my mind toward a generalization of views." [30] The novelist's range is by no means all-inclusive, for, as George Orwell says, there are whole worlds that Dickens does not touch.[31] But his observations are reliable within the limits of his horizon. David Copperfield, in a combination sightseeing trip and classificatory study, travels over a sizable area of human nature, recording his generalizations partly for his own pleasure and partly for the benefit of other students of nature. Some of his specimens are curiosities and deviations from the norm; but showing through all the variety is the personality of Mr. Everyman calling our attention to human nature as one great systematic whole.

With Dickens' generalized view of mankind one should associate the concept of separateness, which is of fundamental significance in relation to the static, pre-evolutionary perspective of the Dickens world. The characters cohere in neighborly side-by-sideness, or sharply repel each other, but they give no indication of how one aspect of nature fuses with another, such as occurs in the transfer of personality traits through association. They harmonize with their surroundings and sometimes appear to be the products of their environment, but they are not seen to develop out of it. Little Emily, after her life with Steerforth, possesses the same gentle goodness of her girlhood. What she is obliged to suffer for is the stain on her reputation and not the effects of experience upon her personality. The author's interpretation of character is not for this reason invalid, though our more realistic tastes may now find it somewhat removed from strict probability. The important consideration is that his view of nature, comprehended in its wholeness, is an

29. Concerning the application of this statement to Humboldt, see a review of his *Cosmos* in the *Westminster Review*, September, 1845, p. 78.
30. *Cosmos* (New York, 1851), I, viii.
31. *Dickens, Dali and Others*, p. 68.

aggregate or clustery summation of independent parts rather than a blending of one element with another.

The philosophical significance of the clustery, static vista of nature found in Dickens can be further appreciated by reference to the debate carried over from the eighteenth century concerning the senses, perception, consciousness, and other psychological phenomena, which basically is also a debate on whether the world is governed by unitary or dualistic principles. An illustration is provided by the argument of William Belsham, an "immaterialist," who maintains in opposition to materialistic psychology that consciousness ("perception") cannot develop out of any organic "combination of impercipient particles" and that consequently the whole can never be more than "the united powers of all the parts."[32] This means that the whole of a personality is a mechanical juxtaposition of fixed traits and not an organic development. Belsham clearly recognizes, as Bergson does a century later in his discussion of time, that transition and growth are impossible in a chain of being made up of separate and independent sections. Unlike Bergson, however, he does not as a result reject mechanism. He solves his problem, as most of those with religious faith did in his day, by appeal to a source apart from the natural machine. Hence perception was for him, in its relation to the body, a property "wholly foreign, superinduced and adventitious." Here is a belief in the separateness of nature and God that allows for freedom from the dominion of matter — not an absolute freedom that has no destination save by its own decree, but such as might be visualized in a community of mutually independent spirits watched over by a Supreme Spirit, to whom they are all bound in co-operative action.[33]

In this "fatherly" organization of the world, which is the

32. *Essays, Philosophical, Historical and Literary* (Dublin, 1791), III, 3-7.

33. A similar conception of mechanistic order is expressed, it seems to me, in the following reference to Dickens' novels: "A coherent and balanced structure which exhaustively illustrates a single broad theme, the idea that through all human experience, interwoven as it is for good and evil, the health of an organism — an individual . . . or human kind — depends on the responsibility of the parts one to another and to the whole": Harold F. Folland, "The Doer and the Deed: Theme and Pattern in *Barnaby Rudge*," *Publications of the Modern Language Association*, LXXIV (1959), 417.

world of Dickens, the distribution of parts finds a balance in a dualistic arrangement that divides people and circumstances, for the most part, into camps of good and evil and corresponds to the concept of separation between mind and matter. Evil is taken for granted without heavy concern as to its source and, together with good, stands out sometimes like the objectification of an abstract idea; as, for example, in the situation (chapter 51) in which one woman tries to lead Emily into prostitution and another (Martha) rescues her. Evil thus decidedly interferes with the lyrical rhythm of life, but it is obliged eventually to bow before a Supreme Will that provides a system of checks and balances and measures out rewards and punishments. One could use as an appropriate description of this anthropomorphic role of divinity the following statement of the reviewer, cited earlier, of Chambers' *Vestiges of the Natural History of Creation*: "The only *sure* mode of acquiring sound ideas of our relation to the Creator is to begin with the study of ourselves, and to view God as a Father and Friend, dealing with us in precisely the same way as we would deal with others over whom we exercise authority. Conscience ... tells us that we are responsible beings; and in the domestic, as well as the social circle, we speedily feel the discipline and learn the lesson of rewards and punishments." [34] The Creator stands ever ready to chastise His children, but at least He is not dissociated, in some impersonal form, from the beings He has created.

Dickens' essentially traditional adherence to an old faith which conceives of God as an attentive Father able to ensure the triumph of good over evil could hardly produce less than an optimistic outlook, regardless of personal unhappiness. The consoling influence of old loyalties is one of the most prominent aspects of the novelist's literary personality. *David Copperfield*, in particular, illustrates this allegiance to the past. In this novel the world is not only seen through the eyes of a child; it is perceived in retrospective mellowness that removes the roughest edges and the sharpest sting of unhappiness. The nostalgic backward glance thus is charged more with loyalty to what has been lived than with sadness for the vanity and cruelty of life. "What an idle time! What an unsubstantial, happy, foolish time!" Davy

34. Chambers, p. 341.

declares (chapter 33). The words, which are expressive of the novel's basic mood, are not words of disillusionment. There is no denying that such a mood indicates a certain wistfulness for some unrealized ideal, but it does not suggest gloomy preoccupation with the question of man's cosmic position. It has been said that Dickens' outward show of gay spirits was a mask for a deep-lying loss or want of something that drove him forward always in a desperate effort to escape a feeling of futility.[35] This is a very strong statement which bears primarily on the novelist's personal affairs and the obvious social criticism that runs through his writings. It is hardly justifiable, however, as a statement of underlying philosophical outlook. One must admit, of course, the possibility that Dickens may have unconsciously voiced the somber disillusionment that accompanies Western man's contemplation of himself in fusion with all nature. This attitude could logically be associated with his epoch, as witness Flaubert in the novel, to say nothing of various poets. But this supposition would be much more difficult to support than the belief that the novelist's melancholy is an irrepressible fondness for childhood and a child's outlook, colored no doubt by the memory of certain unhappy episodes in his own life.[36] For Dickens, the tragedy of life is the absence of love in personal experience, not the absence of love in the universe (as with Flaubert), nor the baseness of the material world, nor the prospects of the loss of individuality at death. Most readers must surely agree with André Maurois that the heart of Dickens' message is "a tremendous optimism, both national and personal," [37] and one could expand the scope of optimism to include, in the words of Newton, "This most beautiful system of the sun, planets and comets," which can "only proceed from the counsel and dominion of an intelligent and powerful Being." [38]

A storyteller of the old school, exponent along with Cervantes

35. Edgar Johnson, *Charles Dickens. His Tragedy and Triumph* (New York: Simon and Schuster, 1952), I, 4.

36. Especially the time when as a boy of twelve he had to work in a blacking warehouse and his father was in prison for debts. See John Foster's *Life of Charles Dickens*, ed. J. W. T. Ley (New York, n.d.), p. 26. Cf. Johnson, pp. 39 ff., and Edmund Wilson, *The Wound and the Bow* (Boston: Houghton Mifflin Co., 1941), p. 8.

37. "The Philosophy of Dickens," *The Forum*, January, 1929, p. 56.

38. *Newton's Philosophy of Nature* . . . , p. 42.

and Fielding of the cult of the marvelous, Dickens might aptly have declared his motto to be: art is life, and life is joy, even if it has to be leavened with sorrow and supported with a bit of wishful thinking. The world view that he leaves us is one of stability and unchanging values, combined with youthful exuberance and the spirit of adventure. In this world of faith and traditions David Copperfield was born and grew up, admiring its wonders, facing its dangers, finding his allotted place in it, and proclaiming its soundness. To this world the man of today — and of tomorrow — will undoubtedly return periodically in fond remembrance. He may also return in quest of equilibrium. For, although the static, mechanistic vision of the cosmic order which Dickens reflects can hardly be expected to reassert itself, we must not forget that his philosophical outlook embodies another component of undying appeal. This is the personal element in the concept of divinity, in pursuit of which modern man has displayed some of his most painful striving.

JOSÉ MARÍA DE PEREDA
1833-1906

Devotees of Spanish literature esteem Pereda above all as a regional artist, whose vivid pictures of customs and types in and around Santander are superlative examples of genre painting. Possibly because of this strong local focus they have overlooked the affinity that exists between the Spaniard and Dickens, while frequently naming the latter in speaking of Pérez Galdós, Pereda's contemporary. There is, of course, a sound basis for associating the names of Dickens and Galdós, especially in connection with their attitudes of sympathetic amusement toward a wide variety of human specimens; and there is no question that Galdós greatly admired Dickens, as have many other Spanish novelists. But in a fundamental intellectual sense these two writers belong to radically different worlds. Galdós was very alert to developments in science and philosophy, as we shall have occasion to see in a later chapter, and in his own independent way left a substantial novelistic interpretation of the most advanced thinking of his day. Pereda, on the other hand, would have liked to turn the clock back and recapture the rhythm of living that preceded the appearance of railroads and all the noisy progress of an industrial age. Like Dickens, though not specifically from the same motives, he resurrected his childhood days and reconstructed a world that contrasts sharply with the modern world of questioning search into the uncertain meanings of life.

During the years of heated controversy that followed the revolution of 1868 in Spain, Pereda was an outspoken opponent of the skepticism and materialism which many Spanish traditionalists were quick to read into new ideas coming from abroad, especially from France.[39] But the militant aspects of his conservatism are of less relevance to our subject, and are decidedly of less interest artistically, than his nonargumentative depiction of a way of life free of any challenge to his traditional interpretation of man's place. The desire to revive the past is more noticeable in his novels than in those of Dickens, who was historically in closer intellectual proximity to the world vista that he presents. Yet at his best Pereda provides a thoroughly contemporaneous view within the range of an old perspective. It would be difficult to find anywhere in literature stronger support for Newton's contention that the universe proclaims the greatness and wisdom of an omniscient Creator than Pereda's descriptions of sea and mountains. Nor could one find anywhere a portrayal of personal relationships more suggestive of a "fatherly" arrangement in the world order.

Upon the broad basis of this traditional outlook the comparison of Pereda and Dickens should be made. At the same time it must not be assumed that the two novelists have a close affinity in all respects. There is, indeed, a certain curious interest attached to the fact that two personalities very unlike in several ways present fundamentally the same philosophical outlook and do so apparently without the least intention of being philosophical. Pereda was a person of aristocratic bearing from the well-to-do middle class, a retiring person content to live apart from

39. Pereda's conservative attitude and traditional beliefs are so well known that I am dispensing with documentation. Also, as regards the intellectual environment in Spain in his day, I am deferring the mention of details, since I shall return to the subject when discussing Alas and Galdós, for whom the consideration of specific ideas will be more necessary than it is in Pereda's case.

society, an orthodox Catholic, and a believer in an authoritarian social structure. Dickens, though by no means affiliated with the proletariat, was more a man of the people, socially an extrovert, and in religion an anti-Catholic and rather indifferent to the formalities of worship of any kind. He was, also, much more personally involved in questions of social welfare than the Spaniard, although the latter often engaged in caustic satire of social flaws. But when the two novelists rise above the level of controversy and attack they occupy positions close to each other in so far as their vision of the world order is concerned; and in their spirited and picturesque record of this vision rests their major claim to recognition. Surely Dickens' survival value derives not so much from his social indignation as from the warmth and colorfulness with which he portrays the human species, especially as seen in the neighborly relationships of friends and families. The same can be said of Pereda, whose regional sketches and novels combine with a vivid local color a sympathetic delineation of people in broad and simple strokes.

Sotileza (1884)

Pereda is at his best in *Sotileza*, probably because it is the novel in which he becomes most enthusiastically involved. Like *David Copperfield*, it is a personal composition; for it recalls the days when the author was a boy in Santander, associating with the children of the fisherfolk and taking great delight in all activities relating to the sea. Like *David Copperfield*, also, *Sotileza* leaves us with the impression of having been on an excursion. The English novel, however, as we have interpreted it, is the record of a youth's journey over a large area of the human community; while the Spanish novel is more aptly described as a visit to a chosen place of recreation, since it localizes its record of youthful experiences within the confines of a single city. In a very real sense it can be called a novel of customs, for Pereda clearly shows that in so far as narrative technique is concerned his main inspiration is the *costumbrismo* or depiction of customs in which Spanish writers have always displayed special talent and which enjoyed great popularity in Spain in the first half of the nineteenth century. At times the author gives himself whole-heartedly to the delineation of scenes, seemingly more interested in what can be seen at any given moment than in what the action or the situation may lead to. Consequently, the narrative progression, in the early part of the novel at least, appears to be merely a chronological succession of episodes.

The narrative structure of the Spanish novel thus is even looser than that of *David Copperfield.* The explanation is that in the beginning of his story Dickens concentrates pretty much on one person. The old way of life that he evokes gradually assumes broad dimensions as his hero, once his security is established, is drawn into a large group relationship, the picaresque aspects having to do with an orphan boy's hardships meanwhile fading into the background. Pereda, on the other hand, as he explains in his foreword to the reader and in the conclusion of the first chapter of *Sotileza,* proposes to re-create scenes, people, and customs of the fishing town of Santander that he had known as a boy.[40] He therefore sets about his task of reviewing "the good old days" by visualizing a collective picture at the outset and centering his attention on a group of children.

Having this objective in mind, Pereda jovially begins his novel with a descriptive dialogue scene in which *pae* Apolinar, a fussy, good-natured secularized priest, tries with little success to drive information into the thick heads of his clientele of ragged urchins, who are assembled in a dilapidated schoolroom. The scene, which sets the tempo for the first part of the narrative, is typical of the spirit in which *Sotileza is* written; and Pereda probably would have been glad to compose the entire novel in this manner, placing together a series of loosely connected scenes. He realized, however, that a novel cannot be constructed with description alone and he turns, seemingly with reluctance, to the problem of creating a central plot interest. For this pur-

40. Pereda apparently had little thought of the picaresque kind of narrative when he wrote *Sotileza.* He was sympathetic with picaresque literature, however, especially in a stylistic way, and wrote one novel (*Pedro Sánchez,* 1883) that is quite plainly modeled on the pattern exemplified by *Guzmán de Alfarache,* in which the narrator looks back with melancholy regret on the folly and mistakes of his youth. *Pedro Sánchez,* incidentally, has one definite mark of similarity with *David Copperfield* apart from the picaresque aspect: the hero finally settles down in happy marriage, after losing his first wife, with the girl who had loved him silently for many years.

pose he decides to involve in a major difficulty the small circle
of friends with whom he is to deal, allowing one of them
(Sotileza) to become the focal point in the group. The major
complication will center upon the problems of youthful love,
and since the children are only ten or twelve years of age at the
beginning of the narrative, the author can take his time in leading up to any kind of climactic action. With an abundance of
time at his disposal, therefore, he enters with full freedom into a
presentation of the setting, though keeping in mind always the
complication that will eventually arise. The setting consists just
as much of people, fisherfolk for the most part, as it does of
places and things; and the people blend into one harmonious
whole with their dwellings and their physical surroundings.

Sotileza is an orphan girl living with the harsh family of Tío
Mocejón, who is surpassed only by his wife (la Sargüeta) and
daughter (Carpia) in griminess of appearance and perverseness
of character. The son of the family (Cleto), though quiet and
hard-working, shows scarcely more consideration for Sotileza
than do his venomous mother and sister. The family lives on the
small fifth floor of a tenement house whose balconies are covered
with fishing equipment, dirty clothes, and refuse that proclaim
the trade of its numerous occupants. Sotileza maintains in general a stoic impassivity toward favorable and unfavorable circumstances alike, but she leaves the Mocejón abode one day determined not to return. One of her friends is Andrés, a boy from
a well-to-do middle-class family, whose father is the captain of
a merchant ship. Although his is a society where class distinction
is sharply drawn, he has a particular liking for the sea and finds
his closest friends among children of the humblest fishermen. He
is quite conscious of his socially superior position, though not in
an unpleasant way, and possibly for this reason takes it upon himself to aid Sotileza, leading her to Padre Apolinar while the latter
is engaged in the classroom activity already referred to. Here
he promptly transfers his responsibility to the harassed padre
and marches off to watch his father's boat come in, followed by
several playmates, including Sotileza herself and Muergo, a
brutelike urchin with whom the priest was having much peda-
gogical difficulty.

From the reader's expanding acquaintance with the general situation it is apparent that Sotileza and Andrés are going to be the two main characters, for they are continuously in view, the one becoming established in the friendly home of Tío Mechelín and his wife, direct opposites of the Mocejón family, who live in the same building; and the other looking on with pride for having had a part in aiding his friend. A suggestion of difficulty thus appears, for if any kind of "romantic" interest should later develop between these two, the serious question of class barriers would arise. This is the complication that the author has in mind as he proceeds leisurely, devoting himself wholeheartedly to sketching portraits and scenes. He does not intend, however, to concentrate on the relations between one couple, either by way of psychological portrayal or by the study of a social problem. Even before he skips several years in his narrative account, resuming the story when his principal characters are approaching maturity, he lays the foundation for a broad plot structure that will involve two other characters in important secondary roles. One of these is Cleto, who, we are led to believe, will become seriously interested in Sotileza. The other is Luisa, daughter of the wealthy merchant employer of Andrés' father, who will be a determined competitor for Andrés' attention. Included, also, in a minor role is Muergo, whose very animality and ugliness seem to hold a fascination for Sotileza and who to some extent complicates the network of relationships. The group, therefore, remains always the subject, and although the ramifications are confined within a smaller and more compact circle of acquaintances than is the case with *David Copperfield*, the narrative unity in similar manner depends on the significance of the collective experience, and not on the fortunes of an individual.

For purposes of supplying dramatic action, the author creates a disturbance around Sotileza which involves almost all the other characters in the story and which — as in *David Copperfield*, we may say — represents an interruption of the balance assumed to be characteristic of the universal order. The disturbance arises when Cleto reveals to Andrés his concern over the vicious insinuations made by his sister Carpia concerning the relationship between Sotileza and Andrés. The latter denies with complete sincerity the false rumors and determines to make less frequent visits to the home of Tío Mocejón. But the diabolical power of suggestion sets him to pondering Sotileza's charms and impels him to behave in a way exactly opposite to what he had intended. Now, for the first time, he resorts to devious action, contriving to call on Sotileza and make love to her when Tío Mocejón and his wife are absent. Class distinction is so much a part of the young woman's environment that she has never even considered as a possibility the love of anyone above her social level. In Andrés' presence she has been circumspect, never allowing herself any of the liberties of familiarity noticeable in her treatment of Muergo, whose mentality and animal appearance make him her inferior. She is therefore more surprised and angered than tempted by Andrés' advances. Her reprimands, however, only make the youth more determined, and he visits her a second time when she is alone. On this occasion Carpia, who is always on the alert for an opportunity to hurt Sotileza, manages to lock the young couple in the Mocejón apartment and proceed to broadcast the "scandal" to the entire neighborhood.

Notwithstanding the fact that Sotileza vigorously affirms her innocence, engaging Carpia in violent hand-to-hand combat after finally emerging from the trap, the scandal has been created; and Andrés finds himself in an embarrassing predicament, which is further aggravated by his father's severity. He is sorry for his folly and is upright enough to offer to marry Sotileza merely for having brought upon her the appearance of dishonor. Such a marriage, of course, is strongly opposed by his father, and by Sotileza as well; and Andrés, confused and yet rebellious, stays away from home one night and departs with a fleet of fishing boats on the following morning. External nature now enters the picture, bringing to a climax the social disturbance and contributing to a restoration of order by hastening the solution of a problem which, in the logic of the situation, must be solved in conformity with social tradition. A tremendous storm arises at sea, which Pereda describes with almost as much talent and enthusiasm as he exhibits in the portraiture of local types. A number of fishermen lose their lives, among them Muergo, but

Andrés returns safely, now completely sobered and docile.[41] An episode in the life of a community thus comes to a peaceful and orderly conclusion, as marriages are planned for Andrés and Luisa, and for Cleto and Sotileza.

In a novel of this kind the question of plot may seem unimportant as compared to the general panoramic view of the locale and the collective view of a humble but heroic people. Yet a novel cannot be considered simply as a picture of something, even though the scenic material may be its most enjoyable part. It inevitably tells a story, and the story in turn inevitably gives meaning to the scenes recorded. Realizing this, Pereda accepts his narrative responsibility and in fact becomes intrigued by the possibilities surrounding the dramatic episode that he invents. As a result, he leads us into a potentially tense study of character and situation and almost forgets his major objective in favor of a psychological handling of the Sotileza-Andrés relationship. The major objective, however, which is to revive imaginatively a way of life by way of a group experience, reasserts itself decisively in the conclusion and gives finality to the narrative movement. This can now be defined as an account of the rather usual experiences, including the complications of youthful love, of a group of children who grow up in the Santander of the author's boyhood days. When viewed in its completeness, the novel thus becomes a colorful and sympathetic presentation of the ageless story of childhood blossoming into maturity, stumbling and bruising its collective nose, but emerging at last on an even keel in accord with the traditions of old and the lessons of experience handed down from generation to generation.

In subject and comprehensive narrative development, therefore, *Sotileza* bears a marked resemblance to *David Copperfield*, even when we grant that the latter reaches beyond the problems of young people to a larger extent than the Spanish novel. The similarity in the basic narrative concept is found in the fact that each story is something of a conducted tour over youthful pathways marked with mishaps, amusing incidents, and pic-

41. The storm in *David Copperfield*, one will remember, also helps to bring the narrative to a close by disposing of two of the characters (Ham Peggotty and Steerforth), although it does not have as much of a climactic function as in *Sotileza*.

turesque people, and terminating in a peaceful synchronization with the even rhythm of life. The Spanish tour, restricted to a smaller area, is much like a visit to a beach where a crowd is gathered for a day of recreation. Acting as guide and commentator, the author directs us toward a youthful group at play, which becomes a special point of interest within the larger setting. After a while the group stirs with excitement, entangles in its problems some of the people nearby, and finally resumes its allotted role in the tranquil movement of the total scene. Pereda has, in effect, selected and elaborated upon one portion of an extensive tour, such as that conducted by Dickens, and has done so with a kindred spirit of gaiety appropriate to a sightseeing trip. Both writers find it difficult to pass up an opportunity to create a kind of circus entertainment by enlarging upon a promising incident. Both writers, also, have an eye for the poetry of little things and both indulge in humorous extravagance, seemingly able to lose themselves in the art of narration and the art of description without worrying about grave questions relating to human destiny. Compare Dickens' comment on Ham Peggotty's hat, "and you couldn't so properly have said he wore a hat, as that he was covered in a top, like an old building, with something pitchy," [42] with the following from Pereda: "A Catalan cap placed in just any manner on top of his tangled hair, like a dirty rag spread out on a thatched fence." [43] The novelists' pleasure in description is even more vividly evident in their sketching of scenes. Recording the incident when the waiter at an inn eats Davy's meal, Dickens makes a game of his narration:

So he took a chop by the bone in one hand, and a potato in the other, and ate away with a very good appetite, to my extreme satisfaction. He afterward took another chop, and another potato ... He entreated me more than once to come in and win, but what with his table-spoon to my tea-spoon, his despatch to my despatch, and his appetite to my appetite, I was left far behind at the first mouthful, and had no chance with him.[44]

42. *The Personal History of David Copperfield* (New York: Charles Scribner's Sons, 1924), p. 31.
43. Translated from *Obras completas de D. José María de Pereda* (Madrid: Libería General de Victoriano Suárez, 1923), IX, 58.
44. Ed. cit., *The Personal History of David Copperfield*, p. 73.

Pereda, lustier in his manner and more intent on physical detail, indulges in a similar exercise of playful extravagance while describing the rough Mocejón family eating a meal:

Each spoonful was maneuvered by Mocejón like a cartload of hay. Only his wife surpassed him, not so much in the loading as in the unloading into her mouth, which came out to the encounter with lips spread back over the angular and half-open jaws ... and then ... then it was all over, because Silda, observant as she was, could never determine whether it was the mouth that sprang upon its prey, or whether it was the prey that jumped, from midway in its journey, into the mouth.[45]

Both novelists, in short, survey the human species with the amusement of sympathetic observers and with a sense of responsibility for leaving descriptive and classificatory records. The records which they leave, moreover, are characteristic of a pre-evolutionary outlook upon the world. In Pereda, as in Dickens, the total collection of personages is a balanced assortment representing in separate categories the variations in nature. The kindly, courageous Tío Mechelín and his patient, industrious wife (compare the Peggottys and Wickfields) and the vitriolic Mocejón family (compare the Murdstones and the Heeps) are stationed in the same milieu and are almost exact opposites, because they are meant to be primary classifications within a static order and not blends of successive stages in nature's continuous process. The assortment, too, includes some of the oddities of nature which add color to the collection. Muergo, for example, who might as well have been a horse or a good-natured dog, is included more for his curiosity value than for any other reason. Pereda is less abstract than Dickens in his method of characterization, for his portraiture relies heavily on details of local surroundings. His characters are nonetheless typical and fixed quantities that represent general patterns of behavior. The personal motivations, social and moral, reveal the virtues and weaknesses that make up a cross section of human traits applicable to all people from time immemorial.

Even in his handling of Andrés and Sotileza, whose portraits are freer than most of the others from the limitations of type depiction, Pereda is interested primarily in generic traits. The

45. Translated from *Obras completas* ..., IX, 68.

characterization of Andrés comes near being a psychological study, but the youth is still a typical son of a middle-class family, who behaves in a typical manner as he listens to the temptations of the devil, gets into troublesome complications, is reprimanded by his elders, displays a momentary rebelliousness, repents, and quietly follows the path that he is expected to follow. In portraying Sotileza, the author deliberately tries to envelop her in an air of mystery, pointing to her lofty detachment, her obsession with cleanliness amidst sordid surroundings, and her seeming fascination for the brutish Muergo. In general Pereda professed little interest in the why of personality traits and was openly hostile to the newfangled school of realists who indulged in psychological analysis and emphasized the importance of environmental influence on character. While trying to make his heroine seem mysterious, however, he was more of a psychological realist than he supposed; for Sotileza's personality can logically be explained in terms of adjustment to her environment. Her cool aloofness is a defensive shell against harsh surroundings, and the unemotional acceptance of her lot, including marriage with Cleto, is a rather passive, though not unhappy, adjustment to social circumstances. A more positive, self-assertive adjustment is seen in her extreme cleanliness and neatness, which are an expression of rebellious reaction against surroundings; just as her familiarity with Muergo is a comparatively safe relaxation from the firm discipline with which she has managed her emotions. These socio-psychological aspects individualize Sotileza but they appear as the static result of environment and not as a process of growth. Nor do they give the heroine's characterization any special importance in the narrative development. The author is less interested in her as an individual personality than he is in the group activity for which she is responsible. Hence, despite the nominal position of heroine, she is scarcely more than a representative local element in a corporate body of mutually independent parts, on equal terms with all the other elements.

We have in Pereda, therefore, a picture of neighborly separateness similar to what we find in Dickens, as regards both the relationship between one personality and another and the rela-

tionship between personality and environment. In the Spanish
novel the characters seem to be on no better than an equal footing with their material background, since they are enveloped
in a world of things almost as prominent and interesting to look
at as they. In this respect, however, they are somewhat like
children playing in the dirt — attached to it but independent of
it. The reader is interested in what happens to each person, but
there is no reason for any particular interest in what happens to
each personality. Consequently, the narrative effect in its wholeness leaves us thinking about the disposition of an assemblage of
parts that must find their allotted places in an ordered system.
Operating within the limits of a freedom granted by a Supreme
Father, the persons move about in friendly independence of
each other, accepting the regulations of the universal order, like
children who trust and obey their elders, and adopting the viewpoint that the most important questions are already settled or
will be settled without the necessity of anxious searching for
new interpretations. "Niños grandes" (big children), Pereda
affectionately calls a group of friends who visit Andrés' father
on one occasion, and he himself would hardly aspire to a philosophical outlook more complex than theirs.

Sotileza, then, is a serene composition, seemingly untouched
by the provocative questions raised by modern science. Pereda
was very conscious of contemporary religious skepticism, and
his orientation to the past may in part be a consequent reaction.
But, as in the case of Dickens, his loyalty to the old is a spontaneous manifestation of intellectual equanimity whose explanation is found not simply in religious faith but in its harmony with
rational and scientific interpretation. The stand taken by both
novelists is, fundamentally, the extension of an eighteenth-century outlook in which science, philosophy, and religion agree
in their conception of a stabilized, mechanistic universe, whose
earthly compartment is for the most part a robust and healthy
order that operates smoothly in conformity with the rules of
its separate Creator. Holding such a vision of the world, one
might wholeheartedly repeat the declaration of Manzoni: "We
ought to thank God and be content; do whatever we can,
work industriously, help one another and then be content, be-

cause it is no disgrace to suffer and be poor; the disgrace is to do evil." [46] Essentially, the philosophical outlook of Dickens and Pereda can be appreciated if we combine with Manzoni's words an expression of admiration for the enduring wonders of nature found in Alexander von Humboldt's hope that "an attempt to delineate nature in all its vivid animation and exalted grandeur, and to trace the *stable* amid the vacillating, ever-recurring alternation of physical metamorphoses, will not be wholly disregarded even at a future age." [47]

The tranquil, compartmentalized view of the world found in *David Copperfield* and *Sotileza* contrasts sharply with the uneasiness that surges in the naturalistic novels of the nineteenth century as a result of the scientific and philosophical insistence on the identification of man (and God) with nature. In these twentieth-century days, when the gloomy preoccupation with man's position in the universe is even more intense, the novels of Dickens and Pereda may seem far removed from actuality. It is natural to look on them as friendly companions of childhood, to be recalled occasionally for a moment's innocent pastime but not to be taken seriously as subjects of philosophical contemplation. Yet they stand as reminders of more than the simple faith and simple tastes of long ago. For in their interpretation of harmony between science, religion, and philosophy they illustrate in the history of thought the attainment of a goal that man seems to prize above all else. The desperate striving on the part of other modern novelists, within radically different intellectual perspectives, bears testimony to the significance of an intellectual orientation in which both science and religion allow for the ideal of a divine personality.

46. These words from Manzoni's *I promessi sposi* (1825-1827) are quoted by Philo Buck, Jr. (*The World's Great Age;* New York: The Macmillan Co., 1936, p. 92) as being characteristic of the Age of Dickens.
47. *Cosmos,* p. xii.

3

In Quest of a God of Love

Gustave Flaubert   Leopoldo Alas

GUSTAVE FLAUBERT
1821-1880

IF WE THINK of Dickens as representing a philosophical outlook that was already retreating into the past at the time he wrote, we may in comparable manner regard Flaubert as an interpreter of the encroaching ideas that caused the retreat. It would be difficult to find a novelist more deeply involved than Flaubert in the intellectual turmoil of an age in which old beliefs were reluctantly laid aside in the face of a gradual entrenchment of more modern scientific and philosophical views. Burdened with the reversal that science had dealt traditional ideas concerning a personal God, Flaubert tried to make a stoical adjustment, grimly disciplining himself under the banner of impersonal truth. While a student at the collège in Rouen, he spent long hours in metaphysical discussion with his close friend Alfred Le Poittevin, an ardent admirer of Spinoza. One can easily imagine the painful restraint of emotion with which the two young romantics reflected upon the cool sublimity of Spinoza's God, who allows small comfort both for private passions and for the ideal of personality.

A comparable intellectual disturbance is found in the person of Leopoldo Alas, whose most important work, *La Regenta*, has often been said to recall *Madame Bovary*. The two novels are generally associated in connection with formal similarities having to do with narrative situation, but there is also an underlying common bond bearing on the man and God relationship and traceable to certain powerful currents of nineteenth-century thought. The important common motivation is found in the notion that love, as it is humanly known, is excluded from the concept of divinity. A God of love is replaced in the literary imagination by a cold impersonal Idea untouched by human emotions. The theme of unsatisfiable longing in individual man thus is focused on the impossibility of deifying love. In order to appreciate the significance of this theme as a basis for comparing the novels of Alas and Flaubert, it is necessary first to consider briefly the philosophical atmosphere of the mid-century in France, which, in broad terms, may be described as the challenge of a positivistic age overlaid with the influence of Spinoza.

The one indispensable fact to keep in mind is the tendency which became ever stronger in scientific and philosophical circles in the first half of the nineteenth century, to encompass nature, God, and all existence in a unitary and evolutionary view of the universe. Notwithstanding the opposition of influential biologists (notably Cuvier), the evolutionary viewpoint was gradually entrenching itself, and in combination with early nineteenth-century sensation psychology produced a great impact on philosophical thought. The idea of mind's evolvement out of matter [1] gave rise to much troubled and acrobatic reasoning with regard to the role of God in the universe and the position of self-consciousness or the sense of personality. The basic problem was — as it is today — how to avoid completely undermining the human ego. If Cartesian dualism was to be abandoned in favor of a single reality manifest within nature, where was a home to be found for the self? If animism had to be rejected,[2]

---

1. It is worth noting that in the first half of the century there was a widely held belief among scientists in the possibility of spontaneous generation of life from inorganic matter, and that the subject was debated sometimes with reference to the original, primordial generation of life. Flaubert himself apparently was a "partisan convaincu de la génération spontanée": Roger Veillé, "Madame Bovary a cent ans," *Europe*, June, 1957, p. 23, note 2.

2. The most idealistically inclined among biologists and psychologists wavered uncertainly in compromise positions, trying to take neither a ma-

the notion of "free" individual souls must give way, it seemed, to the unpleasant thought of a mass consciousness identifiable with purely natural states of being. In the language of positivism, man differs from animals only in degree of complexity.[3] Hence there is no fundamental difference between a physical sensation and the intellectual understanding of it, and no difference between a state of mind and consciousness of it as being a state of mind. Self-consciousness or the sense of personality, therefore, is in Comte's view a wholly subordinate phenomenon, scarcely more than a state of equilibrium in the organism (II, 273, 279). Though conceding a "reasonable liberty" within the laws of nature, Comte opposes the unruly energy of the self "asserted by the German school" (II, 281) and declares that true liberty is nothing more than rational submission to the laws of nature (III, 61).

In this climate of naturalistic emphasis, Spinoza's thought occupied a prominent position, commanding the attention of those who respected the scientific information on which the positivist took his stand yet were unwilling to replace their metaphysical inclinations by the positivistic viewpoint.[4] Under the heavy shadow of the natural sciences, however, the philosopher's metaphysical support afforded small satisfaction; for popular interpretation carried to unpleasant extremes both aspects (physical and mental) of his One Substance. By one route God was brought into the world of minerals, plants, and animals; Spi-

---

terialistic nor a dualistic stand. Cf. William McDougall, *Body and Mind. A History and Defense of Animism* (London: Methuen, 1915), pp. 80-84. Flaubert took the position that body and soul somehow form a unity but he assumed something of an agnostic attitude toward the question. Compare the following, dated 1859: "Et d'ailleurs je ne sais (et personne ne sait) ce que veulent dire ces deux mots: âme et corps, où l'une finit, où l'autre commence": *Correspondance* (Paris: Louis Conard, 1927), IV, 314.

3. *La Philosophie positive* [of Auguste Comte], résumé par Émile Rigolage (Paris, 1910), II, 277, 280. Numerals in parentheses will refer to this edition.

4. Flaubert spoke derisively of Comte's *Philosophie positive*: letters to Louis Bouilhet, Sept. 4, 1850 (*Corres.*, II, 238) and to Louise Colet, July 2, 1853 (*Corres.*, III, 259). It should be noted, however, that he was objecting primarily to the socialistic content of Comte's doctrine. Actually, he sometimes talked like a positivist himself. Consider: "La science deviendra une foi, j'en suis sûr. Mais pour cela, il faut sortir des vieilles habitudes scolastiques: ne pas faire ces divisions de la forme et du fond, de l'âme et du corps, qui ne mènent a rien; – il n'y a que des faits et des ensembles dans l'univers. Nous ne faisons que de naître. Nous marchons encore à quatre pattes..." (*Corres.*, IV, 357).

noza was converted into a pantheist of the rankest sort, and self-consciousness was relegated to dissolution in a world Soul of a decidedly earthy, if not materialistic, quality.[5] If, on the other hand, emphasis was placed on the rational aspect of the One Substance, the implications were hardly more satisfactory in so far as individuality is concerned; for human personality could find no ultimate home in a realm of pure, abstract intellect.

There were those who sought to effect a compromise between dualism and monism by trying to comprehend a God who is two different things at the same time, one real and one unreal. An example of this curious ambidexterity is Etienne Vacherot, who thought that he could reconcile science and metaphysics in the spirit of a "métaphysique positive," [6] which amounts to a dualistic extension of Spinoza's two aspects into separate and incompatible somethings, one of them pervading the world we know and live in, the other residing in the pure "geometry" of our imagination. In answer to the demands of individuality, he tries to avoid the unpleasant alternatives of exclusion from God's perfection and absorption in a World Spirit by recourse to a God of reason (614-16) who is rescued from both matter and abstraction by being located "in the always accessible heaven of Thought" (586). He thus approaches a solid footing by identifying God with actual experience. But no sooner does he place Deity within reach of the individual mind than he declares that the Ideal so conceived is impossible of realization (587); since, as he argues, when we try to realize God, He becomes either an idol or an empty abstraction. In this essentially posi-

---

5. Among those who followed such a line of reasoning was the youthful Hippolyte Taine. In his *Les Philosophes français du xixe siècle* (Paris, 1857) the passage which concludes his essay "De la méthode" sounds like an interpretive epitome of Spinoza's *Ethics*, with the word "nature" taking the place of "God." Gustave Planche, in a review of Taine's essays ("Le Panthéisme et l'histoire," *Revue des Deux Mondes*, VIII [1857], 667-91), asserts that Taine has taken Spinoza as a guide and has consequently embraced all the evils of pantheism. The term "pantheism," it must be remembered, was very loosely used and was directed as a term of opprobrium at philosophers in general. Thus Victor Cousin condemns pantheism in connection with the German idealists ("Promenade philosophique en Allemagne," *Revue des Deux Mondes*, XI [1857], 534-60); Taine, *op. cit.*, p. 126) accuses Cousin of being a pantheist; and Planche accuses Taine of being the same thing.

6. See the preface to his *La Métaphysique et la science, ou principes de métaphysique positive* (Paris, 1858). Numerals in parentheses will refer to this work. Translations are my own.

tivistic perspective God's ideality costs Him His reality, and He turns out to be little more than "man's shadow projected against the sky." [7]

There were also some few spirited minds, like Ernest Renan, who could take the age in their stride, embracing poetry, science, and religion in one harmonious whole, welcoming the erasure of myths and superstitions while maintaining a love of mystery and faith in a glorious destiny of mankind. Renan possessed a fortunate adaptability to that borderland of skepticism in which one surrenders traditional beliefs without surrendering faith in the traditional affections associated with those beliefs. Flaubert, by contrast, could not visualize the unknown in such pleasant perspective. Like Vacherot, he accepted the idea of God's inaccessibility, but he did so without trying to deceive himself by playing with the concept of Deity as an ideal that slips in and out of sight like a will-o'-the-wisp. Instead, he reflected fatalistically on an unknowable God, before whom he bowed, not in bland resignation but in bitterness.

Flaubert's thoughts on Deity were undoubtedly colored by his reading of Spinoza, whose initial influence on him is manifest in its pantheistic suggestiveness. An important example of this is *La Tentation de Saint Antoine* (first written in 1848-1849, revised and abridged in 1856, and finally published in 1874, after another revision), whose central motivation is the crushing effect of science and reason on religious beliefs. Since man's quest of divinity is a basic idea in this novel, we are justified in looking to it for its possible bearing on *Madame Bovary*. The narrative recounts the saint's temptation at the bidding of carnal desires and rational argument, including parades of ancient, transitory religious and philosophical creeds. Probably the two most important aspects of the thought content, however, pertain to scientific and philosophical subjects having special prominence in Flaubert's lifetime. The scientific subject is the evolvement of life and intelligence out of matter, and the episode in which a vision of prehistoric monsters appears to Anthony presumably represents the stage of animal existence between

7. As E. Marras says of Vacherot's God, reviewing E. Caro, *L'Idée de Dieu et ses nouveaux critiques* (1864), in *Revue de Paris*, II (1864), 614.

man and the most primitive of organic forms.[8] The philosophical subject, presented through the Devil as spokesman, is the Spinozist concept of One Substance, which holds that God is present in all things and yet indivisible. The result of the philosophical and scientific mixture is the saint's mystic urge to enter into and become one with matter. In the two early versions of the fantasy, this pantheistic demonstration concludes the second of three divisions. In the last version, which underwent considerable technical reconstruction, the same episode comes at the end of the story (now divided into seven parts). The author thus finally chooses the most climactic position for the grotesque scene in which Anthony lies in the dirt flat on his stomach, watching the minute globules of animated matter that represent the last step in a retrogressive view of evolution, and expressing with mystic fervor his desire to fly, swim, bark, bellow, and howl.

The major change made by Flaubert in this his favorite composition, over a period of some twenty years, has to do with organization rather than ideas, but there is one significant modification bearing on the metaphysical subject. In the early versions the allusions to Spinozist thought leave primarily the impression of a Deity diffused in all things, the loss of human individuality being implicit in the pantheistic fusion rather than specifically stressed. In the final version the concept of personality is placed in sharper focus by association with the emotions. The thought that God is a cold impersonal perfection, untouched by the human sense of person, comes clearly to view. To Anthony's assertion that there is above everything a Lord and Father "whom my heart adores, and who must love me," the Devil replies, "You desire that God be not God; for, if He experienced love, anger, or pity, He would pass from His perfection to a greater or smaller perfection. He cannot descend to a sentiment, or be contained in a form." [9]

8. Cf. Jean Seznec, "Science et religion chez Flaubert d'après les sources de *La Tentation de Saint Antoine*," *Romanic Review*, XXXIII (1942), 364. The sources are discussed in a great deal more detail in another article by the same author: "Saint Antoine et les monstres. Essai sur les sources et la signification du fantastique de Flaubert," *PMLA*, LVIII (1943), 195-222.
9. Translated from *La Tentation de Saint Antoine* (Paris: Louis Conard, 1924), pp. 174-75. Cf. Spinoza's *Ethics*, Part V, Proposition XVII: "God is free from passions, nor is He affected with any affect of joy or sorrow";

In this very personal composition of Flaubert's, then, we are brought face to face with the two aspects of Spinozist thought that had the greatest suggestive potency in the nineteenth century, one bearing on the pantheistic merging of spirit and matter and the other on the exclusion of individual personality from communication with Divinity. That both lines of suggestion preoccupied Flaubert during the long years that he worked on *La Tentation de Saint Antoine* seems evident, and it is only logical if we take them into account as we ponder the essential nature of *Madame Bovary*.[10] The second aspect, in particular, appears to be a significant element in the thought background of the novel. The important thing is to visualize the Spinozist persuasion as a broad factor in combination with the mood of an epoch in which the cold impersonality of the scientific attitude seemed to decree for individual consciousness a lonely position in a world of sentient matter. In such an atmosphere the image of Spinoza's Deity hovered over all like a ready-made symbol indicating God's remoteness from the sentiment of love and giving rise to a kind of popular protest, whose refrain is concisely stated in these words: "We demand a God who loves." [11]

The general philosophical attitude which had plainly received stimulus from Spinoza in the mid-nineteenth century continued to disturb the popular mind after his name receded from its once conspicuous position. Some two decades after the composition of *Madame Bovary* was begun, the unpleasant thought of man's exclusion from God's love found expression in intellectual circles in Spain. The following statement in 1870 by a Spaniard who decried the trends in the philosophical thought of the day,

---

and under the "Proof" of the proposition: "God cannot pass either to a greater or to a lesser perfection." Translation of the *Ethics* by W. Hale White and Amelia Hutchinson Sterling (New York, 1894).

10. Spinoza's influence on the youthful Flaubert is generally recognized. Understandably, it has not been observed in *Madame Bovary*, where the indications of influence are much less clear than they are in the novelist's youthful writings. My principal purpose, of course, is to show how Flaubert's novel reflects the mood of an epoch which Spinoza's ideas helped to determine.

11. The quotation (translated) is from an article by Mme. Clarisse Cogniet, "Études philosophiques. Panthéisme, Spinoza," *Revue de Paris*, XXXIX (1857), 270. Referring, presumably, to this article, Flaubert calls Mme. "Coignet's" discussion of Spinoza "bien insuffisant," though he does not state his reasons: *Corres.*, IV, 233.

is relevant here because it testifies to the kind of intellectual environment from which *La Regenta* came, and which is essentially a continuance of the kind of thinking that formed the background for *Madame Bovary*. The reference is to Jean Reynaud's *Terre et Ciel* (1854), from which the writer extracts in particular the idea of a perfect and unapproachable God:

and for another thing, our infinite smallness disappears in the abysses of His infinity. If as a result of His omnipotent wisdom He deigns to distinguish us, we are before Him no more than a nothingness that cannot provoke an act of any kind on His part toward an unworthy thing in which He can take no pleasure. It is, consequently, a delirium of our pride to persuade ourselves that God can love us, when it is more in conformity with His nature to ignore us and cast us aside.[12]

The protest registered by this writer is fundamentally akin to the motivation that delineates Emma Bovary's repulsed love. Flaubert found himself in the unhappy position of emotionally rejecting the concept of a Deity incapable of recognizing human passions, while rationally accepting it. The conflict emerges in his masterpiece in the form of chastisement, including self-chastisement, in which scorn of the mediocrity of collective humanity joins with a stern philosophical restriction of individual aspirations.

Madame Bovary (1857)

The personality of Flaubert's heroine rises timidly, yet challengingly, out of its material medium. There is in Emma's undefinable uneasiness far more than a residue of girlhood dreams issuing from an isolated existence in a convent and on her father's farm; and Flaubert manages to impart the suggestion of a mysterious inner drive that will eventually become a violent storm. To establish contrast between his heroine's sensitivity and the world in which she is imprisoned, and thus to set the stage for her compulsive restlessness, the author surrounds her with a drab

12. Translated from Nicomedes Martín Mateos, "El catolicismo y la filosofía alemana," *Revista de España*, XVII (1870), 99. Note that the German idealists, rather than Spinoza, are now blamed.

environment and condemns her to a dull succession of uneventful days. With the same deliberateness he marries her to Charles, who appears, even as the narrative begins, like an omen of doom. For Charles is a personification of the average level of sensibility, in short, a synthesis of the human capacity for imaginative attainment and hence an exemplification of the human species when viewed in the aggregate; just as various other characters in the novel typify other unattractive aspects of mass humanity, including the nobility: the father of the marquis to whose home Emma and Charles are invited eats like a pig, letting gravy drip from his mouth. This aggregate view of the species finds humanity in its abstract or composite form to be much closer than individual beings to the primitive impercipient stage of animal existence. Under this imagined mantle of drabness and vulgarity the heroine's longings become more and more intense. Sharpened by environment, but not caused by it, they can be only temporarily quieted by changes in external circumstances, such as Charles resorts to when he moves to a larger town.

In this introductory section of the novel (Part I) the author establishes an essentially tragic theme and adopts a predominantly tragic tone. He plants a strange passionate longing in his heroine, he burdens her with a monotonous existence in a materialistic atmosphere, and he watches the inner fire begin to grow. The rapid summary narration, even when recounting simply how day follows day with the humdrum sameness of the "eternal" garden and the dusty road, contributes to the expectancy of an inexorable end; and the stylistic coolness of the author's simulated detachment adds to the impression of a grim destiny.[13] The tragic tempo is interrupted periodically by satirical attacks on the milieu that imprisons the heroine, and the satirical mood is more in evidence after the Bovarys move to Yonville, where the circle of acquaintances expands. The heart of the narrative development, however, follows consistently the course of a progressive intensification of Emma's inborn restless-

13. The tragic quality of *Madame Bovary* is unmistakable, and we can agree with Robert J. Nelson ("*Madame Bovary* as Tragedy," *Modern Language Quarterly*, XVIII [1957], 323-30) as regards "the tragic rhythm" which characterizes the novel's structure. Nelson speaks of the heroine's perception, through suffering, of a limited creature's position in an ultimately unknowable universe. I am trying in my own interpretation to draw attention to the heart of the tragedy more specifically.

ness, which is something independent of her surroundings and would have disturbed her regardless of local circumstances. At first "an unseizable *malaise*, which changes aspects like the clouds, which eddies like the wind" (57),[14] takes hold of her violently, filling her "with desires, with rage, with hate [for her husband]" (149), and drives her toward her lovers as though she were propelled by an irresistible force.

The inner drive, or conatus, at work in Flaubert's heroine may appropriately be called "desire," to use Spinoza's terminology,[15] who considers it man's very essence and the manifestation of an effort to persevere in his own being. The frustration that accompanies such an effort may be regarded as the inevitable suffering to which the human personality is doomed for carrying within it a sense of lack. For a feeling of privation, to continue with the Spinozist view, is something impossible of divine recognition, since God cannot experience imperfection. The tragedy for the individual, therefore, is that the ungodlikeness or unreality of desire costs it all chance of fulfillment. This is not to say that the human being is untouched by divinity, but simply that he cannot expect to find divine reality in his personal emotions, which in Emma's case are focalized on the passion of love and directed toward persons who she thinks might possibly be the means to celestial realization. The first of these — if we do not count the hopelessly unresponsive Charles — is Léon, the timid notary's clerk, with whom Emma discusses sentimental literature while her husband plays dominoes with the garrulous and pretentious druggist Homais.

In the dramatic presentment of his theme, the author adds to his heroine's unfortunate situation by investing her striving with a satanic cloak that contrasts with the celestial nature of her aspiration. It is as though a divine inner spark were thwarted by a demon who carries the heroine toward an abyss while she seeks to attain to heaven. Constantly thinking of rapturous experience, she grows thin and pale, taking a martyr's pleasure in nursing her suppressed emotions and accumulating an ever-greater scorn for her husband. When Léon, unable to declare

14. Page references are to *Madame Bovary* (Paris: Louis Conard, 1921). Translations are my own.
15. *Ethics*, Part IV: "Of Human Bondage."

his love, moves to Rouen in order to escape from an uncomfortable situation, Emma sinks again into a quiet boredom, which
she tries in vain to alleviate by aimless activity and an indulgence
of whims. With the unanswered longing still burning deep
within her, she falls an easy prey to Rodolphe Boulanger, one of
the major shams to whom the author subjects his heroine with·
an inflexible resoluteness that deepens the demonic coloring of
her predicament.

Flaubert thus includes a diabolical ingredient in a way somewhat comparable to the situation in *La Tentation de Saint Antoine* where the Devil prepares Anthony for his defeat; and
while doing so he keeps in mind always an opposite extreme.
For Emma's longing, with all its madness, bears definite marks
of lofty fineness. Her love, except for an occasional show of
tenderness toward her daughter and her father, is clearly self-
centered; but it reaches out toward the highest level of ecstatic
refinement. "Did she not seem," the author reminds us, "to be
traversing existence scarcely touching it, and to bear on her brow
the vague impression of some divine predestination?" (149)
The continuous shifting between the divine and the demonic,
between elation and despondency, traces an increasing awareness that the celestial goal sought after can neither be reached
nor forgotten; and the consequent desperation constitutes at
the same time the psychological solidity of the narrative development and the forecast of its outcome. In the long illness that
follows her abandonment by Rodolphe, Emma's mystic desire to
be immersed in God's love is but the quiet preface to a final mad
attempt to pacify her gnawing unrest, which is once more given
a satanic reception when she happens to meet Léon while in
Rouen with her husband to attend an opera.

As the author comes to the last act of his drama, his mood
becomes noticeably more caustic. Part III begins with drily
humorous comments on Emma's halfhearted attempts to ward
off the advances of Léon, whose open tactics now contrast with
the timidity he had shown in Yonville. The humor expands into
sardonic laughter with the account of the seduction episode, in
which the author sends Emma and Léon on a frenzied cab ride
through the city, marking the route of their long journey by
naming some thirty-five place names in the brief space of a

couple of pages. The harshness of mood is relaxed as the lovers enjoy a few weeks of happiness, meeting each other regularly in Rouen. But it reasserts itself sharply, emerging finally with the bitterness of a cruel farce after the heroine's entanglement in indebtedness and unreliable love drives her into an unyielding trap.

In this last feverish episode of her striving, Emma is still trying in good faith to satisfy the burning desire that impels her toward transcendent attainment. She seems more reckless than ever before, and Léon wonders whence comes "this corruption almost immaterial" (384). The change, however, is not a degeneration in personality under the weight of environment, as one might expect in a typically naturalistic novel. It is, rather, a climactic development of frustration in reaction to the consciousness of failure. Even when, in a last desperate effort to raise money, Emma tries unsuccessfully to sell her attractiveness to the tax collector Binet, she does so scarcely conscious of self-debasement; and when finally she decides to commit suicide she acts in an ecstasy of heroism, silently affirming the loftiness of her desires as she approaches death, with her lips glued "to the body of the man-God." The strange force that has driven her is thus clearly associated at the end of her journey with a desire to experience the love of God. The progressively intensified frustration of this desire is the "story" of Emma Bovary.

The celestial impulse, which has been concentrated in the love of man, has operated through the instrumentality of sex. In this way, primarily, it has acquired its demonic distortion, and one cannot escape the impression that the subject of sex weighs heavily on the author's mind. We are reminded of Schopenhauer's assertion that the sexual instinct is the instrument by which illusory individuality is made to serve the interests of the species.[16] There is, certainly, a strong suggestion of Schopenhauer's outlook as regards the insatiable "striving forward in boundless space without rest and without end," [17] including the idea that the striving is meaningless. Compare, for example: "Whence came this insufficiency in life — this instantaneous

16. "Supplements" to *The World as Will and Idea*, in Schopenhauer, *Selections*, ed. De Witt H. Parker (New York: Charles Scribner's Sons, 1928), p. 337.
17. *Ibid.*, p. 92.

decay of everything on which she leant? . . . nothing, moreover, was worth the trouble of seeking it; everything was a lie" (392).[18] When the novel is viewed as a whole, however, the Schopenhauerian color appears to be only an aspect, though certainly an important one in its reinforcement of the tragic failure of a person who sought to deify the emotion of love.

Before *Madame Bovary* was begun, Flaubert pondered for some time what to write about, and a letter in 1850 to Louis Bouilhet named three possible subjects, all bearing on love and mysticism.[19] One of the subjects in particular, the account of a woman who wished to be loved by a god, clearly points to the theme of his novel. For the quest of divinity and the enjoyment of love are inseparably joined in Emma Bovary. One could say that the author stands impartially to one side and observes the rashness of a representative of the sex that readily thinks of an Adonis when in mystic mood, thereby confusing material appetites with bursts of idealistic longings.[20] In a way Flaubert is reprimanding — as Spinoza would do — the will to worship a corporeal Jehovah who manifests His divinity in corporeal form. But, although he could wholeheartedly reject a crude anthropomorphism, he could not be content with thoughts of a God who has to be comprehended in terms of Truth or Principle and who presumably can take no cognizance of human personality.[21] His unmistakable sympathy with his heroine is evidence that he himself is emotionally involved in his portrait of a person who is faced with the impossibility of deifying human sentiments. It is precisely the thought of this impossibility or — what in Flaubert's mind is the same thing — this nullification of personality that enters into the heroine's desperate striving to lift herself above the earth by the sheer force of passion. Unconsciously, in her own intensely private way,

18. Cf. also Flaubert's letter to Louise Colet, 1853 (*Corres.*, III, 403), in which he calls Emma's quest of love and happiness the devil's own invention to drive man to despair.

19. *Corres.*, II, 253.

20. "Ne voyez-vous pas qu'elles sont toutes amoureuses d'Adonis? C'est l'éternel époux qu'elles demandent," Flaubert says of women, in a letter to Mlle. Leroyer de Chantepie, Feb. 18, 1859, while speaking of idealistic impulses: *Corres.*, IV, 313.

21. There is no need to think that Flaubert's viewpoint is the same as believing in no God at all. Of Spinoza's religious view he says, "Les gens qui l'accusent d'athéisme sont des ânes": *Corres.*, II, 233.

Emma Bovary aims at the absolute; and she fails because she cannot validate the idea of an eternal self as understood in terms of human emotions. The author not only is aware of the cause of Emma's disaster, but he strongly protests against it and shares in it while depicting the grim farce of a world concept that denies human personality the right of immortality and forces the alternative of disappearance into the nothingness of inert matter.

The final chapters of the novel are especially dedicated to this protest. As Emma lies in mystic dreams upon her deathbed, she is violently reminded of vile, earthbound reality when the diseased beggar whom she had frequently seen in Rouen happens to pass by her window singing. She "raised herself like a galvanized corpse, her hair untied, her gaze fixed . . . and began to laugh, an atrocious, frenzied, despairing laugh, thinking she saw the hideous face of the poor wretch standing out against the eternal darkness like a terrifying threat" (448-49). The repulsiveness of matter is further impressed upon the reader by reference to Emma's corpse: "A kind of white dust dotted her lashes, and her eyes were beginning to disappear in a viscous pallor that resembled a thin gauze, as if spiders had spun it over . . . and it seemed to Charles that infinite masses, an enormous weight, bore down upon her" (454). Even Charles was aroused to fury by thoughts of the emptiness beyond the grave. At the funeral service he tried to force upon himself the hope of a future life in which he would see her again, but "when he thought of her lying there, and that all was over . . . he was seized with a fierce, gloomy, despairing rage" (464). When he finally discovers his wife's letters from her lovers and experiences further bitterness, he dies, an example, like his wife, of human futility. Their young daughter, who goes to live with an aunt, has to do menial labor in a factory; while Homais, a personification of superficiality, is awarded the cross of the Legion of Honor. The farcical visage of mediocrity, which throughout the novel has served as a base from which the heroine attempts to take flight, thus joins with a vacuous world of matter in mocking farewell laughter at a sensitive self-consciousness that dared in its own right to claim the recognition of Divinity.

Skepticism drives Flaubert almost to the point of visualizing a Deity, who, like Vacherot's ideal God, exists only in one's mind as a beautiful and empty symbol. But it is diverted under the force of an irrepressible mysticism into the contemplation of a real but seemingly unapproachable God, like that of Spinoza. The literary result is *Madame Bovary*, whose basic motivating idea is the unhappy thought of man's inability to experience divine reality consciously and emotionally. This feeling of exclusion from God's presence is an alternative to the pantheistic impulse that took possession of Anthony (*La Tentation de Saint Antoine*), whose urge to become one with matter has little counterpart in Emma Bovary. The latter, it is true, on one or two occasions seems impelled to seek a fusion of consciousness with all creation. On one of her visits to Rouen she looks mistily upon the city, and a "giddiness seemed to detach itself from the massed existences, and her heart swelled as if the hundred and twenty thousand souls that palpitated there had all at one time sent to her the vapor of the passions she fancied theirs. Her love grew in the presence of this vastness. . . . She poured it out upon the plazas, upon the walks . . ." (364). Though indicating a desire to feel at one with all existence, this passage expresses above all an urge to deify the passion of love. Emma's dominant attitude toward the natural world, in evidence throughout the novel, is that of an imprisoned spirit seeking to break out of bonds that close in upon her like a contracting vise.[22] The author's thoughts thus turn away from the fusion of consciousness and matter toward an immaterial Deity so far removed from matter that it has no place for human sentiments.

The contrast between these two possible interpretations of Spinoza may seem clearer if we think of the distinction between saying that all is God and saying that God is all.[23] The second statement can be taken to emphasize exclusiveness and is quite applicable to Spinoza, because in his view nature is God only in so far as it is an indivisible essence neither originated nor destroyed.[24] Hence God's reality appears to be something like an

22. Cf. Georges Poulet, "La Pensée circulaire de Flaubert," *La Nouvelle Nouvelle Revue Française*, July, 1955, pp. 30-52.
23. A writer in the *Revue de Paris*, XL (1857), 539, makes this distinction, applying the first statement to modern "naturalistic" pantheism and the second to Indian pantheism, and locating Spinoza somewhere between the two.
24. See his *Ethics*, Part I: "Of God."

impersonal mathematical truth, whose abstract perfection has no place for human passions. In bondage to these, man gains freedom only through the power of intellect over his perishable imagination, which is the source of his suffering.[25] In other words, the human being seems to be a victim of God's perfection and doomed to the nullification of what he considers his personal reality.

For Spinoza, this kind of fatality was not a misfortune, at least not as expressed in his own words, because he could behold in the God and man relationship an "infinite intellectual love" — an impersonal love, if you will — to which man can attain through intuitive knowledge.[26] Flaubert apparently appreciated the potential grandeur in Spinoza's conciliation of science and religion, and he could wholeheartedly reject a crude anthropomorphism that beheld in the supreme reality "an old fellow of a God ... who lodges his friends in the belly of whales," as Homais would say (106). But he could not achieve a satisfying interpretation of impersonality. A person as fond of his affects as he was could not be content with the thought of their exclusion from God's mind. Together with other of his contemporaries, he longed for a God whose love is an emotional experience. He could, therefore, very logically be expected to portray the suffering that derives from a will to deny, while actually believing, one of Spinoza's most suggestive and tantalizing assertions: "He who loves God cannot strive that God should love him in return." [27]

A tragedy of the finitude of personal sentiments, *Madame Bovary* stands out prominently in the vanguard of modern novels that wrestle with a unitary concept of being and interpret the implications as they pertain to individual personality. Its philosophical attunement with modern thought is found especially in its handling of the subject of human aloneness, which has become an ever-louder accompaniment to man's lack of confidence in his divine relationship. Still, its nineteenth-century marks are conspicuous in its emphasis on love and its inter-

25. See especially the *Ethics*, Part IV: "Of Human Bondage," and Part V: "Of the Power of the Intellect, or of Human Liberty."
26. *Ethics*, Part V: Propositions XXXV and XXXVI.
27. *Ethics*, Part V: Proposition XIX.

pretation, in terms of love, of the human predicament as an entrapment in the natural order.

Small wonder, then, that *Madame Bovary* should have stimulated the imagination of other nineteenth-century writers who also expressed their uneasiness with regard to human finitude and chose the sensitive self-consciousness of woman as the vehicle for an attempted celestial flight. Examples of this kinship with Flaubert could probably be found in several well-known novels of the century.[28] Of such an affinity in the case of *La Regenta*, by Leopoldo Alas, there is no doubt.

LEOPOLDO ALAS
1852-1901

One can always expect to find a greater portion of traditionalism and less outright skepticism in Spain than in France, but in the last third of the nineteenth century the intellectual climate in the two countries was very similar. During the mid-century years of 1840 to 1860, the strong Catholic reaction to the excesses of Romanticism, together with the deadening political atmosphere that characterized the reign of the incompetent Isabel II, had a stifling effect upon intellectual activity. The dull mid-century, however, was followed by a virile liberal movement which, for one thing, resulted in the overthrow of the monarchy (1868) and a brief though unsuccessful experiment with a republic and, for another thing, brought an influx of ideas from abroad. From 1868 on, Spanish interest in scientific and philosophical ideas is particularly noticeable. One has only to examine an important magazine like the *Revista de España* (1868-1895), in many ways comparable to the *Revue des Deux Mondes*, to see how closely the Spaniards were keeping up with intellectual developments in other countries. The major source of information was Paris, whence came

28. Tolstoy's *Anna Karenina* and Thomas Hardy's *The Return of the Native*, it seems to me, can be placed in this category, though as far as I know the comparison has never been made. In addition to *La Regenta*, there are several Spanish novels of the late nineteenth century that recall *Madame Bovary* in some significant way: *Genio y figura* of Juan Valera, and *La Desheredada, Tristana,* and *Realidad* of Pérez Galdós.

not only works by French writers but French translations of German and English works as well.

For a number of years preceding and following the revolution of 1868, the dominant philosophical influence in Spain was the syncretistic idealism of Karl F. C. Krause, which was espoused by Julián Sanz del Río, professor at the University of Madrid (1854-1867), after having studied for a long time in Germany. Krause was credited with supplying the formula for a unified concept of the universe that avoided the errors of both dualism and pantheism.[29] Sanz del Río, too, emphasized the necessity of clinging to a vision of oneness. His influence on the "generation of 1868" was very great, but the broad, liberalizing effect of his teachings was more instrumental in establishing a respect for philosophy in general than for any particular system,[30] and his doctrines gave ground gradually to the stancher kind of rationalism found in Kant and Hegel. The former, especially, came into prominence around 1875,[31] in association with a positivistic trend, and was blamed by the most orthodox religious believers for all the negative systems of the nineteenth century: for the "positivismo puro" of Littré, as one writer declared, the "positivismo naturalista" of Taine, and the "positivismo panteístico" of Renan and Vacherot.[32] French "materialism" (positivism)

29. Cf. Rafael Montoro, "La polémica sobre el panentheismo," *Revista Contemporánea*, V (1875), 246. Because of Krause's indebtedness to Schelling and other German idealists of the early nineteenth century, his defenders were accused of pantheism. They replied by substituting the term "panentheism," making a distinction between the beliefs that "All is God" and "All is in God": See F. de Paula Canalejas (in reply to Ramón de Campoamor), "El panentheismo," *Revista Europea*, IV (1875), 361-64, 526-32. It is interesting to observe that these discussions have to do with the same fundamental question of God's allness with which Spinoza's name was prominently associated in France in the 1850's.

30. For historical accounts of Krausism in Spain, see Pierre Jobit, *Les Educateurs de L'Espagne contemporaine* (Paris: E. de Beccard, 1936); and Juan López Morillas, *El krausismo español* (Mexico: Fondo de Cultura Económica, 1956). For a good brief discussion, see Joaquín Xirau, "Julián Sanz del Río y el krausismo," *Cuadernos Americanos*, No. 4 (1944), 55-71.

31. See Manuel de la Revilla, "El neo-Kantismo en España," *Revista de España* (hereafter referred to as *Rev. de Esp.*), XLVII (1875), 145-57; José del Perojo, "Kant y los filósofos contemporáneos," *Revista Europea*, IV (1875), 85-89; López Morillas, pp. 100 ff.

32. Nicomedes Martín Mateos, "Las corrientes filosóficas del siglo," *Rev. de Esp.*, LVI (1879), 313. Worthy of note in this connection is Eduard von Hartmann's assertion, in his preface to the ninth edition (1882) of *Philosophy of the Unconscious*; that Kant rather than Schopenhauer was the father of his pessimism.

and German rationalism were thus sharply felt in Spain and, though ardently combated by some, left definite marks on many who reluctantly surrendered some of their traditional beliefs.

Among those adversely affected by the skepticism of the time was Leopoldo Alas, who sometimes appears determined to retain the beliefs of his childhood days despite his rational inclination to doubt. Novelist, short-story writer, literary critic, and tireless contributor to periodicals, Alas was in a substantial way a reporter for a positivistic age. Prior to his appointment to a law professorship at the University of Oviedo in 1883 he had lived some ten years in Madrid, where he had studied at the university and associated with the leading intellectuals of his day. Moreover, he was a voracious reader and, although his acquaintance with the sources to which he alludes in his writings was sometimes superficial, he was well posted on many of the most influential thinkers of the nineteenth century; particularly the French, including the novelists Flaubert, Zola, Hugo, Balzac, and the critics and historians Taine, Brunetière, Renan.[33]

Some indication of Alas' uncertain orientation in an environment of skepticism can be found in his comments on Ernest Renan, for whom he felt a profound admiration. He was by no means as much of a freethinker as the Frenchman but he saw in the latter the magnanimity of a truly religious spirit combined with the sensitivity of a poet and the rational capacity of a philosopher.[34] There was no doubt a desire on his part to align with a Catholic viewpoint one of the most likable personalities of the nineteenth century. But there is also an indication of divided loyalty with regard to traditional beliefs and the liberal intellectualism of his day. For, although Alas may be considered to have been an orthodox Catholic in his later years, there was a period, in the 1870's and 1880's, when his religious faith seemed decidedly shaken.[35] Speaking of his friend Menéndez y Pelayo,

33. See William E. Bull, "Clarín's Literary Internationalism," *Hispanic Review*, XVI (1948), 321-34.
34. A combination, incidentally, which must have appealed to Flaubert, for he also spoke highly of Renan (*Corres.*, IV, 314, 339). For a good example of Alas' opinion of Renan, see "Un drama de Renan," in *Nueva campaña* (Madrid, 1887), pp. 375-76.
35. See Albert Brent, *Leopoldo Alas and "La Regenta"* (Columbia, Mo., The University of Missouri Studies, XXIV, No. 2, 1951), 74; Marino Gómez-Santos, "Sobre la religiosidad de Leopoldo Alas y sus evoluciones,"

he says (in 1881), "Menéndez y Pelayo is a traditionalist, a 'hard-bitten' Catholic; I am almost a demagogue, and *in matters of religion* — mine is *the natural* kind." [36] An allowance must be made for a certain mischievous pose of skepticism in the youth-ful writings of Alas,[37] but it is undoubtedly true that he experi-enced a religious conflict and it is probable that he found in Renan an optimistic enactment of his own problem.[38] He would not discard his Catholic beliefs, but he could admire — and perhaps he secretly envied — one who, like Renan, was able to maintain an enthusiastic attitude toward life in the face of a growing materialism.

What must have caused Alas considerable concern, at least enough to elicit his protest, were the gloomy implications of developments in the natural sciences: man's seeming insignifi-cance in a vast universe, the finiteness of his destiny, the ultimate disappearance of the human species in accord with the laws of natural selection; and with all this, the positivistic dependence on the testimony of the senses and the rejection of metaphysical objectives. Alas expresses these sentiments in an article (1876) on Emilio Castelar, which is worthy of being quoted at some length since it not only reveals the young writer's own state of mind but also reports on the intellectual climate in Spain at that time:

This youth which is growing up in Spain today, eager for intel-lectual exercise, almost ashamed of our scientific backwardness, seeks, with more zeal than discernment, after new theories, the last word of science.... Positivism, or what is popularly re-garded as such, that aggregate of theories which, perhaps con-tradictory among themselves, agree with each other in rejecting the possibility of all science of the absolute and any communi-cation with the metaphysical, is gradually gaining ground among

---

in *Leopoldo Alas, "Clarín"* (Oviedo: Instituto de Estudios Asturianos del Patronato José María Quadrado, 1952), chapter 3.

36. Translated from *Solos de Clarín* (4th ed.; Madrid, 1891), p. 29.

37. Cf. W. E. Bull's observation ("The Liberalism of Leopoldo Alas," *Hispanic Review*, X [1942], 332) that Alas' calling himself a freethinker was "a sophistic gesture to confound his opponents"; also Gómez-Santos (*Leopoldo Alas, "Clarín,"* p. 146) to the effect that Alas donned the Krausist philosophical garb to keep up with the styles.

38. Cf. Carlos Claverías, " 'Clarín' y Renan," in *Cinco estudios de litera-tura española moderna* (Salamanca: Colegio Trilingüe de la Universidad, Consejo Superior de Investigaciones Científicas, 1945), p. 42.

us, and even those who began their philosophical studies in the most exaggeratedly idealistic schools are now looking for agreement and relations with that experimentalist tendency which threatens to become universal ... humanity inhabits the infinite. .... This belief comes down to earth: we are worms, we are told, of this planet; and our ephemeral lot is joined with the soil as though we were slaves to lumps of dirt. The human heart, then, on feeling that its wings are cut, on hearing in the name of science the terrible prediction "you will not fly," looks with sadness at the heavens; and in the stars, those promises of eternity, sees only sarcasm ... another great dejection is common among us also: most people think that our race is dying. Every day we hear of historical fatality, of the laws of selection.[39]

Alas was not of a disposition that would enable him to make an optimistic adjustment to doubts, such as a person like Renan could make. On the contrary, there was in his personality an element of bitterness that antagonized others and darkened his own outlook. An introvert, aloof from people in general, and scornful of mediocrity, he had much in common with Flaubert, including a kind of mystic yearning for suprahuman attainment. *La Regenta*, the work for which he is most remembered, is permeated with social acerbity but, of greater significance, it possesses an underlying metaphysical unrest that provides it with a philosophical base. It is a forceful example of an unhappy adjustment to skepticism, in which a disillusioning vision of nature — in the form of love, specifically — is colored with religious austerity.

La Regenta (1884)

Choosing as a setting the city of Oviedo (giving it the fictional name of Vetusta), the author builds up an oppressive environment of mediocrity and places in its midst a sensitive and refined woman who longs for liberation and wants above all to be loved. In general outline, then, *La Regenta* plainly recalls *Madame Bovary*, and there is little question that Alas had Flaubert's novel in mind when he mapped the basic framework of his narrative. He was writing, however, at a time when the real-

39. Translated from *Solos de Clarín*, pp. 90-93.

istic technique was at its height in popularity, and he indulged in an elaborate use of detail and collateral material, showing a greater interest than Flaubert in the relationship between environment and personality. In other ways, too, he engaged in a more ambitious task than Flaubert had undertaken. For one thing, he was interested in painting on a grand scale the portrait of an urban society in a materialistic age,[40] and the sharpness of his satirical mood indicates how strong a motivation his antipathies were. In a leisurely, deliberate manner he presents numerous personal sketches that emphasize the trivial interests of almost everyone, including the clerics. The attention given to the activities of the numerous minor personages is so great that the community itself appears at times to be the protagonist, and has been so designated.[41] In a further ambitious move, Alas introduces a second major character, a priest, to share with the heroine the burden of the narrative development. The subjects of religion and love are in this way brought into specific relationship. The scope of *La Regenta* is therefore broader and the technique less concentrated and precise than we find in *Madame Bovary*, but the fundamental ideas in each novel center on essentially the same subject: the heaviness of the material world and the failure of love as a means of liberation.[42]

As the narrative begins, the reader is introduced to Don Fermín de Pas, *magistral*, or "master," of the Cathedral of Vetusta and the most powerful ecclesiastic in the city. A man of great strength, both physical and intellectual, he has gained his influential position at the early age of thirty-five by dint of hard work and a grim determination to erase the unpleasantness of his poor and obscure peasant origin. His ambitious drive has

40. The urban society happens to be provincial but, as is also true in *Madame Bovary*, provincialism is subordinate to a broader range of human mediocrity.
41. Albert Brent, p. 25.
42. The resemblance of *La Regenta* to *Madame Bovary* has long been recognized. A few years after his novel was published, Alas was recklessly accused of plagiarism by one of his countrymen: Luis Bonafoux y Quintero, *Yo y el plagiario Clarín* (Madrid, 1888). Since then various similarities have been discussed, though little has been said of the philosophical outlook in the novels. Since I am interested primarily in this aspect, I shall make no special effort to point out resemblances in plot and situation. A number of these will, in any case, no doubt be obvious to those familiar with both novels. For a discussion of the subject, see Carlos Claverías, "Flaubert y *La Regenta*," in *Cinco estudios...*, pp. 11-28.

been reinforced and in good part directed by a mother of iron will whose compensation for an insecure place in society has been even more fierce than that of her son. De Pas feels a proprietary pride in his ecclesiastic command of Vetusta, ancient city of noble and honored past, but the loneliness and lack of affection that darkened his childhood persist with an intensity that can be pacified only by a woman's love. Sexual satisfaction alone will not suffice; the servant Teresina is available for that. Nor can De Pas be interested in an ordinary woman of high society, such as the frolicsome widow Obdulia, who was "exaggeratedly endowed by nature with the attributes of her sex" (I, 38),[43] and who throws herself at men acquaintances, priests and laymen alike. Rather, he scorns the commonplace, holds himself aloof from the gossipy, envious clerics around him, and aspires to a companionship that will allow him to realize his emotional self at the highest possible level. The opportunity for such a companionship arises when the aged Don Cayetano withdraws as the confessor of Ana Ozores and recommends De Pas as his replacement.

The characterization of De Pas is from the outset a solid psychological portraiture and an excellent example of modern realism that takes into account the relationship between personality and environment while observing fully the special features that make the person stand out as an individual. The author is less fortunate in the portrayal of his heroine, apparently because he is less able — possibly less inclined — to measure than to cauterize the ethereal nature of her aspirations. Nevertheless, he relies on the contrast between her idealistic impulses and her material medium as the basis for his story. Ana Ozores is an aristocratic person, beautiful, refined, of spotless reputation. Like De Pas, she suffers the effects of a lonely youth devoid of affection. For she had never known a mother and had been left for the greater part of her childhood in the care of a hostile governess, whose major contribution had been to impress on the child an indelible sense of guilt for having on one occasion unavoidably spent the night in a boat on a river with a boy of

43. Numerals in parentheses (from here to end of chapter) refer to volume and page of the edition of *La Regenta* published in Madrid by Librería de Fernando Fe, 1900. Translations are my own.

twelve when they were unable to make their way back to shore. In her lonely adolescent years she withdrew into herself and sometimes, in a feverish physical state, felt strange mystic longings that caused her more uneasiness than peace, confused as she was by thoughts of the sinfulness of sex and the relationship of love and beauty to the idea of God. Receiving little sympathy from her aunts, with whom she lived after her father's death, she drifted into marriage with the ex-judge, Don Victor Quintanar, an upright and kind person but some twenty-five years her senior, rather careless in his appearance, and more alert to details pertaining to hunting than to the emotional — and sexual — needs of his wife.

Married to a neglectful husband and having no child on whom to lavish affection, Ana is lonely and bored, oppressed by the gloom of the Vetusta climate, and unable to find anything in common with the trivial acquaintances in her social circle. As she had done in her childhood, she caresses the pillows of her bed, feeling voluptuous pleasure in the touch of cold sheets and soft rugs, and daring now and then to think of the physically attractive Don Alvaro Mesía, skilled Don Juan of Vetusta. But the sense of guilt resulting from the boat episode of her childhood weighs on her still, and she lives in constant restraint of her natural impulses. Though rebellious at times, she actually increases her self-discipline to the point of taking a martyr's delight in it, determined to resist the threat to her soul, which "was beginning to become infested" with the perfume of love left by the proximity of Mesía. Torn thus between spontaneous emotional-physical demands and the necessity for moral restraint, she is especially amenable to the thought of converting carnal love into spiritual love under the direction of the *magistral*, De Pas.

As the author brings the two principal characters together, then, he has prepared the way for a relationship that could become a tense psychological experience centering on an attempted sublimation of human love. Both persons are suffering from the absence of love, both are oppressed by the mediocrity of their surroundings, and each sees in the other an opportunity to rise above the immediacy of their prosaic existence. Hence the personal relationship which the author places in the forefront points to a struggle on the part of two people to liberate themselves from the bondage of circumstances by way of a Platonic partnership. In Ana's case the conflict will be essentially an effort to divert the demands of erotic instinct into an abstract mystic channel with the aid of a priest who, because of his profession, causes her no temptation in a physical sense. In the case of De Pas, the conflict will be more complicated. For in his burning desire to make Ana his exclusive spiritual possession there is a strong carnal attraction which he has to suppress, not only in deference to his profession but in bitter concession to the fact that Ana is not interested in him as a lover and is, instead, physically attracted to Mesía, the Don Juan. Conspiring against both persons are numerous gossipy "friends," a low level of moral values, and above all a social atmosphere redolently suggestive of carnal love. In this way support from the outside is assured for the interference of the third party, Mesía; and before the prospects of this uneven contest the reader finds himself pulling for De Pas to win. The latter, at least, is a man of flesh and blood, a troubled soul of complex emotions; while Mesía is merely a hollow symbol embodying little more than sartorial correctness and pride in the conquest of women.

The lurking presence of the third party tends to convert a potential drama of character into a contest for the favors of a woman, whose designation of a winner soon assumes more plot interest than the resolution of psychological complications. Ana wavers between the two men somewhat like a feather tossed to and fro by the wind, aspiring under the priest's tutelage to a mystic refinement of love and regarding her sensuous impulses toward Mesía as temptations befitting a test of her ability to achieve her exalted aim. Unfortunately, she tends more to caress the temptation than to nourish the aim, and her honest efforts to curb her physical impulses repeatedly produce in her a psychophysiological cycle that traces a predominantly physical path.

A brief summary of chapters 16 to 19, inclusive, will illustrate this cyclical process, which constitutes the author's "psychological" method. Lonely, oppressed by the gloomy weather, pondering the monotony of her existence, Ana is inclined to forget the careful coaching of the *magistral*, feeling, rather, the

strong pull of nature toward a danger that religion has somehow seemed unable to cope with. When Mesía happens to pass
her balcony one day on a fine white charger, she is more desirous than ever of enjoying life and justifies her mental waywardness in the light of her unhappy past and her boredom in
Vetusta. Encouraged by her husband and Mesía, now a welcome
visitor in the Quintanars' home, she attends a performance of
Zorrilla's *Don Juan Tenorio*, which she watches with a sensuous
delight faintly refined by mystic sentiments. As she thus nears
entrapment by a calculating Don Juan who needs only a pro-
pitious occasion to claim his prey, her sensuous deviation is
brusquely interrupted by her spiritual adviser. De Pas is angry
with his protégée for having gone to the theater on All Saints'
Day without his permission, but he controls himself and sets
about patiently trying to win her back to a religious path. Ana
dutifully follows his directions, even accompanying him in
some of his charitable enterprises. But neither charity nor the
recommended religious readings provide the "poetic" experience that she longs for, and, confused and frustrated, she ends up
by falling ill. Her husband watches over her solicitously for a
while but misinterprets, or disregards, the sexual import of her
nervous state and leaves her to tearful reflection on the cruelty
of a world without love. When after a relapse and a long illness
she recovers she accedes again to the ministrations of De Pas,
who continues to be a counterbalance to the routine of the
drawing room and the attentions of Mesía.

The drama of stifled, sex-laden love, which is thus enacted in
the heroine is really more of a situational than a psychological
conflict. It is, in fact, a tug of war between two men for a
woman, who acts as a kind of physiological barometer indicating
the fluctuating influences of the rivals. The Ana-De Pas relationship reaches an idyllic peak in the summer following Ana's long
illness. Continually the *magistral* has conducted himself with an
excruciating self-discipline, curbing his rebelliousness at the
domination of his mother, at the restrictions of his profession in
general, and particularly at the necessity for refraining from
open conflict with an insignificant rival, whom he could easily
vanquish in either physical or intellectual combat. Now, for a
short time during the summer, when both his mother and Mesía

are out of the city, he enjoys the luxury of freedom at home and the pleasantness of a peaceful relationship with his spiritual partner. The happy situation, however, is sharply disturbed by Mesía's return, and under the tension of the renewed contest De Pas makes the mistake of disclosing his love to Ana. Revolted at first, Ana feels compassion for her religious adviser and forcibly increases her zealousness, going to the extreme of walking barefoot in an Easter procession, only to react against this excessive display of self-punishment by an indulgence in the pleasures of a gay house party at the country estate of friends. Here, in an atmosphere of frivolity and pent-up sexual passion, the priest's rival has a tremendous advantage. After an episode in which De Pas is made to look somewhat ridiculous as he searches madly in the woods for Ana and Mesía, the attraction of the latter becomes irresistible. On the very last night of her stay in the country Ana finds herself alone with Mesía on a dark balcony. At last the *tenorio* has found the long-awaited coincidence of mood and circumstance.

The outcome of the tug of war, of course, has from its beginning been a foregone conclusion, discernible from obvious hints and especially from the repeated postponements of the decision. The author, in fact, has conducted a prolonged cat-and-mouse game which, for its continuous sameness, seriously taxes the reader's patience. That he has thus allowed the psychological quality of his story to become obscured by the elements of satire and suspense in a long drawn-out situational plot can be considered a technical weakness. Our complaint becomes less severe, however, when we realize that the narrative method is designed to enhance the farcical aspects not only of the local social scene but of life in general. The laughable features, therefore, belong to the life described and not to the description itself. For it is the author's intention to burden his heroine with the crassness of her situation; and in carrying out his plan he indulges in his own self-punishment, deriving a certain bittersweet pleasure from displaying the cruelty of a world in which love is either missing or debased. One cannot help remembering in this connection the circumstances, grim and farcical at the same time, attending Emma Bovary's love experiences. Probably the major distinction between *La Regenta* and *Madame*

Bovary, to be found not so much in theme as in literary manner, lies in the preponderance (in the Spanish novel) of the comic element over the tragic — a fundamental distinction between the Spanish and the French literary genius.

This important difference, however, should not cause us to overlook the deep-lying similarity between the two novelists' motivations. As in *Madame Bovary*, the concluding section of the Spanish novel leaves a heavy impression of the meanness of the flesh and the futility of human aspiration. For a while after her surrender Ana experiences an ecstasy of physical love, becoming ever bolder in her relations with her lover. But De Pas, now consumed with anger and a desire for vengeance, contrives to reveal the love affair to Ana's husband, thus driving him to a duel and to his death. With the resultant scandal, the city of Vetusta turns against Ana. The women who have envied her beauty and reputation now gloat over her shame, and the typical reaction in her social circle is to condemn her for letting the situation get out of hand. "Nauseating," says the Marqués de Vegallana, who "kept in a country village all his illegitimate children" (II, 580). Thus deserted by almost everyone, including Mesía, who has fled to Madrid, Ana begins to think again about religion, and one day goes to the cathedral, hoping to gain the pardon of De Pas. The latter, still burning with the anger of frustration, rebuffs her in bitter silence, refraining with difficulty from striking her. As she lies on the floor after fainting, a sordid acolyte happens by and with lascivious impulse kisses her lips. She awakens, thinking she has felt "on her mouth the cold viscous belly of a toad" (II, 592).

The author thus concludes his story with emphasis on the wretchedness of the human situation after having followed the efforts of two people to rise above it via the idealization of love. The long tug of war has been, after all, only a means of displaying the human predicament. A lonely woman, unhappy in her marital relations, has tried in vain to convert erotic impulse into an intellectualized experience, only to be vicitimized by the bestiality of sex. Sharing with her the futility of this intellectual and aesthetic endeavor is the priest, himself wholly unable to disregard the physiology of love. And surrounding both of them is a hostile aggregate of humanity that looms like a diabolical conspirator breathing triviality and lasciviousness. The feeling of frustration, which has permeated the main narrative action and the psychology of the two principal characters, acquires in the end a climactic bitterness that underscores the tragic farce of an attempted exaltation of love. The final impact of the story thus recalls *Madame Bovary*. The similarity, of course, does not mean necessarily that Alas imitated Flaubert, but simply that he chose a basically similar problem as subject and followed it to its logical conclusion.

The particular kind of frustrated idealism found in *La Regenta*, which is inseparably linked with the question of a divine recognition of human love,[44] can best be appreciated by thinking of a naturalistic philosophy colored with an ecclesiastical viewpoint that underscores the sinful aspects of love. Two considerations seem especially appropriate. If nature and God are one, the One recognizes only animal love and hence looks indifferently upon any attempt to idealize it into a fine sentiment suggestive of the word "divine." If God is independent of nature, He opposes human passions and chastises the human impulse to deify them. Both views, separately or together, exclude aesthetic and spiritual values from the concept of love.

The character portrayal of the heroine in *La Regenta* is particularly indicative, for it is in large degree a physical analysis in which sex satisfaction is the chief personality need. In this respect Alas was following naturalistic trends in the novel, possibly influenced by Zola, whom he greatly admired. *La Regenta* is, in fact, commonly considered one of the foremost examples of naturalism in Spain and may properly be so regarded if we think of the author's preoccupation with the heaviness of the natural world. As regards the fundamental question of relationship between environment and personality, however, it is scarcely more naturalistic than *Madame Bovary*; for Ana is neither a product of her environment nor a degeneration because of it. She is the victim of an irrepressible urge to love and be loved, which is only superficially explained by the absence of love in

44. There is always the probability that Alas' personal experiences had something to do with the feeling of frustration so noticeable in his novel (see Albert Brent, pp. 80 ff.), but we must remember that frustration is inherent in the intellectual atmosphere in which the novel is situated, just as it is in the case of *Madame Bovary*.

her childhood.[45] Alas nevertheless occupies himself with physiology much more than Flaubert does, and his technique of portraiture reminds one at times of a clinical study that attaches great importance to the close relationship between the physical and the psychical. In this particular he reflects the prominence of an interest in physiological psychology, which was probably the most widely discussed scientific subject at the time *La Regenta* was written.

In view of the tendency in scientific circles to identify "soul" with the activity of the brain and nerve centers, it is understandable that one as alert to current intellectual trends as Alas should be affected to the point of depicting the suppression of love's sentimental and aesthetic aspects. Such a depiction, however, is carried out in a spirit of protest, and the protest is enacted in the heroine. Though falling prey to animal instinct, Ana wanted to believe, like Emma Bovary, in a divine love big enough to embrace all creation: "love for all men and all creatures — for birds and beasts, for the grasses of the field and the worms of the earth" (II, 289).[46] That she had in mind at the same time a personalized kind of love can be seen from her desire to believe that "God was in heaven presiding over and loving His marvelous work, the universe; the Son of God had been born on earth and for this honor and divine proof of affection the entire world was gladdened and ennobled" (II, 289). The fact that Ana's mystic longings are more obscured by carnal desires than is the case with Emma Bovary means simply that the delusiveness of sex, which is an unmistakable idea in Flaubert's novel, is given more space by the Spaniard.

The notion that love is merely a delusion working in the service of a "life force" was an attitude superimposed on biology by philosophy, and we should keep in mind that Schopenhauer and Von Hartmann were much discussed around 1880, in Spain as elsewhere. Some of Von Hartmann's remarks, in essential agreement with Schopenhauer, are relevant in the present connection; particularly his assertions to the effect that love is an

45. W. E. Bull rightly calls attention to the nondeterministic psychological method of Alas: "The Naturalistic Theories of Leopoldo Alas," *PMLA*, LVII (1942), 536-51.
46. Cf. the somewhat pantheistic passage quoted above (p. 65) from *Madame Bovary*.

evil to be endured for the sake of perpetuating the race: "The goal of the demon, then, is really and truly nothing but sexual satisfaction, and with a particular individual, and everything therewith, as harmony of soul, adoration, admiration, is only weak and false show, or it is something else, something next door to love." [47] In the realm of self-conscious individuality, an aversion arises to sexual union as being "inadequate to the infinity of longing and hope, and unworthy of the unapproachable sublimity of the dreamt ideal." (I, 232). But, as Von Hartmann reminds us, alluding to Schopenhauer, the instinct of love performs its function as a "deceptive bait, by means of which the Unconscious deludes conscious *egoism*, and leads to the sacrifice of self-love in favor of the succeeding generation, which conscious reflection could never effect by itself" (I, 234). Von Hartmann's assertions take on a tone of harshness as he speaks further of the wretched consequences of love in general — the betrayals and sufferings, the bitterness and degradation associated with it (III, 33 ff.); and though he would admit to being neither a Christian nor an ascetic, his attitude reminds one of asceticism when he lapses into an emotional discussion of sex.

Whether or not Alas was influenced by Von Hartmann,[48] it is of interest to observe the parallel in which a philosopher, who called on the sciences, especially physiology, to support his theory, and a novelist, who showed respect for the sciences, assume an attitude toward love which harmonizes with a religious view that looks upon sexual enjoyment as sinful. Assuming that Alas was adversely affected by the implications of modern science, and was at the same time determined to cling to some kind of religious belief, he could logically be expected to make an adjustment by way of ascetic austerity. To such an

47. Eduard von Hartmann, *Philosophy of the Unconscious*, trans. William Chatterton Coupland (London, 1893), I, 231. References in this paragraph are to this edition.
48. The following articles discussing Von Hartmann and the philosophy and the psychology of the unconscious are typical of the kind of literature that Alas could hardly have failed to see: Guillermo Graell, "El pesimismo. Hartmann, su sistema filosófico, religioso y moral," *Rev. de Esp.*, LIX (1879), 327-55; Alfred Fouillée, "La Vie consciente et la vie inconsciente d'après la nouvelle psychologie scientifique," *Revue des Deux Mondes*, LIX (1883), 879-906. The *Philosophy of the Unconscious* was not translated into Spanish before *La Regenta* was written but it did appear in French in 1877 (see Lorenz, *Catalogue de la librairie française*, 1876-1885).

unhappy compromise position he seems to have been driven, judging from *La Regenta*. For his heroine is trapped between asceticism and an urge to dignify her natural state with an aura of divinity. The idea of sinfulness in the relation between male and female, which was impressed on her in her childhood at the time of the boat incident, is combated by a constant desire to find, on the part of a "natural, affectionate, artistic religion," the sanction of "the profane emotions of love, of youthful joy" (II, 289).[49] But she is forced to believe instead that life is all vanity and wretchedness, a view which she would be willing to accept if she could only visualize her distress in terms of beauty and emotion, unsoiled by "the prose and falsity and evil" of the world (II, 4). Her husband, also, in his unhappiness over her infidelity, is driven to reflection on the wretchedness of life, recalling declarations of Thomas à Kempis on the necessity for suffering and mortification (II, 529). Yet he affirms that nature is beautiful when free of the baseness imposed on it by man. It is as though the doctrine of original sin were merged with the theory of man's animal origin.

The attempt to sublimate nature thus becomes resignation to suffering, from which the artist, like his heroine, tries to extract the poetry befitting the lofty aim.[50] The author's satirical, moralistic tone is the rougher aspect of this bittersweetness,[51] which

49. In Alas' early compositions one can detect a preoccupation with the conflict between spontaneity and religious austerity, expressed with a mild rebelliousness couched in youthful impishness. For example, in the brief fantasy *El diablo en Semana Santa* (published in *Solos de Clarín* in 1881), the devil interrupts a solemn worship in a cathedral, producing an outburst of hilarity, much to the relief of everyone, including a judge's wife and the *magistral* of the cathedral, the first shadowy sketches of Ana Ozores and Fermín de Pas. The novelist's maturer writings in various places reveal his inclination to glorify suffering and death in the name of religion; cf. W. E. Bull, "The Liberalism of Leopoldo Alas," *Hispanic Review*, X (1942), 334, in particular reference to *Un discurso* (1891). *La Regenta* can be considered the first major manifestation of this austerity.

50. In this connection we should remember that Flaubert also had a certain ascetic strain in his outlook. The evidence is found not only in an impression of the sharp bittersweetness of suffering in *Madame Bovary*, but also in Flaubert's correspondence. Note the following: "Il arrive un moment où l'on a besoin de se faire souffrir, de haïr sa chair, de lui jeter de la boue au visage, tant elle vous semble hideuse. Sans l'amour de la forme, j'eusse été peut-être un grand mystique" (to Louise Colet, Dec. 27, 1852: *Corres.*, III, 77). Alas was less able than Flaubert to hammer his asceticism into the cool impersonality of literary form.

51. A revealing expression of Alas' "ascetic-aesthetic naturalism," clothed in a mellowness that contrasts with the sharpness of *La Regenta*, is found

envelops the total narrative development in an expression of disappointment at not being able to validate the concept of love as a pleasurable, poetic sentiment by making it an attribute of the Supreme Being. The basic problem dramatized in La Regenta, therefore, seems unmistakably to be the human desire for a personal and sympathetic relationship with Deity. The problem is complicated, if not actually created, by the tendency in science and philosophy to emphasize the impersonal. Alas says of his heroine: "Perhaps this was the profoundest part of Ana's religious faith; she believed in God's direct, open, and individual attention to the acts of her life, to her destiny, to her pains and pleasures" (II, 28). This, at least, is the belief that Ana wants to embrace in the face of a skepticism that has originated she knows not where, perhaps in childhood while in the company of her father, a freethinker who associated with "philosophers" and scientists (II, 109). Science and reason, the author indicates, have led to the replacement of a benevolent Father by an unfeeling, indifferent Power. Defeat thus leaves Ana in a state of sickening helplessness and De Pas in a mood of bitter resentment. Both are victims of a "universal indifference" which, as De Pas feels (II, 541), envelops all things and all people.

It is appropriate here to recall the quotation from the *Revista de España* (1870) given above (p. 58) in connection with our discussion of *Madame Bovary*, referring to the concept of a God who, in the isolation of His own perfection, is shut off from human affections. In the immediate background of *La Regenta* the ghost of Spinoza still seems to haunt the popular imagination, imbued more than ever with a suggestion of divine impassivity. With an expression of bitterness even more trenchant than that of Flaubert, Alas captures a mood befitting the vision of an indifferent Deity. The modernity of Flaubert's novel, it

---

in the following comment on Zola's *La Terre:* "Después de leer la última página de *La Tierra* de Zola, quedó mi espíritu, este pobre espíritu de que hoy no se atreve a hablar muchos, por vergüenza, dulce y tristemente impresionado. Eso que podría llamarse lo bello doloroso, fecundo fermento formado con miles de esperanzas e ilusiones disueltas, podridas, germen de una vaga aspiración humilde, en mi sentir *cristiana*, a lo menos cristiana según el cristianismo de la agonía sublime de la cruz; esa tristeza estética, eterno *dilettantismo* de las almas hondamente religiosas, era el último y más fuerte aroma que se desprendía de aquel libro..." (*Ensayos y revistas* [Madrid, 1892], p. 31).

will no doubt be agreed, is particularly impressive at the present time; for Emma's anguish at being cut off from God's "personal" attention is fundamentally similar to the anxiety underlying the twentieth-century existentialist estrangement from Being. The same observation is not so clearly applicable to *La Regenta*, probably because Alas' metaphysics is less pointed in its implications and more complicated by religious attitudes. Nevertheless, the major dramatic force of Alas' novel originates in a conception of an impassive God out of reach of human love. The Spaniard bitterly scorns mass humanity while chastising himself, even more openly than Flaubert, with thoughts of the nullification of individual personality. The impression of cruelty in his novel, in fact, reminds one not only of Zola's naturalism but of certain twentieth-century novels in which Divinity is converted into an unfeeling — and terrifying — Force (see chapter 8).

4

The Deification of Unconscious Process

Emile Zola   Emilia Pardo Bazán
Vicente Blasco Ibáñez

ÉMILE ZOLA
1840-1902

FLAUBERT AND ALAS, who were antagonized and chilled by the materialistic trends of their epochs, reflect the impact of scientific developments in a general rather than a specific way. They represent what may be called the initial thuds of nineteenth-century skepticism, characterized by an essentially static visualization of the problems raised by science. Although Alas was clearly attentive to the contemporary emphasis on physiological psychology, his character analysis is actually restricted to the stationary situation of people trapped in a feeling of dispiritment. With the writers now to be discussed, Zola and Pérez Galdós especially, we witness a dynamic engagement of the characters in the life process as seen from the viewpoint of the life sciences.

The naturalism demonstrated by Zola made a great impression on a few Spanish novelists, among them Pardo Bazán and Blasco Ibáñez, because of its literary vigor; and they followed his lead primarily because of his strong artistic appeal. In discussing these writers, therefore, one must not forget that the naturalistic thought discernible in their works is in a sense borrowed. In the case of Galdós we face an entirely different situation; he rises independently of Zola, speaking for a different kind of naturalism and standing in a category by himself in Spain in the last quarter of the nineteenth century. It is true that he occasionally exhibits some of the marks of Zola's literary manner, such as the description of crude physical and moral conditions. But his naturalistic philosophy stands out in bold competition with Zola's, even though it too is closely related to the implications of scientific developments. Today, as we look back on the nineteenth century, these two novelists appear to us as literary giants exemplifying parallel yet contrasting channels of thought. An examination of the intellectual perspective of each should be, indirectly, a valuable commentary on the philosophical outlook of the other.

Physiology and psychology are unquestionably the two fields of scientific inquiry most closely related to the novel in the second half of the nineteenth century. Chronologically first, as an experimental science, physiology at one and the same time forced metaphysical psychology into disrepute and laid down conditions for the experimental psychology that was to replace it. The physiological emphasis made a great impression on man's imagination, particularly in reference to the question of human personality as visualized in unity with physical processes. The inseparability of body and soul, which by the middle of the century had become a predominant belief in scientific circles, seems to have had the effect of causing "soul" gradually to fade into "body" and hence to lose some of its most valued connotations. The course of man's thoughts on the subject may be sketched as follows: Soul is not something independent of the body; it is mind. Mind is not a substance apart from the brain and the nervous system; it is simply their total functioning and is known as consciousness. Self-consciousness, or the sense of personality, is merely an extension of consciousness to the point of rational understanding and is therefore a subordinate part or appendage. Having no status except as belonging to a total field of consciousness, the self is destined, paradoxically, to continuity in an unconscious state. The soul thus ends up in the realm of the unconscious.

This odyssey of modern man's soul, which in the novel of the twentieth century has acquired a heavy vestment of abstractness, bore in the day of literary realism deep imprints of attention to the bodily substratum of mind. The scientific background of the biological emphasis may be visualized as an inclined plane seen in evolutionary perspective rising from inorganic matter to the higher faculties of intellect. Herbert Spencer, while granting that there may be a primordial element of consciousness, something akin to a nervous shock, explains mental evolution as a graded compounding of these units of shock, similar to the action of molecules carrying their individual rhythms into higher compounds. Progressive mental integration parallels and corresponds always to a redistribution of matter and motion.[1] Taine, following English psychologists as well as Condillac, offers a similar exposition of mind, stating it to be a chain of sensations which can be objectively comprehended either as a group of molecular movements or as a bundle of nervous vibrations.[2] He reduces all knowledge and all ideas to the association of sensations in accord with physiological doctrine and views the human as well as the animal individual as a system of relationships or "liaisons constantes," not as some mysterious entity called "soul."[3] Théodule Ribot, also in the same school of thought as Taine and Spencer, holds that consciousness is merely an accompaniment of nervous activity and that memory itself is primarily biological and only accidentally a psychological fact.[4]

In short, around 1870 psychology was but a chapter in the broader field of physiology, and the individual soul was taken to be nothing more than an ensemble of cerebral and nervous functions.[5] A psychologist-philosopher like Spencer would not presume to place either of the dual aspects of consciousness, physical and psychical, above the other in importance; but it

1. *The Principles of Psychology* (3rd ed.; New York and London, n.d.), I, 150-56, 186-90. First ed., 1855.

2. *De l'Intelligence* [1870] (18th ed.; Paris: Librairie Hachette, n.d.), pp. 5, 7.

3. *Ibid.*, pp. 274, 330, 348-50. This concept of the individual is apparently what Taine considers his own contribution; he had made a similar argument in reference to "la force vitale" in *Les Philosophes français du xix* siècle* (1857), pp. 68, 319.

4. See Alfred Fouillée, "La Survivance et la sélection des idées dans la mémoire," *Revue des Deux Mondes*, LXIX (1885), 357-89 (hereafter referred to as *RDM*).

5. Cf. Victor Egger, "La Physiologie cérébrale et la psychologie," *RDM*, XXIV (1877), 193.

is easy to see how the dominant trend in psychology produced an impression of materialism in the popular mind. It was so regarded by the more idealistically inclined of the physiological psychologists themselves, among them Wilhelm Wundt, who granted the reflective capacity of the mind, by which the self gains its status, a position demanding the dignification of reason. Psychologists in general, however, kept their attention focused on the sensory basis of mentality. It had been demonstrated by experiment that the mind's functioning is not controlled by a single headquarters located, as Descartes supposed, in a specific part of the brain; and it had been easy to go a step further and extend the seat of mental activity over the entire body. Such a broadening of the physical base of mind had the effect of removing man's reflective faculty from a classification of special privilege. Moreover, Kant's influence still contributed toward undermining confidence in the purely rational powers of mind. The dominant tendency in the third quarter of the nineteenth century, therefore, was to emphasize the concept of consciousness in the broadest possible sense, making it more or less synonymous with life. This was equivalent to glorifying the subrational realm of being wherein man and animal are essentially the same.

With the psyche thus virtually identified with the total organism, the problem of personality was primarily a biological subject, more appropriately discussed from the standpoint of vitalism as opposed to mechanism than from the standpoint of spiritualism and materialism. For the believers in mechanism, the sense of personality was simply a state of equilibrium, a unity of composition, about the same in a man as in a cat.[6] In opposition to this conception of personality as being ruled by physicochemical laws, the vitalist biologists proclaimed the idea of an organizing principle or creative force present in the body and distinguishing it from a machine. Early in the century vitalists (Bichat, Cuvier, Müller) supposed the vital force to be separate from and antagonistic to the physical properties of the body,[7] subscribing in this respect to the predominantly dualistic

6. Cf. Comte: *La Philosophie positive* (résumé par Emile Rigolage), II, 279.
7. A. Dastre, *La Vie et la mort* (Paris, n.d.), pp. 18-25.

perspective of the eighteenth century. Later vitalists insisted on the harmonious union, or co-operation, of physical and mental processes, declaring the entire organism to be the "seat" or the fact of unity. Such, for example, were E. Chauffard (*La Vie,* 1878) and the very influential Claude Bernard, whose "physicochemical vitalism" was claimed by mechanistic philosophy and vitalism alike. Bernard, who refused to be concerned about the conflict between spiritualism and materialism, sharply rejected the assumption that some mysterious entity inhabited the body and opposed physical laws. He argued that the phenomena of consciousness and intelligence, with which the idea of "soul" is associated, are the ordinary phenomena of life resulting from the brain's functioning.[8] Yet, not satisfied completely with a physicochemical explanation of life, he granted (in his *Introduction à l'étude de la médecine expérimentale,* 1865) the necessity for an *idée créatrice* or *force vitale,* which he also called *force organisatrice, idée directrice, idée vitale.* It was recognized by Bernard's contemporaries that his determinism does not exclude "mind" from the intrinsic properties of nature [9] nor preclude the possibility that the organizing thought principle works toward an end.[10] But the "end" which is allowable in the views of such vitalists as Chauffard and Bernard is not necessarily consciously sought. It is, instead, rather vaguely conceived as an all-enveloping abstract principle of life, to which all particular organisms are subject.

The shift of the argument between materialism and spiritualism to an argument between mechanism and vitalism has the effect of clothing the concept of individuality in heavy biological color without affording it any real validity. The concept of a rational and free self was perhaps more sympathetically viewed by the vitalists, but even for them the "I" remained without a home of its own and was destined to a vast unknown sea of "life." The soul had to be regarded simply as "l'unité vivante"; and, whether by mechanical or dynamic necessity, the individual

8. "Des Fonctions du cerveau," *RDM,* XCVIII (1872), 373-85.
9. Paul Janet, "Le Problème des causes finales et la physiologie contemporaine," *RDM,* CIII (1873), 865, 876.
10. E. Vacherot, "La Vie et la matière. Le Vitalisme," *RDM,* XXX (1878), 825.

was a mere moment in "a succession of beings and forms in the functions of birth and death." [11]

This atmosphere of anonymity, in which the individual soul was supplanted by a kind of universal mind stuff or something akin to primordial instinct, provided an appropriate setting for a revival of the Schopenhauerian mood, which some fifty years before had arisen, in part at least, as a response to scientific studies. Schopenhauer had, in fact, assumed the role of a philosophical interpreter of biological science, with particular attention to the physiologists' preoccupation with the question of intelligence as a part of the body. He made a metaphysical distinction between will and intelligence similar to the physiological distinction made by Bichat between "organic life," the continuous stream of life to which the passions belong, and animal or intermittent life, to which belong sensations and intelligence.[12] He was an admirer also of Cabanis and attracted by his belief in the existence of an organic sensibility belonging to a universal instinct inherent in matter and hence prior to the external sensibility manifest in the sensations of an individual organism.[13] From these and other early nineteenth-century physiologists who departed from the mechanistic school of Condillac, Schopenhauer found a plausible scientific basis for Kant's unknowable thing-in-itself. Accordingly he postulated the Will as a universal spirit or life force, the same throughout nature, differing only in degree for minerals, animals, and man.[14] In relation to this one enduring source and destiny of all individuality, intelligence is a subordinate and ephemeral manifestation. Combining thus the subjective emphasis of post-Kantian idealism with the physiological realism of his day, Schopenhauer constructed a subterranean view of the human being which proved to be especially compatible with the vitalistic thought so promi-

11. E. Caro, "La Poésie philosophique dans les nouvelles écoles. Un poète positiviste," *RDM*, III (1874), 244-45 (in reference to Mme. Ackermann).

12. *The World as Will and Idea*, trans. R. B. Haldane and John Kemp (London, 1896), II, 488 ff. Cf. Th. Ribot, *La Philosophie de Schopenhauer* (Paris: F. Alcan, 1905), pp. 71-73.

13. See Paul Janet, "Schopenhauer et la physiologie française," *RDM*, XXXIX (1880), 35-59.

14. See Schopenhauer, *Selections*, ed. De Witt H. Parker (New York: Charles Scribner's Sons, 1928), pp. 8, 75-78.

nent in the second half of the century. From an organic view-point, his "god-spirit" may be called an unconscious will to live; in an abstract physical sense, it may be designated simply as impersonal energy.

Von Hartmann, whose philosophy of the unconscious was much discussed in the 1870's and 1880's, also helped to popularize the somber mood having to do with the unimportance of individuality. He had proposed to spiritualize Schopenhauer's "materialism" by bringing the unconscious Will into union with the purposive Idea of Hegel; [15] and although he sought in this way to take the blindness out of the Will, he did little more than enthrone an "unconscious purpose" and call it instinct: "One of the most important and familiar manifestations of the Unconscious is Instinct, and the conception of Instinct rests on that of Purpose." [16] Like Schopenhauer, he draws upon the experiments of physiologists, especially those studying the manifestation of intelligent activity throughout the body; and he concludes that the brain is not at all requisite for the exercise of the Will.[17] From his viewpoint, of course, self-consciousness is secondary in comparison to the superior Unconscious, in whose service nature sacrifices egoism.

Whether or not Von Hartmann drew valid conclusions from the experiments of scientists, in so far as specific facts are concerned, is not particularly important for our purposes. The important thing is that he exemplifies a general tendency to combine biology and philosophy in such a way as to emphasize the subrational rather than the rational man. He enhanced, with somber accouterments, what other scientist-philosophers were saying about the comparative magnitude of reason and feelings. Consider, for example, Spencer's statement that the main part of mind is not intelligence but feelings,[18] and Taine's assertion that "the greater part of ourselves remains out of our reach and the visible I is incomparably smaller than the I that lies in dark-

15. *Philosophy of the Unconscious*, I, 117, 125, 324.
16. *Ibid.*, p. 43. Cf. also: "Instinct is purposive action without consciousness of the purpose" (p. 79) and "I conclude this chapter with the words of Schelling: 'There is no better touchstone of a genuine philosophy than the phenomenon of animal instinct'" (p. 116).
17. *Ibid.*, pp. 62 ff. There is, for example, an independent ganglionic will which gives evidence of intention and idea.
18. *The Principles of Psychology*, I, 190.

ness." [19] The philosophy of the unconscious thus underscored the new kind of dualism that set up a contest between the non-rational, embracing the concept of instinct and its relation to the species as a whole, and the rebellious self-consciousness, with which are associated intellect and the sense of personality.[20]

The part that Darwinism played in establishing the heavy emphasis on the nonrational man, and the accompanying concept of a species or group level of intelligence, can hardly be overstated. *The Origin of Species* (1859) and *The Descent of Man* (1871), generally accepted as scientific confirmation of the theory of human evolution from subhuman forms, contributed an element of grimness to the vision of man's place in nature. Although Darwin himself took an optimistic view of his subject, the effect of his arguments was in some quarters virtually a justification of the Schopenhauerian mood. For, after all, he maintained that all living beings belong together as regards origin; [21] that self-consciousness, intellect, and the moral sense are developments out of simpler aptitudes; [22] and that "there is no fundamental difference between man and the higher mammals in their mental faculties." [23] Coloring this thought of lowly origin is Darwin's basic idea of natural selection by way of fortuitous variation, in a struggle for existence where almost certain extinction awaits the less improved forms of life. The paramount intending of nature, in a word, is concentrated upon the continuity and improvement of the whole and not upon the individual, whose essential role is to transmit through the principle of inheritance the characteristics that are profitable to the species.

Compare with these ideas Schopenhauer's thesis that nature is constantly preying upon itself in a process of life and death, and that man, who is one with all nature, is individually sacrificed to the species. Toward the end of the century Schopenhauer's outlook is most noticeable in its aspect of passive resignation to

---

19. Translated from *De l'Intelligence*, p. 7.
20. Such a dualism of "énergie totale" is specifically mentioned by Auguste Langel, *Les Problèmes de l'âme* (Paris, 1868), pp. 28-29.
21. *The Origin of Species and The Descent of Man*, p. 368.
22. *Ibid.*, pp. 460, 471-72.
23. *Ibid.*, p. 446.

the impermanence of individuality. Around 1875, however, it is more often combined with the dynamism of Darwinian evolution. The biological realism of the novel was the literary manifestation most closely identified with contemporary scientific thought and pessimism regarding man's individual destiny was the most noticeable philosophical attitude. A good portion of philosophical interpretation of science located man's essential reality in the subrational realm of instinct or "will," where individuation is unconscious and immortality is conceivable only in terms of a mass existence of something like "energy" or "will to live." Of this intellectual environment Zola stands out as perhaps the most representative and the most dynamic literary spokesman. It would be difficult to find a novelist who more impressively combined in an awesome reaction a respect for science and an emotional uneasiness at its implications.

As Zola began preparations (in 1868) for his ambitious Rougon-Macquart series of novels, in which he proposed to follow the history of a family through various generations and ramifications, he plunged into the reading of literature on physiology and natural history. Science was for him a kind of newly discovered God, and with youthful optimism he openly embraced the positivistic attitude. It is quite possible that he combined with this enthusiasm a certain showmanship and pugnacity, compensating perhaps for a feeling of inferiority with respect to his more educated literary contemporaries.[24] In any case, he professed little respect for metaphysical speculation and was content — as he thought — to be a positivist and a materialist. Nevertheless, the duality of imagination and objectivity within him gradually attained the proportions of a conflict between sentiment and reason and emerged in spectacular fashion in his novels.

The sources that Zola consulted at the outset of his project were numerous, as he himself testifies.[25] The notes that he took on two of the works (Dr. Charles Letourneau, *Physiologie des passions* [1868], and Dr. Prosper Lucas, *Traité philosophique et*

24. Cf. F. W. J. Hennings, *Emile Zola* (Oxford: Clarendon Press, 1953), pp. 124-25.
25. In a letter published in 1878. See "Notes et variantes" in *La Fortune des Rougon* (Paris: François Bernouard, 1927), p. 352.

physiologique de l'hérédité naturelle [1850]),[26] which are probably representative of his reading and thinking at that time, are significant in their indication of a nonrational view of life to be taken as a basis for portraying the human being. Of special interest in the notes taken on the Lucas treatise on heredity is the subject of atavism as a threat to the individual; and also the notion that crime and vice can be handed down from parents to children by the law of heredity. With reference to Letourneau's book, the interest lies especially in the emphasis on the impulsive aspects of man's nature. Some importance attaches to the distinction between "desire [freely irrational impulse]" and "will [deliberate impulse]"; but still more important is the stress on "impressionability (impression is a feeling of pleasure or of pain)." The human organism is visualized as a physiological machine operating on all levels, from the vegetative to the intellectual, toward the goals of nutritive calm and emotional equilibrium, which may be defined as the attainment of pleasure and the avoidance of pain.[27] This physiological emphasis, of course, is but a version of the widespread tendency to identify man with the mechanism of nature and to deprive the intellect of any special privilege in the unitary system of being. Zola states such a viewpoint through Sandoz, one of the characters in *L'Œuvre* (1886):

Is it not a farce to make a study of the brain's function exclusively, under the pretext that the brain is the noble organ? ... Thought is the product of the entire body.... Furthermore, psychology, physiology mean nothing (as independent terms); the one has penetrated the other, and today both are but one, the mechanism of man comprising the sum total of his functions.[28]

There is little evidence that Zola thought critically about the scientific ideas that he encountered in his reading. He was first of all an imaginative writer, a poet, not a scientist. The vision of

26. The notes may be consulted in Henri Massis, *Comment Emile Zola composait ses romans* (Paris: Bibliotèque Charpentier, 1906), pp. 28 ff.
27. *Ibid.*, pp. 30-33.
28. Translated from *L'Œuvre* (Paris: François Bernouard, 1928), p. 175. This statement, for which Letourneau is cited as the source by Massis (p. 27), could have been prompted by any one of numerous writings, since it was a widespread opinion. In general tenor it sounds very much like Taine and Claude Bernard.

man as an element of the natural world seems to have grown in his impressionable consciousness like a threatening cloud, becoming especially dark in its reference to an evolutionary history reaching far back into an obscure past. In his view of evolution he thought of man, collectively, as a social being as well as an animal, and he visualized a laborious, faltering advance trammeled by the pull of physical heritage and the heavy influence of environment. He was preoccupied with the question of man's linkage with his past, not so much in the specific sense of inherited characteristics handed down from father to son as in the broad sense of a vast indefinite natural and material process. It is this general and uncomfortable impression of material origin that produces the primary tones in Zola's epical depiction of the human species. Metaphysics, for which he professes a scorn at the outset of his grandiose novelistic venture, actually forces its way into his thinking in the form of a vague pessimistic pantheism and creates an effect that largely overshadows his admiration for positivism. The metaphysical disturbance is grounded in the question of the self in the face of a total natural "force" and is aptly described as a contraposition of the two entities, to use Taine's words, which the world comprises: "the I and matter." [29] Taine could calmly believe that the dualism may possibly be resolved in "that deep penumbra where sensation is born," [30] which is virtually the same as saying in matter itself. For Zola, thoughts of such an absorption of the "I" in a mass entity, whether of matter or spirit, creates a serious emotional conflict, which emerges in his novels as a dualistic view (individual and collective) of the human being. With his view of man as an individual are associated the ideas of sentiment and the finer qualities of mind, which, in the language of his day, belong to an ephemeral self-consciousness. With his more dominant and more striking view of man in the aggregate belong ominous aspects of subrational life, which in an imaginative way are most easily associated with the world of matter. This kind of dualism is perhaps nowhere better expressed than in *Germinal*, written at the peak of Zola's career and generally considered his masterpiece.

29. *De l'Intelligence*, p. 347.
30. *Ibid.*, p. 320.

Germinal (1885)

Germinal is rich enough in suggestiveness to admit of various interpretations. In its most obvious aspects it is a socioeconomic picture emphasizing the wretchedness and injustice suffered by the working class. At the same time it is a depiction of man in his relations to the world of nature; and, in union with this view, it brings into focus the question of the individual's position as compared to the human species when regarded collectively. These three views — socioeconomic conditions, man as a product of nature, and man's position as an individual — probably include the novel's major significance in so far as meaning is concerned. The first of these provides the narrative framework and the occasion for the unfoldment of the other two. While expending a great deal of emotion in this social "surface" of the story on behalf of the working class, Zola indulges his liking for the spectacular in his capacity as storyteller. For he was alert to the responsibility of creating a narrative interest, and he carries his story forward in successive steps of intensifying excitement. His style seems to be deliberately designed to this end. Despite all his attention to realistic detail, he was a great impressionist, especially in creating a massive fusion of loud tones and colors, often with sensational effect.

In just such a spirit of sensationalism the story of *Germinal* is executed, with social indignation, the bold painting of animality, and mysticism mingled together. The opening chapter is a quick indication of what the reader can expect, as regards both the potential drama of the situation and the novel's ideational content. The mine Le Voreux, which is introduced as a savage beast "that breathed with long and heavy breath the air troubled by its laborious digestion of human flesh" (19),[31] not only appears as a monstrous instrument in the hands of an indifferent, anonymous power, the Company, but less obviously suggests, in association with the heavy darkness of night, another kind of power that decrees a sinister destiny for man. Following close upon this situational and tonal setting that points toward a story

31. References are to the edition of Le Blond (Paris: François Bernouard, 1928). Translations are my own.

of collective experience is the introduction of a plot of personal relations involving Etienne Lantier, a young man who has come to the mine looking for work, Catherine Maheu, daughter of a typical mining family, and Chaval, Catherine's brutish admirer, who resents her friendliness with the newcomer. The significance of this plot, which most of the time occupies a secondary position in the narrative, acquires a fairly definite contour in the end in connection with the theme of man's fusion with nature. In the first part of the novel, however, it is overshadowed by the action having to do with the miners' unhappy lot. In this subject Zola seems most engrossed, for he loses no time in setting the stage for a miners' revolt against the Company, the overbearing representative of capitalism.

As though constructing a drama, the author presents an explanation or justification for the revolt and follows the rebellious mass movement through its climactic development to its decisive defeat. The Maheu family, which exemplifies the miners' lot and serves as headquarters from which to view an entire community, becomes a concrete nucleus around which to build a dramatic narrative of group action. It is a large family that crowds together in its hovel and counts itself fortunate if all its members have as much as a crust of bread to eat. The mother, La Maheude, tries desperately to provide food with her meager resources and is constantly going in debt to the storekeeper Maigrat, who is ever on the alert to take advantage of his customers' misfortunes. The novel's social coloring, which is heavily stamped on its surface in the form of vivid pictures of living and working conditions, is further expressed by attention to the luxury and ease of certain representatives of capital. The home of M. Grégoire, for example, to which La Maheude sometimes goes in an appeal for help, stands in cool aloofness at a comfortable distance from the workers' huts. By a similar purposeful contrast the author keeps intermittently in the reader's view the family of the mine's director, M. Hennebeau, whose hypocritical and unfaithful wife is a choice target for satire of the bourgeoisie.

For the gradual unfolding of the narrative of group movement, Etienne Lantier is used as a kind of operator *ex machina*, whose portrait is of less interest than the action that he instigates. After organizing a strike and kindling the passions of the miners, he looks on helplessly as the fever of revolt gets out of hand. The mass movement reaches a high mark of mob violence when the miners march through the streets bent on destruction and some of the women savagely mutilate the body of the hated merchant Maigrat. It resumes a slow tempo as soldiers arrive to restore order, and it rises to another peak of excitement when the strikers oppose the move to bring in outsiders to work the mines. Following a skirmish in which some of the miners are killed, among them Maheu, a quiet resentment and a feeling of futility settle over the community and some of the miners start back to work. But the bitterness, which has led only to frustration and defeat, is still a storehouse of undischarged emotion and demands an outlet before the narrative movement is completed. The accumulated tension is released in a final catastrophic episode through the instrumentality of the anarchist Souvarine, who manages secretly to saw part way through some of the structure in the main elevator shaft of Le Voreux. When as a result an elevator crashes against the walls already weak because of neglect, water from a nearby canal pours into the mine, which now seems to disintegrate suddenly and totally. Le Voreux, occupying the spotlight here as it did in the beginning of the story, thus plays out its role of monster on a stupendous scale, trapping in its inhuman clutches a number of helpless beings, including Etienne, Catherine, and Chaval. Of these only Etienne survives.

This spectacular explosion of frustrated emotions technically may be considered the climax, not of a specific miners' revolt — since the uprising had already been defeated — but of an episode in the labor movement in general. By way of epilogue the concluding chapter of the novel points to a renewal of the struggle on a national scale. The author has handled his subject with such a display of energy that we are probably justified in thinking that he has used the violent termination of the episode as an outlet for his own feelings. There is no doubt that his sympathy lies with the miners in the conflict that he dramatizes in *Germinal;* but one must not be too ready to emphasize the novel's social motivation. Zola was neither a revolutionary nor a propagandist. He entered warmly into the spirit of revolt but he did so partly in his capacity as an artist identifying himself with his task. His own emotion, fraternizing with the miners' rebellious anger, thus becomes an important directive force in producing "a good story." There is, however, in the composition of *Germinal* an underlying emotion of broader scope than a mere contest between capital and labor. For in its most fundamental meaning the story is a drama of man's frustrated attempt to rise above his natural genesis. The author's portrayal of man as a product of nature thus must be observed in relation to the novel's narrative structure, especially in relation to the spectacular climax.

As presented in *Germinal,* man's place in nature can best be understood when regarded from two different viewpoints, which correspond approximately to the two levels of consciousness, the subrational and the rational, widely discussed in Zola's day in the fields of physiology and psychology. Taine's discussion of psychology affords an appropriate comparison, particularly as concerns his division of the person into two parts of the hierarchy of sensations: "the physical world," lying below the level of rational consciousness, and "the moral world," which appears above that level. Although in Taine's view the idea of a material substance is as much a phantom as the idea of a spiritual substance, the former occupies a larger place in his speculation because it at least is in the area of "the physical world," where the ultimate homogeneity of being is most likely to be found.[32] Now, Zola is preoccupied with these two levels of being and associates with them visions of man as mass consciousness and as self-consciousness. On one level he sees man collectively as identified with the species and finds him steeped in the physical world. On the other level he sees man as an individual and takes a wistful glance at the refinements to be found in "the moral world," where manifestations of consciousness are fragile wisps of reality. The author's interpretation of man's drama as a product of nature is therefore inseparable from his view of the individual as compared to man in the aggregate.

Zola sees the human being in synthesis with the species through three main avenues of observation: environment, heredity, and sex. When viewed in close relation to his surroundings and especially to his living conditions, man is a heavy, earthbound quantity acting more or less unconsciously in obedience to forces

32. See *De l'Intelligence,* pp. 7-9, 320.

beyond his control. There are in the comprehensive view of people in *Germinal* certain admirable social traits, such as family loyalty, loyalty to one mate, and ability to get along peaceably with others. These are generic traits, applicable to man collectively as they are individually, but they are evidenced primarily in small circles of personal relationships where the people for the most part act independently of group interests. They are not related in a strict sense to group motives or environmental effects. On the other hand, when seen as one with the community personality, the people are animal-like, sluggish, and passive. Even their stoical endurance, which might be called a courageous adjustment to necessity, is a form of passivity, from which they are aroused only periodically, and then only in outbursts of violence and brutality. Zola's portrayal of mob psychology is a vivid demonstration of this fusion of individual personality with mass consciousness. A specific illustration is found in the behavior of La Maheude, who is usually calmly dedicated to her family responsibility but becomes, under the magnetism of group consciousness, one of the most aggressive in opposing the termination of the strike and declares that she would commit murder rather than surrender. A similar synchronization with the mob spirit is seen in the boy Jeanlin Maheu, who takes a fiendish delight in the conflict between the miners and the Company and develops a compulsion to kill, which leads him to stalk a young sentinel at the mine and cut his throat.

The fundamental explanation of Zola's view of man as one with the species is his fascination with the notion of heredity, especially in a broad perspective embracing the long history of the human race. The focus narrows at times to the transmission of traits from one generation to the next. Etienne, for example, is supposed to have inherited a maddening effect of liquor, the curse of his family, which brings with it a desire to kill. Similarly, Catherine's passive attitude appears to be hereditary: "overcome in her hereditary notions of subordination and passive obedience" (52). In a way, Zola's application of the principle of heredity is like saying that one can inherit the cigarette habit or a dirty face. This is not a strange view when we think of the common belief in his day in the inheritance of acquired characteristics, whether these be acquired through adaptation to environment or through chance variation.[33] Agreeing with the assertion of Dr. Lucas that vice and crime are hereditary, the novelist magnifies his own examples in accord with literary requirements. In effect he is presenting an accelerated view of the process of evolution in its reference to heredity, and his exaggeration of the immediate aspects of inheritance may be explained in part as poetic license.

The important consideration in Zola's case, however, is his preoccupation with the great power of the hereditary principle, not as manifest in specific aspects but as a general force linking man with his distant past. The backward glance fascinates him, and the phenomenon of reversion terrifies him, because it not only uncovers occasional anomalies but, more important, it unpleasantly directs our thoughts to the early stages of man's history. If Zola had been a religious believer, he might have blamed Adam for the evil and savagery of man, and it is quite possible that he was influenced by the story of man's fall.[34] But he was decidedly oriented to the general theory of evolution, and the probability of having evolved from some inferior form of life, and from matter itself, weighed on his imagination and caused him to speak of man's ancestry in much harsher tones than Darwin or any other natural scientist used. His comment on Jeanlin's establishing a hideout and storing food in an abandoned mine during the bitter days of the strike is illustrative of his grim view of man's animal heritage: "an abortive degeneration into obscure intelligence and savage cunning, slowly recaptured by ancient animality" (287).

Of primary significance in this retrogressive perspective is sex, the most conspicuous of the elemental motives displayed in *Germinal* — the adult miners after a hard day's work respond as

33. Zola's heavy attention to environmental influence, which he visualizes primarily in collective man, seems to indicate more of a leaning toward Lamarck than Darwin; though it must be remembered that the latter includes adaptation as a secondary factor explaining change and asserts that "changed habits produce an inherited effect" (*The Origin of Species*, p. 18).

34. Zola, of course, made metaphorical use of Biblical stories. The Garden of Eden, for example, quite clearly is recalled in *La Faute de l'Abbé Mouret*. With respect to *Germinal*, it has been asserted that the author uses the theme of the Flood to help express the birth of the contemporary world out of the death of the old order: Philip Walker, "Prophetic Myths in Zola," *PMLA*, LXXIV (1959), 449-51.

quickly to the sexual urge as to hunger, and the young unmarried people have a special place of rendezvous in the open, where on evenings they virtually cover the ground. Superficially it may be regarded as a manifestation of man's animal ancestry. But in his obsession with the subject of sex Zola unquestionably invests it with mystic connotations; for he looks beyond the mere animality of primitive life and seems to pause at that point in the evolutionary process where individuation arises. In a kind of retrogressive mysticism, sex thus becomes symbolic of the place of union with the undivided World Force. This deification — or, to be more exact, this diabolization — of sex is so pervasive in Zola's novels that it is pretty generally felt by his readers and recognized by his critics. What perhaps is not sufficiently noted is the emotion that compels the novelist to look in a contrary direction along the slope of evolution to the heights where exist the refinements and complexities of consciousness that are associated with the sentiment of love and belong to individual personality.

There is, in fact, a marked dualism in Zola, and it corresponds to the opposition between individuation and mass fusion that is manifest in *Germinal* in both plot structure and character portrayal. The narrative impact of the collective experience is accompanied by a definite, though less audible, narrative theme having to do with individual relations. This structural aspect, found in the Etienne-Catherine plot, is grounded in the subject of love and sex and affords touches of delicacy and sentiment in sharp contrast to the dominant impression of material heaviness. The relationship between Etienne and Catherine appears for much of the story to be purely incidental, because the reader's attention is continually directed to the affairs of the community, especially to the miners' revolt. But, while deliberately subordinating this personal plot, the author apparently intends it to have a meaningful part in the whole. The narrative technique establishes the dominance of collective experience, but without losing sight of the love of Etienne and Catherine.

In chapters 5 and 6 of Part IV, for example, a wide variety of happenings is rapidly surveyed, constituting a gradual accumulation of mass movement. Etienne, while wandering through the village, sees that some of the families are selling their furniture to obtain money for food. He finds an old woman lying on the ground, carries her into the house of La Mouquette with the latter's aid, accedes to the girl's begging for sexual intercourse, borrows some potatoes from her for the hungry Maheu family, later calls a meeting of workers in the forest nearby, discovers Jeanlin's hideout and store of food, meets up with La Mouquette again, at the same time being seen by Catherine, and finally makes his way to the clearing in the forest and the mass meeting that will lead to mob violence. In passages of this kind the narration clearly emphasizes the group movement. The love relationship between Etienne and Catherine is barely glimpsed; but in the suggestion of unspoken thoughts as Catherine watches Etienne talking with La Mouquette there is a delicate depiction of human experience much larger in significance than the space devoted to it.

In her relationship with Chaval, Catherine represents the group level, in which woman is forced at an early age into a submissive role as though bound by natural law giving the male right of ownership over the female. In her relationship with Etienne, on the other hand, she represents a hesitant move toward an ideal conception of love, which is evidenced by the timidity and delicacy of feeling that exists between the two. From their very first meeting there is a bond of sympathy and kindness between them, and Etienne feels betrayed when he discovers that Chaval has forcibly taken possession of Catherine and that she laughingly accepts her role of mistress. Subsequently they talk of her relationship with Chaval in a bantering tone, but down deep they both feel a pronounced restraint and a cruel sadness somewhat akin to hate (Part III, chapter 1). When Etienne starts living with the Maheu family, he and Catherine sleep in the same room and, although at times they desire each other, are reluctant to put their love on an equal footing with that of the common herd, restrained instead by a barrier of "shame, repugnances, and delicacies of friendship, which they themselves could not have explained" (183). Their sensitiveness contrasts sharply with the animal-like indifference to intimacy between the sexes on the part of the people in general. After Catherine leaves home to live with Chaval, she becomes more passive in every respect and seems to be indifferent to Etienne, but she still experiences a certain shame and sadness when in his presence, revealing both her feeling for him and a deep sense of self-respect.

Zola has invested this personal relationship with more idealism than he appears to have realized. He affirms in his preliminary notes for *Germinal* that Etienne's love for Catherine is purely and simply a love of male for female, devoid of "Platonic" qualities: "He is not a dreamer, a tender person; on the contrary, he obeys the impulses of a savage, of uncultivated nature," and for this reason "it is absolutely necessary that he have her," though he is restrained for a long time by timidity.[35] There is no doubt that the author wishes to demonstrate an irresistible natural law when he compels Etienne to possess Catherine shortly before her death in the mine. He thus carries out his prearranged scheme, but his plan apparently did not call for as much sentiment as has been in evidence. The portrayal of individual character is handled with greater sensitivity in reference to Catherine than to Etienne, who remains always something of a cardboard figure; but there is about him a definite refinement and even tenderness in his display of love. The two young lovers, in a word, stand at the threshold of a world far above the level of mass humanity, and it is altogether conceivable that Zola lets his secret aspirations with regard to the individual's place in the world be idealistically expressed in his depiction of this relationship.

The merging of the Etienne-Catherine plot with the group drama in the episode of the mine disaster and the resultant combination of love, death, and catastrophe in a grandiose climax give this personal plot a place of importance in a discussion of the novel's philosophical meaning. The basic significance lies in the author's view of sex. Various explanations have been offered for Zola's preoccupation with sex as something fearsome and destructive. It has been suggested that his novelistic handling of the subject may be the liquidation of a traumatic aversion caused when he was a child; [36] or that it may be an antipathy

35. "Fragments de l'ébauche," ed. Le Blond, pp. 560-61.
36. Jean Vinchon, "Un psychiatre relit Zola," in *Présence de Zola* (Paris: Fasquelle Editeurs, 1953), pp. 222-31.

arising from a crude introduction to sexual intercourse as a youth, or possibly from a realization that complete possession is impossible.[37] The fundamental explanation, however, undoubtedly lies in the association of sex and death, a prominent feature in his novels.[38] It is certain that the thought of death weighs heavily on Zola; at least it did in the 1880's before his liaison with Jeanne Rozerot and the birth of his first child, which assured him of a kind of tangible personal survival. Placing great credence in a literal interpretation of biological science and yet desirous of immortality, he could imaginatively combine sex (the agent of continuity) and death (the agent of individual finitude) in an emotional fusion. From this viewpoint, which regards Zola as seriously disturbed by a conflict between science and metaphysics, the love of Etienne and Catherine is symbolic of the sacrifice of individuality on the altar of a universal World Force. Their sentimental attachment to each other is a timid venture on the part of transitory individuality turning away from its disappearance in the total sea of life; and when in their case natural law asserts itself through the agency of sex, it is not simply animal instinct at work but something extrahuman drawing them back to their oneness with the All.

The subject of sex and death in *Germinal* becomes more meaningful when viewed in the light of Schopenhauer's philosophical pronouncements. For Schopenhauer had set the mood for all those of the nineteenth century who were tortured by loyalty to the passions of self-consciousness in the face of an all-absorbing Nature. The picture that he draws could understandably have come from the hands of Zola had the latter preceded him chronologically, particularly with reference to a distinction between the one dominating, everlasting force that runs through all nature and the ephemeral forms in which the force is objectified. Like Spinoza, Schopenhauer finds the eternal only in the One that lies outside all human perception, but he gives the One connotations much more material — or at least unconscious — than rational. He grants that reason, which has its pole in the

37. Hennings, *Emile Zola*, pp. 142, 163.
38. Cf. Angus Wilson, *Emile Zola. An Introductory Study of His Novels* (New York, William Morrow & Co., Inc., 1952), pp. 55, 107.

brain, may be considered the source of freedom and eternal existence (129) [39] but subordinates it and actually has it pass into unconsciousness. Reversing Spinoza's emphasis on reason, he arrives at a similarly vague sea of existence by making a nonrational urge to live the underlying force in nature. The phenomenon of individuation has its connection with this urge, the Will, through a physiological process whose pole is the genital organs (129). The will to live "always seeks the highest possible objectification" (88), and causes a strife in nature by an overcoming of lower by higher grades of its manifestation: "Thus the will to live everywhere preys upon itself, and in different forms is its own nourishment" (90). Birth and death are both in the Will's service (190), and the individual is merely a passing moment objectively representing its continuity, which is an eternal process of birth, death, renewal, and destruction. The vision of a grand rhythmic rise and fall of unending creation, which rises out of Zola's novels and is especially magnified in terms of life and death,[40] had already been philosophically and poetically implanted in the popular imagination by Schopenhauer.

The climax of *Germinal* achieves a loud harmony with this Schopenhauerian vision.[41] Here, in Wagnerian tones, Zola has combined the anger and destruction attendant upon a frustrated collective movement with a personal drama in which are poetized a worship of life and a vision of eternal darkness. Through repetition of the symbolism of night, silence, blackness, he builds up an impression of the horror of death. Trapped in the mine and facing almost certain extinction, Etienne and Catherine are

39. Page references in this paragraph are to Schopenhauer, *Selections*, ed. De Witt H. Parker.
40. Cf. Guy Robert, *Emile Zola* (Paris, Société d'édition Les Belles Lettres, 1952), pp. 103-104.
41. I have seen no external evidence to indicate that Zola read Schopenhauer, but the Schopenhauerian outlook was a part of the climate in which he lived. He could, as a matter of fact, have independently duplicated it, and for basically similar reasons. Benjamin F. Hudson, Jr., in his doctoral dissertation, *Zola and Schopenhauer: The Affinity of Some Aspects of Their Thought as Reflected in the Rougon-Macquart Series* (University of Michigan, 1958; Xerox reprint, University Microfilms, Inc., Ann Arbor, 1960), calls attention to the great popularity of Schopenhauer in France before the date of the first French translation of his main work in 1886 and, though finding no proof that Zola actually read the philosopher, points out the strong parallel in their general attitudes and ideas.

also trapped in the absolute night that is their destiny: "It was complete night, absolute, that earthly night which they would sleep without ever opening their eyes again to the brightness of the sun" (524). Yet, "before this menace, their instinct struggled, a feverish desire to live animated them"; and in the very embrace of death and eternal darkness they have their wedding night, feeling the stubborn need "to live, to produce life one last time. They loved each other in the despair of everything, in death" (531).[42] Thus is consummated the love of Etienne and Catherine, even as she is on the point of death and the corpse of Chaval floats in the water at their feet.

In this scene, which is perhaps the most striking scene in the novel and, for purposes of philosophical interpretation, the most significant, we are regaled with a sharp juxtaposition of opposites: the tenderness of love and the savagery of brute combat, the fierce desire to live and the certainty of death, passion for freedom and entrapment in sepulchral darkness. Freedom, love, immortality, and the ideals or "values" appropriate to self-consciousness are absorbed by the absoluteness of an undivided natural force, and sex is the ritual wherewith the mystic union is celebrated. The impression of material heaviness and the symbolism of death as victorious matter cannot be disregarded,[43] but it would be a mistake to think of the picture left by Zola as outright materialism. That is, he is hardly more materialistic than Schopenhauer, let us say. For, like Schopenhauer, he advances beyond the physical to the mystical; and the atomistic movement of matter gives way before an abstract life principle, unindividuated, which governs all, including the death of individuals.

42. Undoubtedly, more could be made of the imagery in *Germinal* with regard to its philosophical meanings. Marcel Girard ("L'Univers de *Germinal*," *La Revue des Sciences Humaines*, January-March, 1953, pp. 59-76) points out, for example, the impression of ennui and despair associated with the flatness of the countryside where the story has its setting and designates black as symbolic of a kind of material night and white as symbolic of *le néant*. The concept of nothingness, it seems to me, at least in so far as it is associated with the thought of individuality, belongs with night and darkness.

43. Referring to *Germinal*, Zola declares in a letter of July 22, 1885 (*Correspondance*, II, 641): "Mon rôle a été de remettre l'homme à sa place dans la création, comme un produit de la terre, soumis encore à toutes les influences du milieu; et, dans l'homme lui-même, j'ai remis à sa place le cerveau parmi les organes, car je ne crois pas que la pensée soit autre chose qu'une fonction de la matière."

What we have, in short, is an unhappy exaltation of the unconscious over the self-conscious, of life en masse as compared to the outer fringes of evolutionary development where the more delicate attainments of individual personality have not established their permanency.

In his youth Zola had the intention of writing a long poem (*La Genèse*) about the birth of worlds and the human race, thus singing a hymn to universal life in its march out of a supposed chaos.[44] Apparently the image of an "enfantement d'un monde" lingered in his mind when he composed *Germinal*, giving rise to the vision of a primordial Creative Force groping its way forward. The resultant picture of the life process is something like that of a seething pool converting itself slowly into a moving stream without allowing any of its inner stirrings to assert themselves independently of the whole. Emerging timidly on the surface of the stream, a bubble appears which seems to glimpse a glorious evolutionary development for itself, only to surrender its dream by force of incorporation in the total process. The bubble is the illusion of individuality, which fades into a vision of mass humanity that knows only a blind urge to live and destroys itself in internecine warfare [45] while ever serving the principle of continuity by propagation of the species.

One gets the impression that Zola unconsciously mixed in a witch's brew remembrances of such writers as Comte, Taine, Darwin, Marx, and Schopenhauer, and that in the act he was carried away by the sensational narrative possibilities of his intellectual concoction. But an emotional conflict is unmistakably present and provides the major impetus for the artistic accomplishment. Zola's novels after 1890 may be more tranquil and optimistic in tone,[46] but they lose in forcefulness. At the height of his career, as represented by *Germinal*, the emotional conflict is the very heart of the dynamic narrative movement; and underlying the narrative impulse is an awesome vision conjured up in imaginative contemplation of the contributions of

---

44. Maurice Le Blond, "Notes et variantes," in *La Fortune des Rougon* (Paris: François Bernouard, 1927), p. 351.

45. Etienne recognizes "the people," collectively, to be a "force de la nature qui se dévorait elle-même" (p. 535).

46. Cf. Hennings, p. 235, and Wilson, p. 122.

biological science. In a broad, fundamental sense, the gloom of Schopenhauer's outlook is superimposed on the dynamics of Darwinian evolution. *Germinal*, thus, is an outstanding example of stimulation in the presence of modern science combined with a dark uneasiness prompted thereby. The combination results in what is unquestionably some of the most remarkable prose fiction of the nineteenth century.

EMILIA PARDO BAZÁN
1852-1921

Los Pazos de Ulloa (1886)

Despite the fact that Spaniards in general opposed French naturalism when it first became a prominent subject in literary and intellectual circles around 1880, there were a few leading writers who defended it and imitated it to some extent in their novels. The most important of these were Emilia Pardo Bazán and Leopoldo Alas in the 1880's and Blasco Ibáñez in the next decade. Pardo Bazán's sympathetic discussion of Zola in *La cuestión palpitante* (1882-1883) was the most intelligent appraisal of naturalism in Spain at the time. She did not approve of Zola's proposal to use the novel as an instrument of science, and being an orthodox Catholic she opposed the philosophical implications of his view of life; but she recognized his great literary merit and found it easy to admire the rough forcefulness of his realism. For artistic reasons, also, she was attracted by Zola's grim vision of man's place in nature. But, since she could not wholly identify herself with his ideas, her adaptation of naturalism turned out to be almost exclusively literary, having some of the weakness inherent in the pursuit of a goal in which one does not fully believe. It is no doubt unjust to say that she was simply following her womanly inclination to keep up with the styles, as Juan Valera intimated in 1887,[47] but the opinion expressed by several of her contemporaries and repeated from hearsay by

47. "Apuntes sobre el nuevo arte de escribir novelas" (*Obras completas* [Madrid, 1913], XXVI, 27).

Zola is surely correct: "the naturalism of that lady is purely formal, artistic, and literary." [48]

Because of her disinclination to embrace even in an imaginary venture the underlying philosophical ideas in Zola's fiction — and this fact should be remembered in comparing her with Blasco Ibáñez — Pardo Bazán's naturalism leaves us with a decided impression of separateness between a world of the flesh and a world of the spirit. Visualizing clearly the standpoint which sees man identified with nature and dominated by natural and environmental forces, she holds the grim specter of nature at arm's length and actually plays with it as though engaged in a literary game. The great God Unconscious which, as both will and idea, flows through the very veins of Zola's characters is personalized by Pardo Bazán and placed outside her own intellectual home. Nature thus appears to be more a diabolical creature threatening mankind from the outside than a diabolical unconscious process enveloping all creation in one irresistible stream. An examination of *Los Pazos de Ulloa*, considered by some to be Pardo Bazán's most naturalistic novel, will illustrate.

This is an exuberant tale with romantic overtones, in which the narrative action is really subordinated to the setting. For the author's attention is concentrated primarily on the creation of an atmosphere appropriate to the primitive lushness and unkemptness of a place far removed from the softening touch of civilization. Unifying the whole is the theme of nature as a powerful overlord exacting its toll of human beings. The essential structure is that of a contest in which refinement and ideals prove to be helpless before their natural opponents.

The contest is occasioned when a young priest, Julián, comes as chaplain to "los pazos de Ulloa," an estate deep in the interior of Galicia, hoping to restore order to a place which has gradually deteriorated through the negligence and indifference of its degenerate owner, Don Pedro Moscoso. The latter lives in concubinage with his servant Sabel, whose father Primitivo tacitly sanctions the relationship, motivated by a desire to maintain control of the property. Julián thus tries to restore moral as well as material order. On his advice Don Pedro marries, choosing as

48. "Opiniones de Emilio Zola sobre *La cuestión palpitante*," in *La cuestión palpitante* (4th ed.; Madrid, 1891), p. 25.

wife his cousin Nucha, a girl of delicate tastes and religiously inclined, whose influence might possibly be expected to counteract the brutishness of an animalistic husband. The marriage experiment fails, for when Nucha gives birth to a girl instead of a boy, Don Pedro becomes cruelly indifferent to his wife and resumes his former ways. Julián suffers with Nucha, considering her his spiritual partner and harboring a silent love for her, which is detected by the hostile Primitivo and leads to the priest's being removed from his position. Years later he returns to *los pazos* and finds evidence of a continuing state of cold indifference toward what he had most prized. The evidence is seen in the contrast between the neglect and the care of the graves of Nucha and Primitivo, respectively, and in the ragged appearance of Nucha's daughter as compared to the well-dressed Perucho, natural son of Pedro and Sabel. The finality of the narrative effect thus is identified with Julián's impotence in the midst of hostile surroundings.

The author's interest, however, does not fall particularly on Julián or any other character when regarded as individuals. It lies in the dramatics of a general situation, in which people are representatives of opposing forces, and it centers primarily on one side of the contest. Hence the vivid pictures of "the rude and majestic loneliness of nature" (9) [49] and the brutishness and sensuality of the people, presented at times with a naturalistic focus couched in rhetorical display. The peasant girl whom Don Pedro brings home as nurse for his expected child, for example, is "a huge earthen-colored girl, a castle of flesh, the classic type of human cow . . . let Máximo Juncal observe carefully the basin of the lacteal river of the powerful female beast" (182). The opposition confronting Julián is personalized in Primitivo, whose name is apparently meant to be symbolic though he is more a cunning and heartless schemer than a child of primitive nature. He is the means of supplying the main plot interest, for he it is who bends every effort to hold Don Pedro a slave to inertia. He opposes the latter's marriage to Nucha; his duplicity during a political campaign makes it certain that Don Pedro will not be elected *diputado* and leave his home for Madrid; he leads

49. Quotations (translated) are from the author's *Obras completas* (Madrid: Editorial Pueyo, n.d.), III.

his master to suspect Julián's love for Nucha, and even in his grave he has the role of a victorious opponent.

The sinister force of nature which hovers over all the personages involved in the narrative action not only defeats outsiders who challenge it; it imposes itself destructively on those who are natives of its domains. Its destructiveness is seen both in the barbarous characteristics of its children and in the sequence of happenings. Primitivo, who plans the ruin of others, is in turn destroyed by another savage, "el Tuerto." Don Pedro, who is at the center of the entire action, lapses totally into bondage to a life of sluggish animalistic ease after a feeble effort to break away. And in the conclusion there is a hint of the cruel indifference of nature which envelops Perucho and his half sister (and which definitely materializes in *La Madre Naturaleza*, sequel to *Los Pazos de Ulloa*).

It seems quite clear, then, that the author's plan is to dramatize a contest between nature and man by introducing delicate visitors into a comparatively static situation where primordial natural forces reign supreme. The plan is carried to its completion by tracing the commotion caused by the visit, recounting in sensational manner — as Zola often does — the peaks of excitement (as, for example, where Nucha is terrified in the archives of *los pazos* by a hideous spider "of disproportionate hugeness, a monstrous belly swinging from eight hairy stilts") and concluding with a calm tone consonant with resignation and defeat. The murder of Primitivo has the effect of accentuating the general atmosphere of savagery which surrounds Nucha; and Julián's melancholy contemplation of Nucha's neglected grave, in the end, accomplishes the impression of a grim quietude following the triumph of an insensible, unconquerable force. It is as though a giant prehistoric beast resumed its impassive existence after being aroused momentarily from its sluggish repose. The whole narrative design is planned to make the spotlight play upon one outstanding and awesome protagonist: Primitive Nature.

This personification of an abstract natural power is actually a deification of primal forces, which shows man to be very close to his animal origin. In this respect Pardo Bazán is quite plainly following in the footsteps of Zola, whose intense preoccupation

with the social world was more than matched by his preoccupation with the natural world. The Spaniard could compose a
hymn to forests primeval, endowing them with sinister power,
and she could picture man in a state close to that of animals,
indulging here and there in passages of coarse physical detail,
without going contrary to her religious or aesthetic beliefs.[50]
The brutishness and helplessness of man, however, are not seen
to be in close union with nature, as they are in Zola. The characters in the novel bear marks that in some degree show the
effect of their environment,[51] but we are not led to imagine that
they have grown out of their surroundings like a plant or an
animal.

The degeneracy of Pedro Moscoso, for example, who is a
focal point in the contest between refinement and savagery,
appears to be the result of separation from one kind of influence
rather than of identity with another. In the author's mind his
vulgarity and insensitiveness are attributable primarily to his
isolation from the advantages of urban life. The idea is expressed
as follows by his uncle, Señor De la Lage, citizen of a provincial
town: "The country village, when one is brought up in it and
never leaves it, debases, impoverishes, and brutifies" (24–25).[52]
The author is scarcely less kind to De la Lage when she says of
him: "A magnificent specimen of a race fit for the wild and war-
like life of feudal times, he wasted away miserably in the base
idleness of small towns, where he who produces nothing teaches

50. Pardo Bazán is more inclined to agree with Taine, that man in his
primitive nature is something of a gorilla, than she is with the Rousseau
view that man is naturally good: *La literatura francesa, III: el naturalismo*
in *Obras completas* (Madrid: Pérez Dubrull, 1891-1914), XLI, 390. The
doctrine of original sin comes to mind in this connection, but it does not
seem to have any special significance in the interpretation of *Los Pazos
de Ulloa*.

51. Donald Fowler Brown attaches much more importance to Pardo
Bazán's similarity to Zola in this respect than I do, declaring "the whole
work is a masterpiece of determinism": *The Catholic Naturalism of Pardo
Bazán* (Chapel Hill: University of North Carolina Press, 1957), p. 93.

52. Pardo Bazán's cosmopolitan, antiprovincial attitude is considered an
important element of her intellectual outlook. Cf. Emilio González López,
Emilia Pardo Bazán, novelista de Galicia (New York: Hispanic Institute,
1944), p. 79; also, Ronald Hilton, who looks beyond the novelist's antire-
gionalism to her general dissatisfaction with Spain and regards her in a sense
as a precursor of the generation of 1898: "Emilia Pardo Bazán's Concept
of Spain," *Hispania*, XXXIV (1951), 329; and "Pardo Bazán's Analysis of
the Social Structure of Spain," *Bulletin of Hispanic Studies*, XXIX
(1952), 1.

nothing and learns nothing, is good for nothing and does nothing" (91). It is evident from these passages that Pardo Bazán is thinking unfavorably of two things: provincial isolationism and decadent feudal aristocracy. The first is the more comprehensive and includes the second. Life in *los pazos* is representative of stagnant feudal aristocracy but, in a more important sense, it is exemplary of life in remote communities in general. In "the numb and drowsy life of *los pazos*" (247), a "large ferret hole . . . so dull, so gloomy, so grimly bare" (328), there is much of the animal-like dullness of the "narcotic, perennial, and monotonous rhythm of the farm life" (327) in the distant parish to which Julián is exiled.

The author's unsympathetic attitude is evident in livelier, satirical scenes also, notably in reference to small-town social life and political activities (Pedro's visit to his uncle and the elections). The body of the novel, however, presents a picture of animal insensibility and sluggishness, from which the people are periodically aroused to acts of violence and fierceness. The rational explanation of this sluggishness, from the author's viewpoint, is isolation rather than the fateful oppressiveness of harsh environment. Nevertheless, the latter idea is attractive artistically because it affords a goal for the creation of a dominant effect. So it is that the vision of a deadening existence in the interior of Galicia combines with a naturalistic vision of human brutificaton.

Pardo Bazán thus devotes her artistic energy to the creation of an impression of naturalism without trying to demonstrate man's fusion with nature in historical process. With the grimness of the naturalistic outlook in mind and a favorable disposition toward Zola's literary manner, she gives free rein to her willingness in passages that sometimes reach melodramatic swells of ebulliency. Consider the following reference to the tragic fate of male hares felled by hunters' guns while racing madly in their amorous pursuit:

And if the lady hare is allowed to go ahead, none of the night wanderers pursuing her will stop in his mad race, even though he hear the shot that ends his rival's life, even though he stumble over his blood-covered corpse, even though the puff of smoke may say to him: At the end of your romance is death!

No, they will not stop . . . at the first scent of the female that is distinguishable from the odor of resin emitted by the pines, the fiery pursuers will spring forward with renewed determination, blind with love, convulsed with desire, and the hunter who lies in wait will stretch them out one by one at his feet, on the grass where they had dreamed of having their nuptial bed (237 - 38).

Pardo Bazán seems quite clearly possessed of a characteristically Spanish spirit of comedy in the presence of harsh reality; and one may feel that in certain passages, like the one above, the lighthearted handling of naturalistic subject matter produces an unintentional burlesque. But we must grant that the dominant impression left by the novel centers on the vivid portrait, actually the personality, of a place: *los pazos* and environs.[53] Investing a specific locale with an atmospheric cloak appropriate to the vision of a primitive world, Pardo Bazán justifies the gusto with which she embarked on her adventure into a literary movement. In the act, she comes about as close as one can to writing a naturalistic novel without an underlying naturalistic philosophy.

VICENTE BLASCO IBÁÑEZ
1867-1928

Cañas y barro (1902)

The most thorough adaptation of French naturalism in Spain is found in the early, or Valencian, novels of Blasco Ibáñez, whose admiration for Zola was especially strong as he

---

53. In so far as setting is concerned, Zola's *La Faute de l'Abbé Mouret* (1875), with its extensive description of the virgin forest *le Paradou*, is remotely suggestive of *Los Pazos de Ulloa*; it is more suggestive of *La Madre Naturaleza*, both in setting and in theme. Cf. Donald F. Brown's convincing contention that *La Madre Naturaleza* follows *La Faute le l'Abbé Mouret*: "Two Naturalistic Versions of Genesis: Zola and Pardo Bazán," *Modern Language Notes*, LII (1937), 243-48; see also *The Catholic Naturalism of Pardo Bazán*, pp. 99 ff. Armand E. Singer, "The Influence of *Paul et Virginie* on *La Madre Naturaleza*," *West Virginia University Bulletin. Philological Studies*, IV (September, 1943), 31-43, disagrees with Brown, and sees a close similarity between the Spanish novel and *Paul et Virginie*.

began his novelistic career.[54] Like Pardo Bazán, Blasco Ibáñez was attracted to Zola primarily by the vitality of his art and perhaps to some extent by his sensationalism. In his case, however, it was easier to adopt a naturalistic view of man's place. He was not particularly interested in philosophical ideas, but he was a lover of nature in the raw and personally inclined to co-operate with the spontaneous, natural side of his being.[55] Moreover, he was not restrained by religious convictions from plunging wholeheartedly into the spirit of Zola's exaltation of primal natural forces. As a consequence of this affiliation between intellectual attitude and earthiness of style, he produced a more authentic version of naturalism than Pardo Bazán, at the same time achieving in his novels a stronger artistic consistency than she was able to attain under the handicap of a loyalty divided between art and her philosophical-religious outlook.

The outstanding example of Blasco Ibáñez's naturalism is *Cañas y barro,* of which the author said: "This is my favorite novel ... it is the one that holds for me the most pleasant memory, the one that I composed with most solidity, the one that seems to me the best rounded" *(redonda).*[56] In this story the novelist grasps the malevolent spirit of primitive nature, holds it at close range, and achieves the sharp singleness of effect that one generally finds in a short story. His procedure is to portray a locale and to impart through his portraiture the suggestion of a sinister transcendent· power. The place is the Albufera, a swampy lake region near Valencia, where the inhabitants eke out a wretched existence fishing and cultivating rice. In this setting the people harmonize with their milieu and through it appear to be oppressed by a cruelty that envelops more than their immediate situation. This blending of two levels of reality, the

54. In a letter to Cejador y Frauca in 1918 (included in the latter's *Historia de la lengua y literatura castellana,* IX [Madrid, Revista de Archivos, Bibliotecas y Museos, 1918]), Blasco Ibáñez expresses his indebtedness to Zola, though apparently wishing to make his borrowing seem less conspicuous than it was. Cf. Jeanine Modave, "Blasco Ibáñez et le naturalisme français," *Les Lettres Romanes,* XII (1958), 300-301.

55. Cf. Eduardo Zamacois' appraisal of Blasco Ibáñez' personal characteristics: *Vicente Blasco Ibáñez* (Madrid: Sucesores de Hernando, 1910), pp. 22-26.

56. See Camille Pitollet, "Cómo escribí el libro sobre Blasco Ibáñez," *Boletín de la Biblioteca Menéndez y Pelayo,* XXXIII (1957), 345-46. Cf. Ramón Martínez de la Riva, *Blasco Ibáñez, Su vida, su obra, su muerte, sus mejores páginas* (Madrid: Editorial Mundo Latino, 1929), p. 119.

harsh earthiness of immediate surroundings and a fateful overtone of transcendent implications, is maintained throughout the
novel. It begins in the initial chapter, where we are introduced
first to the filthiness of the mailboat and the brutishness of its
occupants, "a nauseating mixture of gelatinous skins, scales of
fish that have been raised in the mud, dirty feet, and grimy
clothes" (8); [57] and then to the awe-inspiring La Dehesa, "the
almost virgin forest . . . where fierce bulls pasture and huge
reptiles live in the shadows" (13), habitat of the serpent Sancha
who, according to legend, had crushed its one-time friend and
companion, a shepherd boy home from the wars.

Within this milieu of coarse physical immediateness veiled
with an ominous suggestiveness, Blasco Ibáñez constructs a plot
of personal relations, a love story between Tonet, son of the
hardworking rice farmer Tío Tòni and grandson of the fisher-
man Tío "Paloma," and Neleta, his erstwhile childhood companion. The latter has grown up determined to escape from her
poverty, and while Tonet was away at war she has married
Cañamèl, well-to-do but sickly tavern owner. The author makes
a concession to the subject of environmental influence on personality in the second and third chapters, where he gives a retrospective account of Tonet and Neleta's background. This
explanatory information, which is dull reading in comparison
with the vivid scenes of customs, such as the drawing of lots
for favorable fishing positions (chapter 4), is unnecessarily long
and may be considered the novel's one technical flaw; for the
novel is after all not so much a story of character as it is of situation, in which human beings are pitted against destructive
natural forces. Circumstances explain in some degree the spirit-
less drifting of Tonet and the fierce ambition of Neleta and
hence contribute to the plot complication. But they are really
secondary to the stronger factors of sex and instinct, which
operate at the bidding of an all-powerful Nature that works its
will through the medium of local conditions.

In the climactic outcome of the narrative action we are led
first to the crisis of the illicit love affair between Tonet and
Neleta, which includes the emotional breakdown of the former,
the protagonist, and then to the tonal climax bearing on man's

57. Translated from *Cañas y barro* (Valencia: Prometeo, n.d.).

haplessness in the clutches of nature. Cañamèl dies, specifying in
his will that his widow must not marry or have anything to do
with men if she is to keep his property. Neleta therefore refuses
to marry Tonet or associate with him openly, and when their
child is born she orders her lover to take it to Valencia secretly,
hoping thus to evade the spying eyes of Cañamèl's former sister-
in-law, who has long suspected her infidelity. Fear and remorse
overwhelm Tonet on his way to Valencia, and in desperation
he throws the baby in the lake. Some days later during a bird
hunt, when his dog discovers the baby's corpse, a viscous, formless mass covered with leeches, he flees from the scene and
commits suicide.

In a sense Tonet is a victim of his own weakness, and the
gradual intensification of his moral breakdown is a psychological development of considerable interest in itself. But the dominant narrative effect points to the cruelty in the natural world.
Neleta is in effect an instrument of nature who crushes individual
life just as the serpent Sancha had crushed the shepherd youth.
In his last desperate moments Tonet himself compares his lover
to the serpent. The love story thus is an occasion for the assertion of a malevolent force in a specific manifestation, and the
Albufera is the arena in which the human sacrifice is exacted.
In a similarly grim and earthy arena and similarly through the
instrumentality of sex, individuality is sacrificed to the monster
Nature in Zola's *Germinal*. The tonal theme of human futility,
which has been amplified throughout Blasco Ibáñez' story by
attention to various examples of wretchedness, notably the vaga-
bond "Sangonera," rises to a climactic height in the final scene,
where Tío Tòni buries his son. While his foster daughter, "La
Borda," stands by in silent anguish, still concealing her love for
Tonet, the father ponders the emptiness of existence and the
futility of his struggle with the lake:

The earth would fulfill its mission: like a sea of coppery tassels
of grain the crop would grow over the body of Tonet. But he —
what was there left for him to do in the world?
    The father wept contemplating the emptiness of his existence,
the loneliness that awaited him until his death, a loneliness
smooth, monotonous, endless, like the lake that shone before his
eyes, without a boat upon it to disturb its flat surface. (312)

Identifying his characters with their immediate surroundings, and these in turn with an enveloping philosophical tone, Blasco Ibáñez achieves a close unity between artistic form and philosophical perspective. It is this firm consistency that constitutes a fundamental distinction between *Cañas y barro* and *Los Pazos de Ulloa*. In the contest between man and nature which Pardo Bazán portrays, she brings into an area of primitive nature two persons, Nucha and Julián, who are outsiders and really separate from the world that confronts them. Regarded either as representatives of cultured society opposed by savagery or as representatives of the spiritual realm opposed by the physical, these personages reside in a dualistic vision of the world, in which the two forces of good and evil war with each other. We thus witness the conversion of a literary mode (naturalism) that is philosophically monistic into a personal outlook that is philosophically dualistic. Blasco Ibáñez, by contrast, assumes a monistic viewpoint and produces strong connecting ties between the human being, his natural habitat, and the intellectual perspective that sees them as one. He therefore succeeds in creating the vivid impression that human ideals can rise only momentarily above the earth, which is their source and their destiny. For this reason he is much closer than Pardo Bazán to Zola.

Both Spanish writers understood that a concept of oneness between man and nature underlies Zola's stand, and both give us pictures of man as a victim of nature; but Pardo Bazán preferred merely to get her feet wet rather than plunge into the naturalistic stream. As a result of her aloofness from the grimness inherent in Zola's philosophical outlook, she leaves the impression of observing from the outside a forest inhabited by evil spirits. The portrait of a place which she achieves in *Los Pazos de Ulloa* is no small accomplishment. But Blasco Ibáñez not only creates the vivid portrait of a place in *Cañas y barro*, he combines with it a theme in perfect harmony with the monistic foundations of naturalism. Man is crushed by nature, not in his separateness from it but because he is one with it. On the basis of this oneness the author builds an unusually strong singleness of narrative effect. From an artistic viewpoint, *Cañas y barro* is a gem among modern Spanish novels.

5

The Deification of Conscious Process

Benito Pérez Galdós

BENITO PÉREZ GALDÓS
1843-1920

CONTEMPORANEOUS with the somber view of life so stoutly exemplified by Zola, there was an equally virile manifestation of optimism. It is an attitude that must not be confused with "Victorian complacency," for it was characterized more by determination than by placid contentment. Evidencing respect for but not fear of scientific developments, it was the expression of a frank effort to incorporate the biological, social, and moral sciences in a meaningful whole. The philosophical outlook is appropriately called "spiritual naturalism," a term in wide use in the late nineteenth century.

This "other side" of naturalism finds an unusually vigorous exponent in Benito Pérez Galdós, foremost novelist of modern Spain and one of the most truly representative personalities of the nineteenth century. Although very much a product of his age, Galdós was an independent and poised thinker who occupied a firm middle ground in which he evinced neither a worship of science nor a worship of religion and yet respected both. Like Zola, he was interested in man as a product of nature and of society, but his attention was directed more to the upper reaches of the evolutionary slope and hence showed a greater interest in psychology than in physiology. Moreover, in his conception of man as a social being, however deeply entangled in relations with others, he saw always an individual character rather than a fragment of group consciousness at the mercy of a mysterious vital force or "will." Much more of an intellectual than Zola, he persistently tried to harmonize all knowledge, exact and speculative, in an interpretation of human nature within a comprehensive view of total Nature. At times, especially in his early works, his antagonism to certain excesses of static society, such as religious and social prejudices, led him into the emotionalism of an evangelistic progressive. In his mature and most characteristic posture, however, he contemplates studiously and often with quizzical amusement the relationship between individual personality and its social environment. He thus constructs a novel of character, which typically is a psychological story of struggle, adjustment, and growth.

The age in which Galdós attained his professional maturity — roughly, the twenty years following his arrival in Madrid in 1862 from his home in the Canary Islands — was for Spain a period of intellectual invigoration contrasting with the dull mid-century period of staticism. The age was marked by the growth of liberalism and a lively interest in ideas from other European countries. The major orientation for the Spaniards continued to be France, as it had been since the advent of the Bourbon dynasty in 1700. Paris was, in fact, not only a source of French ideas but a kind of clearinghouse, by way of commentary and translation, for the intellectualism of other lands, notably Germany and England. Of these two major sources of ideas, in addition to France, German thought is especially to be noted in the second half of the century. This influence is no doubt partly to be explained by the personal stature and leadership of Julián Sanz del Río, who took the chair of philosophy in the University of Madrid in 1854 after several years of study in Germany and soon became one of the most influential figures of modern Spain — not so much for the philosophical system (Krausism) that he espoused as for his liberalizing and stabilizing effect on the youthful intellectuals of the 1860's.

In the decade 1870-1880, particularly, there was much controversy between traditionalists and liberals on literary and philosophical subjects, but there was also a widespread attitude of conciliation, which, incidentally, was one of the earmarks of Sanz del Río's philosophy.[1] The attitude was a continuation of the desire manifest in Europe throughout the century for co-operation among science, philosophy, and religion. With some the spirit of conciliation was scarcely more than a willingness to accept a state of peaceful coexistence of independent fields of thought in a compartmentalized world where science could go its own way without intruding on the domains of another discipline. Thus an orthodox religious believer, while trying to keep abreast of intellectual activity, could remain comfortable by dividing the human being, as of old, into body and soul and assigning the parts to different and actually disconnected areas of study.[2] The kind of conciliatory attitude, however, which has special relevancy to our subject is the determination to find within a unitary system of being a co-operative activity that is at one time a natural and a spiritual process. What this intention amounts to is the incorporation of science into philosophy. In the intellectual climate of Spain in the last two decades of the nineteenth century the science most amenable to the merger was psychology. The psychological viewpoint referred to may, in broad terms, be described as a combination in which the physical and the psychical, though apparently independent, are mutually dependent and open to synthesis at a higher level of consciousness.

The subject of psychology seems to have acquired particular importance in Spain around 1880. The Spaniards, who in general rejected any kind of scientific materialism, welcomed a psychology that made room for philosophical idealism. This is one reason why it is worthwhile to look for indications of German ideas in philosophical and fictional literature, and the German

1. This general conciliatory attitude is possibly the most important consideration in regard to Sanz del Río's influence on Galdós. For a discussion of more specific aspects of the Krausist influence on Galdós, with attention primarily to the novelist's early stage, see Walter T. Pattison, *Benito Pérez Galdós and the Creative Process* (Minneapolis: University of Minnesota Press, 1954), pp. 37-58.

2. "Las dos filosofías, la que se ocupa de los cuerpos y la que estudia los espíritus, son en sí buenas, útiles, necesarias," declares Nicomedes Martín Mateos ("Las corrientes filosóficas del siglo," *Rev. de Esp.*, LVIII [1879], 232), a defender of "la filosofía espiritualista," which conceives of an objective spiritual (religious) Law independent of the individual seen as an organism.

psychologist whose natural philosophy would seem most at home in the liberal Spain of 1880 is Wilhelm Wundt. In so far as Galdós is concerned, the way of thinking represented by Wundt has greater interest for us than the systems of other leading European philosopher-psychologists, such as Spencer and Taine. Spanish acquaintance with Wundt apparently was very superficial at first, coming about indirectly, probably through the French. U. González Serrano, prolific writer of philosophical and psychological treatises, opposed the German psychologist in 1879 on the grounds that he was a mechanist who treated the physical and the psychical as one. Referring to Wundt's *Physiological Psychology* (1874), he mistakenly identifies him with the school of contemporary psychologists who place greatest weight on sensation and molecular movement, thus producing a "psychology without a soul." [3] Actually, Wundt was as much opposed as González Serrano to the mechanistic materialism of the eighteenth-century sensationalists and the "psychophysical materialism," as he calls it, of the nineteenth century; and he makes this clear in the Introduction to his *Physiological Psychology*. He refuses to believe that there is any such thing as mind substance — for he believes that mind is process — but he just as quickly rejects any thought of material substance. He makes use of physiology as a necessary basis in experimental science, but he keeps it subordinate by arguing that mental life holds the key to its true interpretation, and he accordingly gives much value to voluntary activity, which is found at the highest levels of life.[4] González Serrano, in some of his statements of later date, shows himself to be in agreement with Wundt in several important respects: the belief that necessity and freedom are complementary rather than contradictory,[5] the belief that the body possesses an unquestionable psycho-

3. "La psicología contemporánea," *Rev. de Esp.*, LIX (1879), 206-20.
4. See *Principles of Physiological Psychology*, trans. Edward Bradford Titchener (London: S. Sonnenschein & Co., 1904), I, 211, and *Lectures on Human and Animal Psychology* (1863), trans. J. E. Creighton and E. B. Titchener (London: S. Sonnenschein & Co., 1901), pp. 3-10, 409. Cf. also Alfred Fouillée ("La Sensation et la pensée selon le sensualisme et le Platonisme contemporains," *RDM,* LXXXII [1887], 422-23), who observes that Wundt seeks the unity of mental composition in the act of thinking itself instead of in something more *vital* than thought.
5. "La psicología novísima," *Rev. de Esp.*, C (1884), 747-71. Cf. Wundt's *Lectures* ..., p. 426.

logical value,[6] and the contention that will, the most complex and superior manifestation of life, which reaches its height in the form of human personality, must be examined in terms of reason.[7]

It is unnecessary — and it would probably be difficult — to prove that Wundt as either scientist or philosopher had a specific and direct influence on Galdós. The latter partook of many fountains, combining them at will and no doubt depending upon popularized presentations of well-known works more than upon primary sources.[8] The important thing, then, is to point out certain ideas prevalent in the novelist's intellectual environment that help to account for his interpretation of character and personality. Wundt and González Serrano represent a psychological-philosophical outlook with which Galdós was in large degree compatible. In broad perspective, it was a mixture of philosophical idealism and scientific realism, which in novelistic art may be aptly termed *idealismo realista*.[9] Psychology was the medium by which this particular outlook was most concretely understandable. "The psychological system," as one writer declared in 1885, offered new hope in the realm of philosophy, for it provided for a synthesis of empiricism and idealism.[10]

In connection with the marked desire to reconcile nature and reason by way of philosophy, the rise of social psychology must be kept in mind and with it the increasing inclination to emphasize the relationship between the individual and society. Sociologists early in the century (Comte and Spencer, for example) had recognized the close relationship existing between the social and the biological sciences, but it took time for the crystal-

6. For which opinion he cites Wundt, Lotze, Ribot, and others: "Valor moral del cuerpo humano," *Rev. de Esp.*, CIV (1885), 27-36.

7. *Estudios psicológicos* (Madrid, 1892), p. 11.

8. As far as I know, there were no Spanish translations of Wundt's works in the nineteenth century and no French translations before 1885. There were, however, numerous treatises on contemporary psychology from which a general view of Wundt's ideas could be had. For example, James Sully, "La psicología fisiológica en Alemania," *Rev. contemporánea*, II (1876), 329-57 (trans. of an article in *Mind*); and Th. Ribot, *La Psychologie allemande contemporaine (école expérimentale)* (1879).

9. González Serrano uses this term based on the German *Realidealismus* (as he calls it), while approving the fact that contemporary art draws on the natural sciences: "El arte naturalista," *Rev. de Esp.*, CV (1885), 41.

10. Mariano Amador, "El fatalismo de Hartley," *Rev. de Esp.*, CVII (1885), 23.

lization of the concept of an active interdependence in which heredity as the natural agent and society as the environmental agent share responsibility in the creation of an individual. The concept of such a creative relationship, however, did assert itself gradually in the field of psychology, and personality came to be regarded as a process of becoming: "personality is not a phenomenon but an evolution, not a momentary happening but a history, not a present or a past but both of them." [11] A viewpoint that visualizes a continuously active combination of natural and environmental factors as an explanation of personality tends to de-emphasize the passive states of evolutionary development, in which man appears to be more or less at the mercy of a nature that looks only to the interests of the species. It allows, rather, for a process of give-and-take, in which the individual uses environment for his own good while being molded by it. A combination of the social and the psychical is thus made to provide a constructive basis for the human situation.

In so far as Galdós is concerned, there is perhaps no more significant phase of nineteenth-century scientific thought than the rise of social psychology; and, as we shall see later, the subject takes on special interest when viewed in conjunction with the spiritual evolutionism of Hegel. The social and psychological synthesis of competing yet co-operative forces, which was a rather common topic of discussion in Galdós' day, is actually suggestive of Hegel and raises the question of his possible influence in the late nineteenth-century novel. Hegelianism had lost ground with the rise of positivism but it regained some of its popularity in the last third of the century and, curiously enough, at a time when Schopenhauer's star was definitely in the ascendancy. Von Hartmann testified in 1878 [12] that the two philosophies most fruitful and decisive in Germany in a period of several years preceding that date were those of Hegel and Schopenhauer, and he himself drew on both in constructing his own system. In the 1870's and 1880's in Spain a number of prominent intellectuals were Hegelians, among them Emilio Castelar, who declared in 1874 that "the real philosophy of

---

11. Th. Ribot, *Les Maladies de la personalité* (1885), as quoted by González Serrano in *Estudios psicológicos*, p. 100.
12. Preface to the 8th edition of *Philosophy of the Unconscious*.

progress is the philosophy of Hegel." [13] In the periodical literature of the epoch Hegel is mentioned at times in a general way only, and at times with reference to the harmony of opposites; and occasionally one finds statements that definitely recall the philosopher without any allusion to him as a source. Such statements give prominence to the idea that progress toward truth is a step of transcendent movement achieved in the synthesis of opposites. For example:

To rise above the objects that experience presents, to dominate this world of oppositions and struggles, of contradictions and antitheses, and to find the truth in which those oppositions disappear, negations are erased, and everything comes together in laws of unity and harmony; such is the science of the essential; such is the object and the usefulness of philosophy. [14]

Or again:

In order that there may be a perfecting, it is necessary that there be limitation; in order to weigh the truth, it is also necessary that there be an opposition of contradictory ideas, and to this conclusion those people will come who allow themselves to be puzzled by the force of antithesis. [15]

Discourses about the necessity of conflict, the transcending of antithetical situations, and the resultant expansion of human personality as an evolutionary expression of Mind are pretty definite indications that certain fundamental Hegelian ideas formed a part of the intellectual subject matter with which the youthful Galdós, alert to ideas of every kind, would certainly have been familiar. [16] When adapted to social psychology, Hegelian theory provides a view of evolution that focuses attention on the later stages of man's history and shifts the emphasis from the past to the future. It is precisely this perspective that be-

13. "La filosofía del progreso," Rev. Europea, I (1874), 1. Cf. also: "Síntesis entre la filosofía y la historia," Rev. de Esp., LXXX (1881), 433. For a brief survey of Hegelianism in Spain in the nineteenth century, see Mario Méndez Bejarano, Historia de la filosofía en España hasta el siglo xx (Madrid, n.d.), pp. 457-61.
14. Luis de Rute, "Breves indicaciones sobre filosofía a los matemáticos," Rev. de Esp., VII (1869), 241.
15. Jaime Porcar, "Observaciones psicológicas," Rev. de Esp., XXV (1872), 266.
16. Such ideas, of course, could be an indirect reflection of Hegel, through Sanz del Río; but Hegel's personality itself was definitely felt in Spain. His Logic was translated into Spanish in 1872.

comes evident in Galdós' novels of contemporary social life once he has expended some of his pent-up rebelliousness against the severe Spanish traditionalism that he opposed both publicly and privately. By 1886 he seems to have developed a firm philosophical outlook; and it was at this time, the most vigorous stage of his career, that he composed *Fortunata y Jacinta*.

Fortunata y Jacinta (1886-1887)

This massive novel is one of the richest and most elaborate examples of nineteenth-century realism. Deeply set in local milieu, it is a broad social record of Madrid life around 1870-1875, and a veritable depository of national types. With all its local color, however, it is an outstanding study of an individual personality and the vital expression of a positive philosophy. Because of the novel's detail and its leisurely tempo, the present-day reader may wish that Galdós had condensed his story into half the space. Yet much of the material that might be classified as background is actually a necessary part of a novelistic method that makes character portrayal the first duty of a novelist and makes social environment an indispensable basis for the portraiture. No better example could be found of a novelist who is also a social psychologist observing the formation and growth of personality in its contact with surroundings. In Galdós' world environment consists primarily of ideas and personal relationships, as compared to the heaviness of physical surroundings found in Zola. Out of a rich background of social relations, the characters emerge slowly, as the author, with a narrative rhythm befitting his leisurely biographical plan, follows the course of personal vicissitudes over a comparatively long period of time. The reader, therefore, cannot expect to find in *Fortunata y Jacinta* a concentration of dramatic action centering on a specific set of circumstances such as Zola presents in *Germinal*. He should look, instead, for a story of gradual psychological development in one or two of the principal personages, and he may expect these sometimes to retreat from view within a large network of friends and relatives, whose activities and speech form a kind of historical record of contemporary Spanish life.

For purposes of a quick introduction, the story of *Fortunata y Jacinta* may be defined as the progress and outcome of a rivalry in which two women, one from the *pueblo* or proletariat (Fortunata) and one from the upper middle class (Jacinta), vie for the love of a man (Juanito Santa Cruz) who belongs to a wealthy merchant family. The outcome of the rivalry, however, when defined in terms of surface events, will prove to be of less interest than the psychological portraiture of Fortunata's efforts to compensate for her inferiority.[17] The feeling of inferiority, which is actually a creative motivation in the central character, is not so much attributable to her social class as to her fall in society's respect after being seduced and abandoned by Santa Cruz. As the author follows Fortunata's psychical agitation and the regenerative development growing out of it, he is deliberately dealing with the problem of morality, viewing it in the light of conflicting demands of natural and social laws. The two women rivals in fact — the author makes clear by repeated allusions to the subject — are meant to be representatives of two great forces, nature and society; and in their relationship, particularly as evidenced in Fortunata, there are definite philosophical implications that will have to be considered an integral part of the story. These have to do especially with the subject of individuality.

The philosophical quality of *Fortunata y Jacinta* will perhaps seem remote to one who begins the novel for the first time, because it is deeply submerged in character and situation as these are handled by an enthusiastic follower of realistic technique. The Spaniards of 1887, themselves, were undoubtedly less moved to philosophical reflection than to enjoyment of a picture of life in Madrid in 1870 revived with the humor and informality of a sympathetic onlooker. Galdós unquestionably took pride in the role of social historian, which he enacts quite openly in volume one of his novel. But he was also concerned with society as a formative influence on personality, and his attention to

17. The essential content of my interpretation of *Fortunata y Jacinta* has been expressed elsewhere: "The Treatment of Individual Personality in *Fortunata y Jacinta*," Hispanic Review, XVII (1949), 269-89; and, rather fragmentarily, in *The Novels of Pérez Galdós* (St. Louis: Washington University Studies, 1954). I feel justified in repeating the main ideas in order to give a comprehensive picture of the novel in relation to its thought background.

background must be considered partly as preparation of the medium in which the main characters are to be observed. Thus, when *Fortunata y Jacinta* is viewed in its totality, volume one is hardly more than a setting for the narrative situation and an exposition of the milieu in which the heroine is to perform.

In this introductory volume Fortunata remains almost altogether out of sight, like the protagonist of a play who comes on stage only after the way has been thoroughly prepared. The reader's attention meanwhile is directed to various minor characters, whom the author treats in a manner reminiscent of Charles Dickens. For Galdós also has the spirit of an amused spectator watching some of the curiosities of the big broad world; and with him, as with Dickens, the most striking curiosities in all nature are people. Purely as an artistic activity the author enjoys describing people, giving us "More and more particulars relating to this illustrious family" (chapter heading, I, vi). Consequently he uses much more time in this pursuit than is strictly necessary for narrative purposes, though he has the incidental characters justify their presence by performing mechanical roles in advancing the central narrative action. One such personage is Estupiñá, a friend of the Santa Cruz family, a former clerk, now eking out a humble existence doing odd jobs and living in one of the poorest sections of Madrid.

It was on a visit to Estupiñá's place, once when he was ill, that Juanito Santa Cruz first met Fortunata, coming upon her as she stood sucking a raw egg on the steps of the apartment where she lived with her aunt, a poultry dealer. This is the only time in all of volume one that the reader sees Fortunata, but the brief glance at an uninhibited, vital, and beautiful girl is sufficient to leave an indelible image of the wholesome primitiveness that was continuously thereafter to exert a magnetic attraction on Juanito Santa Cruz. Juanito is a pampered only son who usually does as he pleases, though the general course of his life is pretty closely watched by his mother, Doña Bárbara. Soon after he meets Fortunata, Doña Bárbara detects signs of waywardness in her son and hastens to arrange his marriage to his cousin Jacinta, a model of respectable middle-class society who carefully observes the approved social and moral standards. On their honeymoon Jacinta's curiosity gets the best of her professed indifference concerning her husband's past, and she finally elicits his confession that he had seduced and abandoned Fortunata. Generous enough to overlook this stain on Juanito's record, she soon realizes that she will have to be even more forgiving during her married life; for after a short time she faces the necessity of competing with another woman for her husband's love. Her longing for a child, attributable partly to a desire to hold her husband, increases when she learns that Fortunata had borne a son to Juanito. She even tries to locate the child and adopt it, invoking the aid of her spinster friend Guillermina, whose charitable activity has led her to an acquaintance with various families of the slums. Jacinta's hopes are thwarted when Juanito tells her that his son has died and her father-in-law asks her to give up the small boy whom she has mistakenly thought to be her husband's. She thus feels with double sharpness the unpleasantness of her competitive position when she detects evidence of her husband's recurring waywardness and suspects that he is seeing Fortunata again.

The first volume, which closes with attention to Juanito's persistent search for Fortunata, has been largely devoted to his part in the triangle and is the one section of the novel in which his characterization has real psychological solidity. His is the case of a young man conditioned in the static ease of middle-class society feeling the attraction of a representative of the virile *pueblo*, intelligent enough to recognize the value of an intermixture of social classes, and yet reacting with the mediocrity of his insignificant companions. Repeatedly he shows this vacillation between two forces (symbolized by Fortunata and Jacinta), between revolution and order, between spontaneity and conventionalism, but he accepts more and more cynically the prejudices of the privileged group and solves his personal problem easily by way of an indifferent, laissez-faire attitude. His characterization is firmly grounded in the general ideational content of the novel having to do with the relative validity of reason and natural impulse and the role of individuality as a medium of interaction between the two. But in so far as our interest in an individual is concerned, Juanito's portrait quickly recedes into the background, becoming of importance only as a mechanical object of reference in the Fortunata-Jacinta relationship.

In all of the novel after the first volume, the rivalry between the two women is presented primarily from Fortunata's viewpoint, and the narrative action records the course of a changing sense of values as Fortunata turns gradually from Juanito to Jacinta as her main orientation. The course is marked off in major steps, in which decisive psychological shifts of emphasis follow climactic happenings, with each new stage being an extension of ideas already at work in the preceding stage. This view of the novel's principal impact, of course, is an interpretation of the story as a psychological development, in which personality change is the most meaningful aspect of the narrative action. It is based on the conviction that Galdós should first of all be understood as a socio-psychological novelist.

When Fortunata comes actively into the story at the beginning of the second volume, some three years have passed since she was abandoned by Santa Cruz. In this time she has drifted from one man to another, and now, temporarily unattached, rests in a rather low trough of indifference. In this state of dulled consciousness a period of reactivation begins, which will become both a process of socialization or adaptation of the individual to the social whole and a moral regeneration or growth in self-respect and sympathetic attitude toward others, including eventually her "enemy" Jacinta. First, the motive of social respectability is stimulated when she meets Maximiliano Rubín and after much persuasion prepares to marry him. Maximiliano is one of the numerous unfortunate specimens of the human race portrayed with humor and sympathetic understanding by Galdós and occasionally, as now, elevated to a major supporting role in the narrative. Physically insignificant, suffering from a chronic nervous illness, held in low esteem by people in general, and dominated by his officious aunt, Doña Lupe, Maxi sees in Fortunata not only a beautiful woman but an opportunity to assert himself and, by reclaiming her, to accomplish something in his own right. Enthusiastically he sets about his plans, gaining with some difficulty the co-operation of his aunt. Fortunata accepts the proposal of marriage halfheartedly, submitting to a transitional period of "moral cleansing" in a convent for fallen women. But, despite all her seeming indifference, she sincerely desires the security of a home and honestly believes that she may someday be able to love the unattractive Maxi.

Even as Fortunata prepares for the marriage, however, certain disturbing thoughts begin to complicate her social reclamation. Through Mauricia *la Dura*, a derelict whom she meets in the convent and who will repeatedly encourage her to return to Juanito, she hears of Jacinta's virtuous reputation and her unfulfilled desire for children. She then learns that Juanito is looking for her. The temptation to rejoin the man whom she has never ceased to love reaches a climactic point on her wedding night when Juanito comes to the door of her apartment and she paces the floor in debate with her conscience as her husband lies sick in bed. Her sense of fair play with respect to Maxi maintains the upper hand on this occasion, bearing eloquent testimony to a restimulated strength of character; but the temptation has been too great, and she soon deserts the Rubín family to live in an apartment provided by Santa Cruz.

Fortunata's attempted readjustment thus appears to be a failure, as the second volume of the novel comes to an end. Pride of possession in a competitive struggle and natural love unmixed with complicating social motives triumph over concern for what people think. "You are my husband," she tells Juanito, defiantly ignoring society, "everything else . . . piffle!" (288) [18] Nevertheless, the seeds have been planted that will cause Fortunata to modify her untamed individualism. Thoughts of Jacinta's spotless reputation will never leave her, looming up first as a cruel obstacle, then as a challenge, and eventually as an object of admiration. Angry when Juanito abandons her a second time, she walks over to the Santa Cruz home, feeling the savage impulse to engage her rival in combat though giving in finally to passive dejection and a liaison with Feijoo, a man three times her age. What follows in volume three is essentially a groping for orientation on the part of one who is bewildered by the conflict between natural, honest impulses and the demands of

18. Quotations (translated) are from Galdós' *Obras completas* (Madrid: Aguilar, 1942), V.

conventional society. Feijoo himself, acting partly as lover and partly as father, contributes toward Fortunata's stabilization. For, although he discusses the subject of compromise between nature and society with the cautiousness of a tightrope walker and the flexibility of one who must justify his own situation, he supplies much-needed kindness and sympathetic understanding. Fortunata, however, is less concerned with Feijoo's moral philosophy and the expediency of social conventions than she is with her relative standing with respect to Jacinta. To be *honrada* like Jacinta, even though she doesn't know exactly what the word means, becomes for her a necessity. For a while she follows a calm, routine existence, showing an acquired veneer of conventionalism, especially after rejoining her husband when Feijoo, because of his age and bad health, urges her to do so and persuades the Rubíns to take her back into the family. A period of intense psychological activity and uncertainty arises again when by chance and for the first time she finds herself in Jacinta's presence, on the occasion of Mauricia *la Dura*'s illness. Here Fortunata again feels the impulse to hurt her enemy and does in fact aggressively reveal who she is.

The conflict now is clearly more than a battle between two persons, one a representative of nature and one a representative of society. It is a psychological conflict between the primitive and the social within the same person, which may also be described as the struggle between a life force that is always surging forward in raw instinctive action and a restraining and directive force that compels halts and periods of stabilization. More important, both elements of the conflict are indispensable to the individual. The "natural" impulse tells Fortunata that the man she first loved belongs to her and that Jacinta "stole him from me" (401). Social motives become gradually more intense, as evidenced by the increasing desire to be accepted in the small circle to which Jacinta belongs. Trapped in a conflict between natural and social interests, like a child groping for understanding, Fortunata climbs a ladder of changing values bearing on self-respect and the respect of others.

The climb, however, is slow and faltering. While in an emotional state of confused aspirations following her unexpected meeting with Jacinta, Fortunata is drawn into the second major climactic happening of the narrative, which proves to be a decisive turn of events and a decisive development in the heroine's personality. Looking for guidance and encouragement, she turns to Guillermina, who has taken a tolerant, even friendly attitude toward her, recognizing that an inherent soundness underlies the rough primitive surface of this representative of the *pueblo*, this "uncut stone." With sincere respect for her "friend's" saintly reputation, Fortunata calls on her one day, nursing the rather astonishing hope that she can gain the gratitude of the Santa Cruz family by contributing a son to Juanito. Jacinta, she argues, may be "as much of an angel as you like; but *she doesn't have any children*," and a wife who cannot have children is not a wife (421). Guillermina is less bewildered by this strange idea than she is embarrassed by the fact that Jacinta had dropped in unexpectedly shortly before Fortunata's arrival and is now concealed in a bedroom. For once in her life the resourceful "virgin and founder" (of charities) finds herself unable to dominate a situation and remains almost completely helpless when Jacinta, at a remark of her rival's, furiously rushes out of her hiding. The hand-to-hand combat and the battle of words that follow end with Fortunata physically the victor and emotionally the loser, at least temporarily; for in an aftermath of despondency she feels more keenly than ever her inferiority. Instrumental in her recovery from this momentary defeatism is her determination to carry out her idea, her *pícara* idea of having a son by Juanito. Volume three thus ends with a re-establishment of relations with her lover in what seems to be another moral relapse: a rebellious defiance of social regulation and the triumph of natural love.

It is quite clear, however, that Fortunata is now merely using nature (the capacity for bearing children) as a means of compensating for a feeling of inferiority caused by society; that Juanito, in contrast with his position earlier in the story, is important to her primarily as a steppingstone to a more favorable relationship with Jacinta; and that defiance of moral rules is in reality an expression of the value attached to approval by others, which brings the ever-increasing need of a more respected moral status. Here is illustrated the paradoxical appearance of life, which Galdós is fond of portraying. Paradox, it should be emphasized, is fundamental in the novel's structure, and apparently so through deliberate design. The turning to Juanito is in reality a turning from Juanito to Jacinta; the attainment of superiority is the expression of inferiority; the desire to triumph over an enemy is a desire to win her respect and friendship; the ascendancy of natural forces is a concession to social forces. In short, Fortunata's seeming reversion to a former state is really an advance to a higher state. The firmness and decisiveness noticeable in her action after the violent meeting with her rival are in themselves an indication of self-direction and self-respect. But the major consideration continues to be her self-enlargement by way of social relations, which is directly attributable to her competition with Jacinta.

The heroine's psychological journey, it must be noted, is a succession of stages, some of which are periods of repose following moments of intense agitation. Her portrayal is characteristic of Galdós' method, by which a protagonist is allowed to rest on a plateau of psychological consolidation after a decisive turn of events. The method is very much in accord with our present-day conception of personality growth as being a fluctuating movement of advances, halts — and retrogressions at times — and consolidations of slowly changing tendencies, rather than an even, uninterrupted flow. Thus in the case of Fortunata there is a quiet period of relaxation and even a display of conventionalistic veneer as she resumes relations with her lover while maintaining appearances as a member of the Rubín family. The author meanwhile devotes a great deal of attention to various secondary characters, especially to Maximiliano, whose bad health and suspicions concerning his wife are driving him nearer and nearer to madness. Some of the personages who receive lengthy attention are altogether minor. Such, for example, are the tragicomic and wretched José Ido del Sagrario and the lonely Moreno Isla, who is hopelessly in love with Jacinta and would have been a much more suitable husband for her than Juanito Santa Cruz. These and other incidental characters contribute to a general impression of tangled and unhappy lives and thus, collectively, give the novel a certain pessimistic coloring, though not enough to obscure the dominant mood of charitable humor on the author's part. Collective human experience, moreover, never assumes a major role in the narrative development. It is, rather, a supplement to the portrayal of a few leading characters, who sometimes appear in harmony with the mass synthesis but are just as likely to present a marked contrast. The explanation is to be found in the author's focus on individuality. Even the mass picture seems to the reader to be an assembly of individual aspirations rather than the fusion of an unconscious urge to live, such as one often finds in Zola. The total picture may be darkened by the shadows of failure and distress, but these only heighten the effect of individual accomplishment; and so it is that Fortunata's struggles and attainments stand out in bold relief amidst a seeming morass of twisted hopes and wasted lives.

As the long narrative approaches its conclusion, the most prominent motive in Fortunata's behavior is her desire for friendship and equality with Jacinta. After a period of quietness she is again drawn into turbulent psychological activity because of accepting as true the assertion of her friend Aurora that Jacinta is unfaithful to her husband. When she tells Juanito what she has heard, he uses the occasion as an excuse for dismissing her, cruelly throwing in her face the lowliness of her moral status as compared to that of her impeccable rival. The fact that she is again abandoned by her lover concerns her much less than her relative moral position, and her desire to attain virtue now becomes a veritable drive to attain partnership with her rival. Formerly she would have delighted in knowing that Jacinta was immoral. Now she begins to have pride in her rival's virtuous reputation, which stands before her like an ideal whose attainment is absolutely necessary to her own happiness. Her preoccupation with this ideal overshadows all other interests, including her domestic situation, and after a quarrel with her husband's aunt she makes a final break with the Rubín family and returns to her childhood home. There she awaits the birth of her child (by Juanito), while Maximiliano, now calm after a period of intense nervous disorder, engages in a long and patient search to discover his wife's whereabouts.

The richest dramatic episode in Fortunata's life and the peak of her psychological journey follows soon after the birth of her son, itself a meritorious accomplishment in her opinion. This contribution of a son is the concrete evidence she has needed to establish her superiority over her rival, but even before the actual event the self-assurance deriving from it by anticipation has already resulted in a feeling of magnanimity toward Jacinta, which she expresses after the birth of her son with a mixture of pride and charity: "now that I have won the dispute [*pleito*] and she is down, I pardon her; I am like that" (524). The "accomplishment" has, of course, a special importance for her as a claim to being accepted, in spirit at least, within the Santa Cruz family circle. She does indeed have the respectable Santa Cruz family in a corner; for, as she muses to herself, "Yes, Señora Doña Bárbara, you are my mother-in-law over and above the head of Christ our Father, and you can jump in any direction you like, but I am the mother of your grandson" (524).

On the basis of this assumed inclusion in the Santa Cruz family, Fortunata takes upon herself the responsibility of the family honor. She is furiously disturbed, therefore, when she learns that Aurora is Juanito's lover, the news coming to her from Maxi, who has found her after a supreme display of logical deduction, of which he, as a person lightly esteemed, is extremely proud. There is in the heroine's reaction an element of anger at Aurora's deception and a good portion of jealousy with regard to the man on whom she has always honestly believed that she held first claim. Juanito as a person, however, is no longer necessary either to Jacinta or to Fortunata. The latter's major motivations are a sense of protectiveness toward her rival and a purely personal need of security; for she sees in Aurora not only a danger to her "friend" Jacinta but a threat to her own hold on the Santa Cruz family. Rising from bed prematurely and fighting for the sanctity of her own and Jacinta's family relationship, she engages Aurora in a violent struggle, which leaves her mortally weakened but one step closer to complete partnership with the woman whom she had once considered her enemy.

The narrative impact of the novel is at its strongest as Fortunata, having willed that her child be given to Jacinta, lies on her deathbed filled with a magnanimity toward everyone, with the possible exception of Aurora. Her desire to be accepted is partially met, because Guillermina, acting in the capacity of friend and counselor, openly recognizes her essential goodness as she tries patiently to prepare her charge for a correct departure from this world; while the author, himself opposed to formalistic religion, mischievously complicates matters by allowing his heroine to die without following the ritual of words pronounced by the priest. Even Jacinta is able finally to admire her rival, and indirectly (through Guillermina) she expresses her gratitude for the gift of the child. The focus of attention in the conclusion nonetheless remains, as it has been through the greater part of the narrative, on Fortunata's preoccupation with her relative position when compared with Jacinta; except that now the standards of comparison reside in a spiritual realm where the approval of God is a necessity. "Both of us are angels," the heroine declares as she nears death, "each in her own way" (545). With the simplicity of a child seeking the warmth of an intimate group, she reaches out in complete sincerity to those around her, at the same time trying desperately to talk herself and everyone else into believing that she, like Jacinta, is a "darling of Heaven" (*mona del Cielo*). The grandeur of spirit that she attains before her death is sufficient to convince a number of her acquaintances, including the author, that she has a good chance of winning God's approval.

The reader who wishes to enjoy the full strength of Galdós' novel must look beyond the situational plot — first to the psychological development that takes place in the leading character and then to the attendant implications of a moral-philosophical nature. The elaborate social background and the large array of secondary characters are not to be disregarded. The portrait of Maximiliano Rubín, who ends up in an insane asylum, is a psychological study that commands a great deal of interest in its own right. But the major significance of *Fortunata y Jacinta*, most critics will surely agree, rests in Fortunata herself, whatever be the method by which the novel is judged. From the standpoint of situation, we have witnessed a shifting course of emphasis within a triangle, where a woman turns gradually from enmity to friendliness toward her rival, virtually forgetting the man involved in the relationship. The final episode, in which Fortunata makes the sacrifice of giving her son to her former enemy, carries a strong dramatic effect when judged purely as situation. The rich emotional quality of the drama, however, derives primarily from the psychology of the heroine, a child of nature, a primitive woman of the *pueblo*, who is increasingly drawn toward ideals of the social whole which opposes her. Fortunata's natural soundness, with all her insistence on the honorableness of natural love, lies at the heart of the characterization; but it is brought to the surface and developed by way of a process in which the socially important (respectable reputation) becomes personally important and growth results through response to challenge. Almost to the last the heroine maintains, verbally at least, that "when that which is natural speaks, men have to keep their mouths shut" (501). But there is no mistaking the value that she places on a sympathetic relationship with those of unquestioned moral and spiritual standing. The Fortunata who in the end is capable of giving her son to her rival is not only far removed from the castoff who had passively agreed to a plan of social regeneration; she is morally and psychologically far beyond the childhood stage where the reader first glimpsed her. Most important of all, perhaps, the advance derives from a contest in which individual impulse and the restraining force of collective humanity continuously counterbalance each other.

The psychological progress, then, may be described as a transcending development arising from the meeting of antagonistic forces. Such a statement naturally brings Hegel to mind, and indeed the developmental process evident in Fortunata's psychology can appropriately be compared to the Hegelian interpretation of self-realization in so far as this is applicable to an individual life. Three aspects, especially, recall Hegel's theory of self-consciousness as set forth in his *Phenomenology of Mind:* the dependence of self upon an otherness (a specific person, for example) for the attainment of its own reality, the necessity of conflict, and a transcending movement in which self emerges from the conflict to rise above its former state. The succession of upward steps by which Fortunata expands her sympathetic attitude toward her antagonist, reverting sometimes to former levels and yet ever acquiring a new and more refined consciousness, could be used as a concrete illustration of Hegel's theory of spiritual evolution. Moreover, Galdós' optimistic contemplation of the paradoxical aspects of experience suggests Hegel's determination to bring meaning into the paradoxes of life. For-

tunata's moral rise is a continuous course of elevation by way
of seeming defeat and moral relapse, and the most dramatic and
significant episode in her personal history is a triumph by way
of surrender (in the gift of her son to her adversary). Maxi's
case also is paradoxical. Though destined finally to an insane
asylum, he is serenely confident of his philosophical and spiritual
rise; and the author, who looks on in smiling fantasy, would
grant that Maxi may be right, because he is willing to look for
wisdom and spiritual grandeur in seeming madness. "The Reason of Unreason" (*La razón de la sinrazón*), the title of one of
the late chapters in the novel, is a favorite theme with Galdós.

There is, further, an unmistakable symbolic meaning, apart
from the psychology of the characters, in the author's contraposition of nature and society as beneficially antithetical. The
representative of nature (Fortunata) and the representative of
society (Jacinta), the one dominated largely by impulse and the
other by the discipline of social regulation, are mutually dependent though constantly engaged in a tug of war. Society may
seem victorious in the end, but Jacinta is no more the winner
than Fortunata; for she must accept the contribution (a son) of
nature's champion. The social woman and the natural woman
(and symbolically, too, the middle class and the *pueblo*) are
each incomplete without the other and by their very conflict
come to realize this fact. Jacinta, whose thoughts are much less
in evidence throughout the novel than Fortunata's, finally ad-
mits that she would like in some ways to be like her rival. Undoubtedly the author meant the two women, when symbolically
viewed, to be mutually complementary in a moral sense; but the
moral import can easily be extended to harmonize with a philosophical concept of universal law. From a comprehensive viewpoint, then, including the psychology of the main character
along with plot situation and symbolism, the story of *Fortunata
y Jacinta* is the account of a co-operative activity on the part of
natural and social forces working itself out in individual psychology along a line of moral invigoration. The personality of
Fortunata is the heart of the process, and the picture of Spanish
society is its framework.

In an earlier study the present writer went to some length
in arguing for Hegelian content in a number of Galdós' nov-

els written after 1885.[19] There seems to be no reason for a change of opinion, especially in the light of further evidence that Hegelian thought, though by no means attaining the proportions of a major movement in Spain, constituted at least a fairly prominent part of the novelist's intellectual environment. Still, we must not overemphasize any one specific influence. Galdós was stimulated by various philosophers, and artists as well, among them Cervantes, with whom he evinces a broad compatibility. But whatever the sources of his philosophical ideas, we can be sure that his outlook is firmly grounded, by way of psychology, in the natural world, which is also a social world. For this reason, while looking for metaphysical meaning in his novels we must look to contemporary developments in the field of psychology. From his viewpoint, nature presents two fundamental aspects which reveal a process of competition and co-operation. In a realistic, practical sense, the process is best described as socio-psychological, since the human being is seen as an interaction of personal impulses and determination from without. The most important consideration, however, is that the psychological process is creative. To borrow a term from Wilhelm Wundt, it may be called "creative synthesis," for it could be used to illustrate the trend in the late nineteenth century in the direction of creative evolution. It is therefore worthwhile to include in our discussion of *Fortunata y Jacinta* the psychological viewpoint of which Wundt is representative.

Briefly, Wundt's concept of creative synthesis visualizes the generation of something new from the combination of distinct elements. It is, in the words of Harold Höffding, "a collection and composition, the product of which possesses properties which neither of the moments possessed of its own account." [20] As early as 1863 Wundt lays the foundation for his theory when he says, "Every remembered idea is really a new formation, composed of numerous elements of various past ideas." [21] By this he is saying that the remembered idea does not exist on its own account like a material substance, but arises out of the act of putting two and two together. In a way, of course, this view

19. *The Novels of Pérez Galdós,* pp. 138-50.
20. *Modern Philosophers,* trans. Alfred C. Mason (London: The Macmillan Co., 1915), p. 6.
21. *Lectures on Human and Animal Psychology,* p. 452.

may be considered an extension of associational psychology, and one should not forget that J. S. Mill, and perhaps others before Galdós' day, had observed that the compounding of parts psychologically often results in a new product. It should be added, however, that Wundt's emphasis rests upon the creative activity in the process of synthesis rather than upon the mere combination of different elements.

For a writer like Galdós, who was inclined always to reflect seriously on current ideas from the field of scientific endeavor, it was almost inevitable that he should give philosophical coloring to the notion of psychological synthesis; and at a time when the theory of evolution was much discussed in both scientific and philosophical circles, it would not be at all surprising if he arrived at a philosophy of creative synthesis independently of Wundt.[22] The process can be seen in operation in the novel under consideration if we think of Fortunata's *pícara* idea of contributing a son to the Santa Cruz family in order to gain their good will. A creature of nature and very much subject to it, Fortunata nevertheless takes charge of her natural heritage for a purpose that produces psychological results quite different from the initial motives. Reacting to her feelings of inferiority, she uses nature (the capacity for bearing children) to satisfy her desire to surpass her rival and actually achieves magnanimity in the process. From either a moral or a psychological viewpoint, there has been a creative synthesis, arising from the meeting and combination of self-centered impulse and social opposition.

Without trying to establish a direct line of influence from Wundt to Galdós, it is profitable to compare their ideas, because the comparison shows how the Spanish novelist reflected in creative art a major contemporaneous development in psychology. Wundt, while maintaining the objective attitude of a scientist, not only conceived of nature as a psychical self-development but considered social psychology the anteroom of ethics.[23]

22. The possibility of Wundt's influence, however, cannot be dismissed, since his psychological theories were discussed in Spanish periodical literature before Galdós wrote *Fortunata y Jacinta*. For example, Teodoro [Théodule] Ribot, "La psicología alemana contemporánea. Guillermo Wundt," *Revista Europea*, IV (1875), 293-304, 339-49. The article is a translation from *Revue Scientifique*.
23. Cf. Höffding, *Modern Philosophers*, pp. 7, 11.

Without the obligations attaching to a scientist's stand, Galdós held essentially the same views. Moreover, both the German and the Spaniard adopt a middle road in regard to the subject of necessity, recognizing that freedom and constraint are reciprocal concepts and both necessarily connected with consciousness.[24] Of special interest is the great emphasis placed by psychologist and novelist alike on individual personality. Wundt looks upon character as the "inmost nature of personality" and, though admitting that we cannot prove that character is not a product of external influences, refuses to assign it to a place in the chain of natural causation:

It has been said that a man's character is a resultant of air and light, nurture and climate, education and destiny; that it is predetermined by all these influences, like any other natural phenomenon. The assertion is undemonstrable. Character itself helps to determine education and destiny; the hypothesis makes an effect of what is to some extent also a cause. And the facts of psychological inheritance make it extremely probable that if our investigation could penetrate to the very beginnings of the individual life, we should find there the nucleus of an independent personality, not determinable from without, because prior to all external determination.[25]

Compare the following statement from *Fortunata y Jacinta*, made in reference to the effort on the part of the Rubín family to re-educate Fortunata by placing her in a convent for fallen women:

In these matters it is necessary to take into account the (particular) disposition, the spiritual skeleton, that internal and lasting form of the person, which is usually stronger than all the epidermic transfigurations produced by instruction (257).

This assertion can hardly mean that Galdós discounts the effect of environment on personality, for he clearly demonstrates its influence in his portrayal not only of Fortunata but of numerous personages throughout his many novels. What he wishes to stress is his belief in a natural "given," the core of individuality, which escapes determinism from without. In this respect he was in line with contemporary psychologists, among them some of

24. See Wundt's *Lectures . . .*, p. 426.
25. *Ibid.*, p. 434.

the positivists as well as Wundt, who recognized in the individual a germ of original character, a primitive "given" containing *l'idée directrice*.[26] The significance of this viewpoint lies not so much in the relative importance of heredity and environment as in the fact that individuality is given a conspicuous place in nature's process; for in conjunction with the outer world it provides the basis for creative activity, which at its best is manifest in the development of human personality.

Nature and society, or natural drives and social restraint, thus are visualized by Galdós as two aspects of a larger whole that depends upon their interaction for its own continuity. The life impulse (nature in a strict sense) that aims always at forward movement is individual, egoistic; the restraining force, necessary as a stabilizer for what otherwise would be chaotic activity, is collective. This is a view almost directly the opposite of what we find in Zola (and Schopenhauer), where the life force is aligned with an unconscious mass entity which uses individuation for the purposes of continuity but otherwise denies it recognition. The comparison between the two viewpoints can better be understood if under the banner of individuality we group the following: life, instinct, love, progress; and under the banner of collective phenomena: mass weight or inertia, discipline, reason, stabilization. In Galdós' case, the role of life and forward movement falls to the individual, and deviation from the collective pattern — or mutation by way of individuation, if you will — is the factor of newness. The fact that there are numerous examples of failures and retrogression does not invalidate the general principle of individual potentiality manifest in some of the main characters. In Zola's case, the two groups mentioned above are merged in one and the responsibility for forward movement falls to a total mass force. As manifest in the form of human species, this force is divided against itself in a destructive way; for the conservative, preservative pull toward the past (heredity and atavism, for example) is stronger than the individual deviation that results in change.

The evolutionary view in Galdós, therefore, as compared to that in Zola, reveals a radical shift in emphasis in which the in-

26. See E. Caro, "Essais de psychologie sociale," *RDM*, XLVII (1883), 530-34.

dividual deserts the position of servant to the species and becomes the leader. The leadership, however, though providing the indispensable impulse toward newness, is possible only in co-operation with the challenging and determining force of the environing world of nature and society. From a social-moral viewpoint, it is effectuated by living example and not by words. Fortunata unconsciously plays the role of leader, because she not only draws all eyes to her, eventually winning the admiration of all, but she demonstrates a constructive process in her personality itself. Compare this version of the individual's place in the total scheme of things with that in *Germinal*, where Étienne Lantier, having (on the basis of the novel's philosophical implications) no rights in his capacity as individual, finds himself trying to control mass humanity, which theoretically has all the rights.

Considerable interest attaches to the fact that Galdós regards reason as a static aspect of the total life process. For him intuition is the true creative factor in life and is to be found perhaps in its highest state of sensitivity among simple folk who, like Fortunata, are more spontaneous than rational. In a fundamental way, therefore, he exemplifies the nineteenth-century tendency to glorify the instinctive. But there is no indication that he was attracted to the philosophy of the unconscious, of either the Schopenhauer or the Von Hartmann kind. His emphasis falls, rather, on the emotion of love, whose biological expression he sublimates in a mysticism which is more suggestive of Bergson's exaltation of creative intuition than it is of Zola's awe before animal instinct. For he makes love the agency for a plunge forward in evolution,[27] rather than a destructive sacrifice of self to an impersonal life force. At the same time, the fact that he allows reason the role of an organizing and directive force clearly shows that he does not disregard its importance. The most accurate view of Galdós, therefore, must underscore his sense of balance rather than his exaltation of one aspect of experience over another. His intellectual outlook embraces probably the most positive and constructive contributions of nineteenth-

27. The view is comparable to that of Bergson set forth in *Les deux sources de la moralité et de la religion* (1932). Cf. my study *The Novels of Pérez Galdós*, pp. 123-24.

century thought: the concept of life as change and growth, the co-operative interplay of self and otherness, the belief that obstacles are but a challenge that leads to progress, and faith in the value of the individual human being. His is unquestionably an optimistic philosophy, but it is free of sentimentalism and complacency. The surface view, in fact, presents much savagery and unhappiness, but the waste and contradictions in nature's total process are not regarded as too high a price for the crowning achievement reached in the creation of an individual personality.

Fortunata y Jacinta is a high mark of the "spiritual naturalism" which was very much a part of the public consciousness in Europe in the 1880's (the author calls one of the chapters in volume four "naturalismo espiritual"). The novel leaves us with a vision of natural law, manifest primarily in the realm of psychology, co-ordinated with, actually incorporated in, spiritual law;[28] and it does so with the indirectness of artistic subtlety. The firm, clear image of frictional though orderly advance transmitted to an imaginary record of human experience in an almost casual way is sure evidence of Galdós' ability to keep his intellectual perspective subordinate to his function as artist. The psychological structure of his story is so deeply submerged in the record of events and the philosophical message is so thoroughly woven into the texture of the whole that the reader can very easily overlook the novel's essential substance. The author's equilibrium, in fact, has contributed to an impression of serenity that lulls rather than excites the reader's emotions. On the other hand, in Zola, whose intellectual perspective is much less equilibrated, emotional turmoil makes itself felt in a great surge of energy, which is directed by artistic sensibility into an organized scheme of dramatic action, the essential drama resting in the sacrifice of the individual to the mass. In Galdós' novel the drama, less spectacular, consists not in the sacrifice of individuality but in its accomplishment within a process that is more psychological than biological. If the Spaniard's view of life had been more terrifying, perhaps he would be more widely known today than he is.

28. Henry Drummond's *Natural Law in the Spiritual World* (New York, 1883), though having no specific likeness to Galdós' novel, is typical in title and content of the general effort at the time to bring the natural sciences into harmony with man's religious impulses.

Whatever the comparative storytelling ability of these two novelists, there is no question that they are outstanding representatives of two of the most prominent phases of nineteenth-century thought. Just as a Schopenhauerian outlook combines with Darwinism in *Germinal* to produce a retrospective view of evolution, so a spiritual perspective of Hegelian color combines in *Fortunata y Jacinta* with a Darwinian look toward the future. Of the Spanish novelist it can be said, as it has been said of Hegel,[29] that he makes the Absolute play a double role: the artificer-deity of the eighteenth century and the organism of the nineteenth century. As to the ultimate destiny of the individual, Galdós does not venture a precise opinion. In a sense he is more scientific in his attitude than Zola, for he examines life as a truth at hand unclouded by fear of the hereafter. Stopping short of the extreme consequence of Hegelianism, which would find individuality absorbed in Spirit or personality lost in Personality, he is willing to leave the question to the imagination, fascinated and perhaps amused rather than frightened by the mysterious unknown. Meanwhile he concentrates on immediate life and produces justification for a belief in individual immortality by creating a personality that has earned it.

29. William Caldwell, *Schopenhauer's System in Its Philosophical Significance* (Edinburgh and London, 1896), p. 55.

6

The Persuasion to Passivity

Maxim Gorky   Pío Baroja

MAXIM GORKY
1868-1936

THE "SPIRITUAL NATURALISM" of the last third of
the nineteenth century was a determined effort to accept nature
as the medium of divine activity; and the doubts concerning
man's divine relationship were counterbalanced by a belief that
somehow the mysterious ways of God conform with reason and
love. The optimism of this outlook finds expression in a potent
outcropping of literary production, including novels by such
stalwarts as Galdós and Tolstoy. In the field of philosophy it
can be found also in the Neo-Hegelianism that extended from
the late nineteenth well into the twentieth century. Buoyancy
of spirit, however, is more than matched by the gloomy impressions that had long attended an awe of the natural sciences and
reached a climax of torpidity as the nineteenth century drew to
a close. Nature as a vast system of mechanical causation had
come to weigh so heavily on man's imagination as to constitute
his "whole world and his whole being." [1] The natural world of
Newton and the natural world of Darwin had in effect been
merged in such a way as to produce an organic mechanism that

1. Rudolph Eucken, *The Meaning and Value of Life* (1908), trans.
Lucy Judge Gibson and W. R. Boyce Gibson (London: A. and C. Black,
1909), p. 26.

seemed to include the worst implications of mechanistic physiology and vitalistic biology. The comparatively new science of sociology fell into step with the general inclination to regard man as a machine,[2] and at the same time tended to enthrone a kind of sociological or group mysticism that overshadowed the individual.[3]

In short, the *fin du siècle*, despite various manifestations of revolt in artistic forms and even in philosophical ideas, was still predominantly a continuation of nineteenth-century naturalism with its heavy biological stamp, in so far as the general outlook was concerned. James Mark Baldwin declared in 1902 that "no philosophy can today deny Naturalism; by Naturalism meaning the recognition of the right of Dame Nature — physical, vital, mental — to be and to do what she really *is* and *does*, with no let nor hindrance whatever from us or from all the tribe of thought." [4] Modifications of earlier scientific beliefs, such as H. De Vries's theory of sudden mutation (as opposed to the gradual change of Darwinian theory), had not basically altered the general current of thought. Two major tenets of modern science — possibly the two principal ones even to this day — remained indelibly impressed upon the collective consciousness: the theory of the conservation of energy and the theory of biological evolution. The contraposition of these two theories created in the minds of numerous thinkers the image of an endless circular movement of rhythmical repetition. For the concept of the universe as a closed system can easily be harmonized with the view of the universe as growth, if evolution be regarded merely as a redistribution of parts involving no increase in the total amount of energy.[5] Nor is the concept of evolution incongruous with an

2. It may be purely a matter of coincidence rather than an indication of basic intellectual trend but it is curious at least that in the 1890's the *Revue des Deux Mondes* had a regular section devoted to "Le Mécanisme de la vie moderne," containing articles on social and economic organization, such as transportation, life insurance, and the like.

3. See Ferdinand Brunetière, "La Religion comme sociologie," *RDM*, XII (1903), 853-77; Alfred Fouillée, "La Science des mœurs remplacera-t-elle la morale?," *RDM*, XXIX (1905), 519-50.

4. *Fragments in Philosophy and Science* (New York: Charles Scribner's Sons, 1902), p. viii.

5. Cf. H. Heath Bawden, "Evolution and the Absolute," *Philosophical Review*, XV (1906), 145.

infinitude of time if there be a cyclical process of continuous repetition.

Now, the vision of a cyclical transformation of things repeatedly into the same substance contributes greatly to a predominantly oppressive intellectual atmosphere around 1900, despite the efforts of Neo-Hegelians to read meaning into the monotonous design. And if one's thoughts turned to the supposition that the total energy of the universe was "running down," that is, passing from serviceable to unserviceable forms, the outlook was even more suggestive of gloom. Perhaps the one feature that most distinguishes the pessimism of this epoch from that of some thirty years before is passivity, and is the more noticeable the more it rests in the shadow of materialism. Even the outward show of spirited rebelliousness which is sometimes in evidence must be considered an indication of resignation to an unhappy fate. The following assertion of the youthful Bertrand Russell in 1903, which is infused with the pessimism aroused by modern science, is a typical reflection at the time on man's place in nature:

... that his origin, his growth, his hopes and fears, his loves and his beliefs, are but the outcome of accidental collocations of atoms ... that all the labour of the ages ... are destined to extinction in the vast death of the solar system, and that the whole temple of Man's achievement must inevitably be buried beneath the débris of a universe in ruins — all these things, if not quite beyond dispute, are yet so nearly certain, that no philosophy which rejects them can hope to stand. Only within the scaffolding of these truths, only on the firm foundation of unyielding despair, can the soul's habitation be safely built.[6]

Philosophical achievement in directing the implications of science into new and constructive channels was slow in developing, although a new orientation was making its appearance before the end of the nineteenth century, notably in the writings of Henri Bergson. Bergson's major objective in life seems to have been a replacement of the currently dominant mechanistic view of the universe by a principle of indeterminate creativity. In this respect he was a prominent figure among those who brought about

6. Bertrand Russell, "The Free Man's Worship," in *Philosophical Essays* (London: Longmans, Green and Co., 1910), pp. 60-61. Quoted by permission of George Allen & Unwin, Ltd.

the twentieth-century break with mechanism. But in his exaltation of primordial instinct and intuition he relegates intellect and
self-consciousness to an incidental role in man's world. Continuity of life becomes for him in effect a veritable stream of unconsciousness, on whose banks the self-conscious intellect lingers
pensively for a moment and then returns to its home deep in the
moving stream. There is much in his view of man, therefore, that
allies him with the very essence of nineteenth-century naturalism, which views all human experience in subjugation to a Life
Force that uses nature as its agent. Bergson was, in fact, a spokesman for the neovitalism that enjoyed considerable support
among biologists at the turn of the century in opposition to the
physicochemical, mechanistic explanation of living phenomena.[7]
Thus, despite the fact that his ideas concerning creative advance
toward unpredictable achievement undoubtedly were influential in determining new directions in philosophical thought, especially after the publication of his *Creative Evolution* in 1907,
the general trend of which he was an outstanding example manifested itself first and most of all as a spirit of protest against
determinism. When this attitude is combined with the negative,
agnostic aspect of Neo-Kantism, which at the end of the century
remained a potent influence,[8] one can see that the intellectual
environment of the age was more conducive to the creation of
moods than to the stimulation of new ideas. Probably the two
most characteristic, most conspicuous moods can best be illustrated by reference to Nietzsche and Schopenhauer, the one
exemplifying the spirit of fiery protest and the other a mood of
passive resignation to suffering.

Nietzsche, the idol of German youths in the 1890's,[9] was well

7. At a congress of learned societies in Cambridge in 1898 a count
showed that nearly all the physiologists present were partisans of the
physicochemical doctrine, whereas the naturalists were for the most part
adherents of a doctrine of vital force and final causes, some of them not
only assuming that the vital force enters the body from without but willing also to invoke Divinity as its source: A. Dastre, "La Physiologie de la
vie et la mort," *RDM*, IX (1902), 201. See also on the subject of vitalism:
A. Dastre, "La Théorie de l'énergie et le monde vivant," *RDM*, CXLVII
(1898), 189-204; and Dr. Grasset, "La Doctrine vitaliste de la vie," *RDM*,
LIV (1909), 629-57.
8. See, for example, Alessandro Chiappelli, "Les Tendances vives de la
philosophie," *Rev. Philosophique*, LXIX (1910), 226.
9. T. de Wyzewa, "Documents nouveaux sur Frédéric Nietzsche,"
RDM, CLIV (1899), 454-55.

known and much discussed all over Europe before 1900. His fundamental appeal apparently rested on his rebelliousness against tradition and his exaltation of the ego in opposition to the growing weight of mass standards. To some he appeared as the champion of individualism and to others as an undisciplined child. Most references to him around 1900 point to his anti-egalitarian attitude and his glorification of power in the individual. He was regarded by some as the *enfant terrible du Darwinisme*,[10] a veritable objectification of Darwinian doctrine of the survival of the fittest. If he exemplifies the destructive consequences of Darwinian naturalism, however, he does so more in protest against it than in agreement with it. The extremism of his reaction, which finds outlet in his cult of the ego and his anarchic attitude, seems to have made a much greater impression on the minds of his readers than his honest opposition to the encroachment of a vast collective personality that swallows all individual manifestation. His influence may have encouraged in many cases a nihilistic kind of rebelliousness, but in justice to him it should be remembered that he was motivated in a fundamental sense by aversion to the unhappy thought that self-consciousness is incidental to an impersonal mass force. In short, he rebelled against what Schopenhauer had accepted — in protest also — as the inevitable lot of individual man.[11]

Nietzsche, however, did not attain the prominence of Schopenhauer and did not capture the imagination of literary artists to such an extent as his predecessor. The Schopenhauerian mood had been compatible with the dynamic evolutionism of an earlier generation. It was even more at home in the atmosphere of naturalistic exhaustion evident at the end of the century, at which time the philosopher apparently was so widely discussed that his name found its way into the comic section of newspapers.[12] For one thing, his exaltation of instinct over reason har-

10. Alfred Fouillée, "Les fausses conséquences morales et sociales du Darwinisme," *RDM*, XXIII (1904), 548.
11. The following excerpts from an appraisal of Ibsen in 1903 can be regarded as typical of the Nietzschean attitude of the time: "Le moi est le parfait pessimiste car il est seul . . . Le moi, c'est l'astre qui compte ses instants et qui se sent descendre . . . Le moi, c'est la mort . . . Le moi est le héros qui désespère" (A. Suarès, "Sur les glaciers de l'intelligence," *RDM*, XVII [1903], 404).
12. Cf. the following statement of William Caldwell, *Schopenhauer's System in Its Philosophical Significance* (Edinburgh and London, 1896),

monized with the "new" tide of intuitionism; but probably more
potent in its effect was his attitude of a lonely spectator contemplating the fleeting natural manifestations of an eternal and
impassible oneness of Will that lies outside time and space and
ignores distinction between one individual and another, or between today and tomorrow.[13] At the fag end of a long and virile
adjustment to the theory of biological evolution, Schopenhauer's
persuasiveness toward a fatalistic sacrifice of individuality settled on the collective consciousness like an anesthetic mantle,
deadening the will to self-assertion and supplanting it by an inclination toward immersion in the whole. One might say that
the evolutionary movement was halted in the mind's image and
the process reversed so as to establish absolute uniformity in
accord with the oneness of reality. It is probably more than a
curious coincidence that a book (*La Dissolution opposée à
l'évolution dans la méthode des sciences physiques et morales* by
André Lalande) appeared in 1899 proposing, in opposition to
Spencer's theory of advance from the simple to the complex or
from the undifferentiated to the differentiated, that the universal
pattern of all things is "development" from the heterogeneous
to the homogeneous. In accord with such a theory, it is man's
duty to conform to the universal by opposing individuality.[14]

There is no doubt that the contrary attitudes personified in
Nietzsche and Schopenhauer, the one exalting the ego and the
other relegating it to oblivion, were two fundamental intellectual tendencies at the close of the nineteenth century. In a discussion of the novelists, Maxim Gorky and Pío Baroja, to whom
we now turn our attention, both attitudes are particularly relevant, and one could argue with conviction that they are more
pertinent to an understanding of the writers than a knowledge
of the local circumstances that saw their rise as artists.

In the case of Gorky (Alexy Maximovitch Peshkov), personal experience undoubtedly helped to color the grim picture
of life that mention of his pen name, which means "bitter," gen-

p. viii: "Nowadays it is almost impossible to escape being brought more
or less under his influence. He has even got into the comic papers of most
countries."

13. Cf. Schopenhauer. *Selections,* ed. Parker, p. 85.
14. See the review of Lalande's book by Fr. Poulhan in his article "Contemporary Philosophy in France," *Philosophical Review,* IX (1900), 54.

erally evokes. Born at Nizhny Novgorod (now called Gorky) of a family of artisans and orphaned at an early age, he had an intimate acquaintance with wretchedness. The internal situation in Russia, of course, provided in itself a pungent realistic background for his novels and stories. The widespread resentment at the oppression of the masses, which at times erupted in erratic violence, tended to replace religious sentiment with revolution and nihilism.[15] The nihilistic outbursts, however, were more than offset during the latter half of the nineteenth century by moderate philosophies of social reform centering on the principle of collectivity. The pre-Soviet concept of collectivity, which is found in the advocacy of a peasant communal system,[16] was an enlightened view of approximate balance in the relationship between the individual and the group. Maxim Gorky would probably have most willingly conformed to this view had he been compelled to systematize his thinking and had not the Revolution swept him along in its course. For his sympathies, his tastes, his whole outlook, reveal a predominantly prerevolutionary orientation and make it seem paradoxical that he should be considered by Communists as a leader of Soviet literature.[17] The ground for Gorky's affinity with the Soviet movement, of course, was his sympathy for the socially unfavored person. With the publication of his first collection of stories in 1898 his fame was immediately established, and he gained great popularity with the masses in the years preceding the abortive revolution of 1905. The revolutionary leaders claimed him as one of their own, and he contributed to their cause with money and influence, trying at the same time to humanize the movement. His alliance with communism during much of his career was not enthusiastic, though he was apparently a dutiful supporter of the party in his last years. The fact is that the religious impulse of the incurable God-seeker that he was would not allow

15. Cf. G. Valbert, "La Situation intérieure en Russie," *RDM*, XXXIII (1879), 700-12; Anatole Leroy-Beaulieu, "Le Sentiment religieux et le mysticisme en Russie," *RDM*, LXXX (1887), 808-42.

16. See the collection of articles by various scholars entitled *Continuity and Change in Russian and Soviet Thought* (Cambridge, Mass.: Harvard University Press, 1955).

17. Cf. Marc Slonim, *Modern Russian Literature* (New York: Oxford University Press, 1953), p. 151.

him to embrace communism wholeheartedly.[18] He was preoccupied with the question of the "superfluous" man as seen under humiliating political and economic conditions, but he was more disturbed by thoughts of superfluous man when seen as an insignificant entity in the universe. For this reason it is especially curious that the so-called leader of Soviet literature and hero of the Communist Revolution was actually a rebel against a philosophy that visualizes individual absorption in mass materialism.

Foma Gordyeeff (1899)

Gorky's preoccupation with the question of man's cosmic position is a salient characteristic of his novels and is so obvious, in fact, that it detracts from their merit as works of art, though not from their significance as the expression of an epoch. *Foma Gordyeeff*, his first novel, is probably his best; although it is burdened with a certain monotonous reflection on the meaninglessness of life, it possesses much of the vitality and spontaneity that characterize Gorky's early short stories, perhaps his major claim to recognition as an artist. The story of a misfit in life, it has a close technical affinity with some of the nineteenth-century psychological novels in which emphasis is placed on the relationship between personality and heredity and environment. In its somber depiction of savagery, untamed passions, and suffering it embodies much of what is considered typical of Russian prose fiction and in this respect recalls Dostoevsky. No one would ever claim for Gorky the richness and depth of Dostoevsky's psychological creations, but *Foma Gordyeeff* is nonetheless an authentic and actually a vivid portrait of an individual caught in the dull spiritual depression of the turn of the century.

The narrative of *Foma Gordyeeff* takes the form of a biography and begins with attention to the family background of the central character. Ignat Gordyeeff, Foma's father, is portrayed apparently to exemplify a philosophy of the survival of the

18. Cf. Avrahm Yarmolinsky, "Maxim Gorki," *American Scholar*, XI (1941-1942), 89-98.

strong. He is an aggressive, self-made man who has attained wealth and influence as a merchant, largely because he knows no law save his own will. A man of violent passions, sensual and cruel at times, he derives a kind of poetic pleasure from a fierce contest with life, feeling such admiration for the savage power of nature that he is able on one occasion to watch enthusiastically as ice in the "Mother Volga" crushes one of his new barges. Although he is religious after a fashion and occasionally prays to God, he seems to have little expectation of surviving the grave and longs for a son who can continue life for him. When his first wife dies without leaving him an heir, he marries Natalya, a silent, melancholy young woman who is possessed of an inner spark of being, something like the fire that burned within Emma Bovary's soul; for there is about her a strange vagueness of character and an otherworldliness that contrast sharply with her husband's blunt realism. Natalya dies at the birth of her son, Foma. The latter inherits from his mother a dreamy, impractical nature, which is nurtured during his boyhood by a kindly aunt who comes to live in his home when he is six years old.

The contrasting personalities of the parents provide the basis of a conflict in Foma's personality, which becomes the focal point of the story. Influenced to some extent by the cold-blooded egoistic realism of his father, yet swayed predominantly by the unfathomed longing that characterized his mother, the son is never able to turn his life with decision in any one direction. The narrative problem thus invites, and receives, a psychological handling, which at the same time becomes something of a philosophical essay.

Foma's first noteworthy experience turns out to be a rude introduction to the problem of adjusting to life. It occurs on a boat trip that the small boy takes with his father, on which he witnesses both the cruelty of human relations and the cold vision of death. In some degree the episode is an opportunity for pondering the immediate Russian scene, with special attention to the lot of the peasants and laborers. Foma's father impresses on his son the necessity for exercising complete mastery over the workers and finds occasion to demonstrate his decisive, if ruthless, methods by knocking down one man who had complained and dismissing two others who had murmured against him. The author's interest in the status of the underdog is plain but it is by no means propagandistic and is always found in combination with a question regarding man's significance in the broadest possible sense. The following description of a river scene leads us to think of the leashed power of the masses but it is also suggestive of something remote from the immediate world, something like the primordial Earth Spirit that we sense in Zola's novels:

> On everything round about rested the stamp of a certain sluggishness: everything — nature and people — lived awkwardly, lazily; but in this laziness there was a certain peculiar grace, and it would seem that behind the laziness was concealed a huge force, an unconquerable force, as yet unconscious of itself, not having, as yet, created for itself clear desires and aims.... Submissive patience, the silent expectation of something new and more active was audible even in the call of the cuckoo.... The mournful songs, also, seemed to entreat aid from some one. And, at times, the audacity of despair rang through them. The river made answer to the songs with sighs (36).[19]

The peculiarly Russian atmosphere brought to life in such passages as this is pervaded by a somberness that arises as much from a contemplation of man's place in the natural order as from thoughts of his social-economic status. The boy Foma, who is sensitive to all manifestations of suffering, is thirsty for an understanding of "what threads and springs regulate the actions of men," and he is especially impressed with the reality of death when a corpse is discovered floating in the river. His father dismisses the incident lightly, but the boy retains vague misgivings concerning man's tragic fate.

The confusion resulting from these first serious thoughts about life comes to the surface only at intervals during Foma's boyhood. He spends a rather monotonous few years in school, where he makes friends with the methodical Smolín Afrikán, destined to be a merchant, and the waspy Ezhóff Nikolái, a janitor's son, who is seen years later in the role of a cynical, starving journalist. At the age of nineteen Foma enters his father's business, still possessing a strange vagueness of character

19. Page references are to *Foma Gordyeeff*, trans. Isabel F. Hapgood (New York: Charles Scribner's Sons, 1921).

and feeling somewhat estranged from the world around him. Given the responsibility of delivering two barges of grain, he enjoys his first moments of independence, giving away a large quantity of grain in a spontaneous outburst of sympathy for the peasants and almost as spontaneously falling in love with a black-eyed woman laborer several years his senior, who unselfishly refuses to take advantage of his offer of marriage. When he returns home he feels more intensely than ever an incompatibility with his surroundings.

Foma's experience now becomes a long drawn-out groping for a stabilizing answer to the gnawing restlessness that keeps him constantly depressed; and it is in this central part of the narrative that the author falls into a disagreeable repetitiousness in his reference to the hero's psychological problem ("O Lord! To what end is such a life?" p. 308). The death of Foma's father leaves him at the head of a prosperous business, and his godfather, Mayakin, partner and lifelong friend of the elder Gordyeeff, tries hard to mold him in the ways of a wealthy merchant. Foma goes through the formality of attending to his business responsibilities but is primarily and continuously preoccupied with the problem of adapting himself to life. In his searching for a solution he has occasion to observe the philosophies that are being practiced by people of his acquaintance. Foremost of these is the creed of Mayakin, who, like Foma's father, is an exponent of the doctrine that life belongs to the strong, that it must be accepted boldly and lived with decision, without question as to a far-off destiny. He obviously believes that individual personality disappears into a sea of nothingness but he refuses to be disturbed by thoughts of the hereafter: "You need have no fear of death . . . do what you were appointed to do. And a man is appointed to organize life on earth . . . in proportion as he circulates in life and absorbs tallow and oil, sweat and tears, mind and soul are created in him" (124). Therefore live intensely, aggressively. Life is war. "Bite everybody, or lie in the mud. (155)"

Foma finds little consolation in the hardened materialism of his godfather, whose repulsive physical appearance adds to the harshness of his ideas. He is equally unsympathetic to the refined aspirations of Mayakin's daughter, Liuba, who is an example of restrained idealism becoming forced conformity to life as it is. Like Foma, Liuba longs for a vague, unattainable something and tries to overcome her loneliness and boredom by reading literature. Her father has long intended for her to marry Foma, but the latter is too primitive to be attracted by her talk of learning and refinement and too rebellious to conform to a prosaic kind of life. The spark of spiritual seeking that causes his unrest thus turns him away from an embrace of materialism and from a quiet resignation as well, and holds him instead on a course of intensifying indecision that results in aimless drifting and disintegration. The principal activity in which he now engages is debauchery.

During the final stages of dissolution Foma continues to grasp for straws of salvation and burns sporadically with fiery aspirations, which include a desire to illuminate all men and an occasional impulse to be one with the workers. On one occasion in a group debauch he finds himself paired with a strange young woman (Sasha) of the proletariat, one of the women of strong will, of deep-lying passions and suppressed longings that Gorky likes to portray. Listening to her and her companions sing Russian folk songs, Foma enters into their mood of anguish. But his momentary impulse of kinship with the humble folk becomes nothing more than a desire to lash out at everyone and is soon spent in an outburst of empty words. Wherever he is he feels always estranged, "exhausted with loneliness," which he tries to escape by carousing. Despite his sincere desire to be delivered from the morass that has enveloped him, he confirms his godfather's declaration of disgust that he is trying "to save his soul . . . in pot-houses" (294).

The climax to Foma's frustration and futility comes when he reluctantly attends a party on the river given by a rich merchant to celebrate the completion of a new steamer. In a surly mood after yielding to Mayakin's insistence that he attend the celebration, he rises at the banquet table and wildly accuses those present of being swindlers and thieves. He is subdued and bound, and becomes completely passive. Mayakin, acting in the capacity of guardian, has him committed to an asylum. Three years pass. Foma now lives in a small apartment in the courtyard of his foster sister, Liuba, who has married Smolín Afrikán, content to exchange her romantic dreams for the stable life of a merchant's wife. On occasion Foma can be seen on the streets, shabby, half-witted, intoxicated, wearing the mournful smile of a religious fanatic and jeeringly called "Prophet" by the passers-by. The narrative thus ends abruptly with emphasis on the pitiable state of one who could not face the question of life's meaning. An inchoate being, almost an inert mass of clay, has shown enough spirit to want to be more than clay, yet has given in to defeat because of assuming in advance an attitude of futility.

One feels that Gorky has caught in this novel a dual vision encompassing the slow stirring of the Russian masses and the frustration of the human spirit in the face of a materialistic, or at least a meaningless, view of the universe. In a sense, Foma's defeat can be attributed to the merchant class. In the conclusion his helplessness stands out in contrast to Liuba's peaceful contentment, which is apparently a deliberate ironic representation of the triumph of bourgeois complacency over the hero's sympathy for the proletariat. But in Foma's story the question of social and economic status is really of incidental significance. His problem is one of general disorientation. "I long for people," he says, "I'd like to go and say: 'Help me, my brethren! Teach me! I cannot live!' ... No one wants it — they're all rabble!" (266) So it is with all men, capitalists and workers alike. Collectively they are like crabs moving aimlessly in a basket; and there is no apparent reason for their being on the earth. This feeling of superfluousness is similar to the existentialist loneliness of spirit which becomes more and more noticeable in the twentieth century. The Gorky protagonist, however, is more easily overcome by the act of reasoning than his more recent kin. Thoughts stick all round his soul, as he says, like resin (266) and overwhelm him. He is, in fact, defeated by mere reflection upon life rather than by life itself, and his tragedy could be described simply as a climactic intensification of the thought that "there is no relief from grief, there is no joy, for him who begins to meditate upon his fate" (368).

The author's intentness on the theme expressed in this quotation no doubt accounts for a certain unpleasant overemphasis, but it should not lead the reader to hasty censure. William L.

Phelps, early in this century expressed a low opinion of Gorky, pronouncing Foma Gordyeeff a dreary character in a dull book.[20] It is accurate enough to say that Foma Gordyeeff is a dreary person, but this is not necessarily the same as calling him a dreary characterization. Certainly he has little of the heroic about him. He has not waged a noble struggle against his bondage to the earth; he has merely drifted, continually unable to engage himself actively or to identify himself with an ideal that would assure his integrity. His portrait is for this very reason the sharply drawn image of a malady — the malady of inaction, which is a veritable paralysis of will.

The philosophical mood that accounts for Foma's paralysis derives from a vision of biological evolution overlaid with a heavy Schopenhauerian color. Darwinian natural selection is taken by Foma's father and his godfather to mean that the supreme law of nature favors the strong of body and will; and they both accept without question the hard material facts of nature, including human life and death. Mayakin, reconciled to his probable absorption in the total natural process, agrees that people must die for the simple reason, if no other, that they must make room for more people. He answers Foma's protests at the sacrifice of the individual viewpoint in favor of the whole by saying, "Your breeches would, certainly, reason in the same manner . . . But you don't heed them — you wear them out and throw them away" (125). Thus, whatever has been used up has served its purpose and should be forgotten: "a live dog is better than a dead lion."

In the face of this primitive, essentially nonreflective embrace of life, and disturbed by an urge to transcend, Foma is tossed about by two conflicting attitudes. Apparently inspired by the Nietzschean ideal of self-propulsion beyond the common level, he wants to rise above the apathy of mass humanity, insisting that he cannot be "reconciled to pettiness" (268); and, Zarathustra-like, he is possessed at times with Messianic fervor. But the flashes of Nietzschean fire are overshadowed by Schopenhauer's vision of an inscrutable Force engulfing the individual in a life stream that moves relentlessly on with no recognizable purpose

20. *Essays on Russian Novelists* (New York, 1922), p. 221 (1st ed., 1910).

other than that of continuing its movement. "What is life, if not people?" Foma asks. "But people are always talking as though it were not they, but something else besides people, and as though it prevented their living. Perhaps it is the devil?" (179) There is always the oppressive thought that people "were not the lords of life, but its lackeys, and that it was twisting them about at its pleasure, driving them and running them at its will, while they apathetically and resignedly yielded to it, and not one of them desired freedom for himself" (290). Foma, assuredly, desired freedom for himself, but in his rational contemplation of the subject he fell victim to the powerful persuasiveness of the Schopenhauerian outlook, and to such an extent as to cause a virtual stoppage of the life process within him.

Whatever our estimate of Gorky's novel, we must grant that it has sharply dramatized in an individual the conflict between an urge to realize life fully and the deadening thought that life, however it may be lived, is to no purpose. The author, very consciously, enters stylistically into the spirit of the conflict by depicting two contrasting moods: the one emphasizing light, buoyancy, and power; the other, stillness and gloom. If one is willing to overlook a certain youthful exuberance, one can appreciate the vitality and spontaneity of the following *tour de force,* in which the mental impression of fluidity — one is reminded of Sartre — symbolizes freedom:

Between them [the cliffs], in a magnificent sweep, flowed the broad-breasted Volga; triumphantly, without haste flow her waters, conscious of their unconquerable power. . . . Above the surface of the water peeped forth the crests of trees, sometimes whole clumps of them, drowned in the spring flood . . . On all sides were space and freedom, cheerfully-green meadows, and graciously-clear blue sky; in the quiet motion of the water, restrained power could be felt . . . (34-35).

In opposition to this surge of movement, the image of darkness and frozen motion asserts itself:

The nocturnal silence appeared to him in the form of a limitless expanse of dark water . . . it had spread everywhere and congealed . . . It was very dreadful for anyone to look down from some height, in the gloom, upon this dead water (61-62).

Consider alongside these contrasting descriptive views of external nature the author's comments on the psychological states of his protagonist, who at times is inspired in the presence of "the loud, cheerful noise of labor, the youthful beauty of nature in spring ... all this ... filled with healthy, kindly, coarse vigor" (80); and at other times is overwhelmed by a sensation of quietness, as for example at the time of his father's death: "tranquillity poured into his soul — an oppressive, motionless tranquillity, which unresistingly engulfed all the sounds of life" (119). The conflict between a view of nature as transcendent movement and a view of nature as a prison of death and emptiness constitutes the broad base on which the novel is constructed. Localized in a Russian setting within this broad arena, the enactment of a particular drama results in the deactivation of an individual life.

We cannot expect to find in Gorky's novels the rich panorama of Russian life, the turmoil of social and moral problems, or the depth of psychological portrayal that characterize the works of Tolstoy and Dostoevsky. He was just as concerned as these predecessors of his, perhaps even more so, with enveloping his portrayal of life in a philosophical perspective; but he was less able than they to move in philosophical depths or to supply the richness of material on which philosophy is based. Though widely read in European literature, he can hardly be considered an intellectual, and he failed to lift his intellectual ruminations far above an incipient, intuitive state. Perhaps it is correct to say, with D. S. Mirsky, "It is his eyes that see through, rather than his mind that understands." [21] Yet, it is hardly appropriate to judge Gorky as a thinker or as a literary psychologist to be appraised in accord with the methods used and the standards set by earlier realists. Let him be judged, rather, as an alert observer who not only was sensitive to the suffering of humble people but grasped, in fact re-created in the form of an individual portrait, the philosophical mood of an epoch. This was the epoch marked by a gloomy passivity, which settled on Europe after a long and dynamic response to naturalistic emphasis in all fields of human experience. It was, moreover, the

21. *Contemporary Russian Literature* (London: George Routledge, 1926), p. 119.

mood that ushers in the anguished existentialist search for meaning. We cannot dismiss lightly one who is moved by the same
troubled spirit that pervades the groping quest for human dignity in the generation that follows his. Consider the following
declaration from *Foma Gordyeeff:*

> The river flows, that men may sail upon it, wood grows for
> use, dogs grow to guard the house — you can find a justification
> for everything on earth. But men, like cockroaches, are alto-
> gether superfluous on the earth. Everything is for them — and
> what are they for? (268)

Is not the following outcry in Sartre's *La Nausée* (1938) an
extension of the same basic motivation?

> We were a heap of living creatures, irritated, embarrassed at
> ourselves, we hadn't the slightest reason to be there, none of
> us; each one, confused, vaguely alarmed, felt in the way [*de
> trop*] in relation to the others... even my death would have
> been *In the way. In the way*, my corpse, my blood on these
> stones, between these plants, at the back of the smiling garden.[22]

PÍO BAROJA
1872-1956

In Gorky the human spirit remonstrates against the
weight of the material world and for a moment declares its will
to spring free, only to fall back apathetic and paralyzed. A somewhat similar state of mind is found in Gorky's Spanish contemporary, Pío Baroja, whose novels also are heavy with mood, like
much of the literature in the early years of the twentieth century. The outlook of the Spanish writers generally grouped together as "the generation of 1898," to which Baroja belongs, is
very strongly colored by unhappiness over Spain's backwardness. Their works are therefore permeated with a strong national
flavor that sometimes expresses harshness with reference to the
present and sometimes nostalgia with reference to the past. Just
as fundamental in their writing as this national orientation, is

22. *Nausea*, trans. Lloyd Alexander (Norfolk, [1949]), pp. 172-73. All
rights reserved. Reprinted by permission of New Directions.

their sensitivity to trends in European art and thought, a prominent aspect of which at the time was the general inclination toward a quiet kind of pessimism.

Among the novelists of the generation of 1898, Pío Baroja is the one most likely to be honored in future histories of literature. Satirist, philosopher, and dreamer, he is a spokesman of his age and as such a very subjective writer who reveals his intense loneliness. A reader on first becoming acquainted with Baroja's work, and following him on his wandering, restless journey over Spanish and European soil, is probably impressed most of all by the author's dissatisfaction with human society, particularly as found in Spain. But scarcely less evident is the more significant note of troubled reflection on man's place in the cosmos. The novelist's outlook, in fact, appears to be an all-inclusive pessimism impregnated with a paralyzing doubt growing out of the scientific and philosophical literature of the nineteenth century.[23] It can be characterized in good part by the following comment on the early years of the twentieth century by Rudolph Eucken, which is clearly an expression of unhappiness over the long and remorseless reign of naturalism:

We are confronted with the vastness and pitilessness of nature, the forlornness of man amid its immensity, the wild whirl of social existence with its passionate excitements and spiritual barrenness, the moral littleness of man with his selfishness, his enslavement to appearances, his entire subjection to natural instincts which he cannot control.[24]

This earth-centered criticism could be extended in Baroja's case to unite with a cosmic view as forlorn as the following:

We shall see that the future of man and his children is to dance for centuries and centuries through space, converted into ashes, into a dead stone like the earth, and then to be dissolved in cosmic matter.[25]

23. Baroja's intellectual orientation is predominantly the nineteenth century. He himself declares as much: "toda la época de formación mía ha transcurrido en la centuria pasada," *Reportajes* in *Obras completas* (Madrid: Biblioteca Nueva, 1949), VII, 1120; and he includes among the personalities in whom he had been most interested: the scientists Darwin, Pasteur, Claude Bernard; the philosophers Nietzsche and Schopenhauer; and the poets Byron, Leopardi, Bécquer.

24. *The Meaning and Value of Life*, p. 77.

25. Translated from *La ciudad de la niebla* (1909) in *Obras completas* (1947), II, 441.

As a partial counterweight to this heavy pessimism, a strong lyrical inclination manifests itself in an underlying strain of wistfulness and fantasy, which shows at its artistic best in Baroja's novels and tales that have their setting in his native Basque region. There are, in fact, two major aspects of the novelist's philosophical outlook, the one indicating a forced acceptance of an unhappy lot and the other expressing an undying aspiration. It is appropriate to say that in Baroja, as in Gorky, a contest is waged between Schopenhauer and Nietzsche: and, as is also true in Gorky's case, the reference to Nietzsche has to do not so much with the latter's aggressive egoism and impertinence as with his earnest aspiration to individual dignity, which was no doubt the real motive behind his exaltation of the ego. The lyrical strain is much more pronounced and much softer in Baroja than in Gorky, although in the final analysis it too is overshadowed by Schopenhauerian melancholy.

From Baroja's voluminous collection of fiction it is difficult to choose an outstanding novel on which his fame might be expected to rest secure. Indeed, the critic is inclined to declare that fragments of gold must be extracted from many of the novelist's works and fused together in order to appreciate his merit. He was a writer of modest ambitions and modest claims, content to express his sharp criticism and his whimsical musings in simple, unpretentious tales. He utilized a great variety of vantage points from which to observe the human race but in no single work did he plunge deeply into a chosen subject. It has seemed proper, therefore, to include in the present discussion two novels which, taken together, may be considered a fairly accurate account of Baroja's essential outlook: *El árbol de la ciencia*, which is predominantly reflective, and *Zalacaín el aventurero*, which is predominantly fanciful. With widely differing emphasis the novels illustrate respectively two fundamental aspects of Baroja the novelist: the gloomy philosopher and the dreamer. The second aspect will best be appreciated if we examine the philosophical emphasis first. Moreover, *Zalacaín el aventurero*, in its attention to the concept of time, has in its suggestiveness an element of newness — for which Bergson may be responsible — and hence may logically be made to follow the older, more biologically colored viewpoint of the other novel.

El árbol de la ciencia (1911)

In this story the problem of personal orientation in life overwhelms the central character, whose quest for a satisfying philosophy is fraught with disillusionment. The story of Andrés Hurtado is in a sense an account of social maladjustment. In a sense, too, the novel is autobiographical, for it reflects the author's own unhappy experience as medical student and practicing physician for the period of a few youthful years. But Andrés Hurtado's basic unhappiness arises from thoughts of his cosmic relevancy rather than from discomfort in his immediate surroundings. As in *Foma Gordyeeff*, but with more sharply defined intenseness, a philosophical mood dominates the protagonist, who as a student of medicine is impelled to view man's place in the universe in the light of knowledge provided by modern science, particularly biological science.

The introductory part of the narrative stresses the local atmosphere of stagnancy and decadence which Baroja so frequently singles out of the Spanish scene. Andrés, acutely aware of the stupidity of his professors, the depravity of the students, and the brutality of the doctors, moves through a curious collection of types which at times assumes the proportions of a human menagerie. He is altogether incompatible with his father and feels little family sympathy except for his young, sickly brother Luisito, whom he looks after earnestly until the boy's death. He has a further outlet for sentiment in his acquaintance with Lulú, a girl of humble background, herself aloof from the crassness of her surroundings. For a long time Andrés scarcely thinks sentimentally of Lulú, being preoccupied rather with gloomy visions of existence and playing the part of a lonely onlooker standing on the bank of the stream of life, "a tumultuous and unconscious stream where all the actors presented a tragedy which they did not comprehend" (471).[26]

In his efforts to solve his problem from a rational approach, Andrés begins with Kant's reasoning on the question of reality. Holding long discussions with his doctor uncle, Iturrioz, which

26. Page references are to the edition of *El árbol de la ciencia* in *Obras completas* (1947), II. Translations are my own.

make the novel seem at times like an essay rather than a narrative development, he arrives at a logical, if uncomfortable, concept of the individual's destiny. He accepts Kant's conclusion that we cannot know what lies beyond phenomena and that knowable reality exists only in the individual mind. But he cannot agree with Kant's insistence upon the necessity for directing one's life as though the presence of a benevolent God or Law were provable. Instead, he declares that "After Kant, the world is blind" (508); and he arbitrarily makes the unknowable bad. Apparently having in his imagination a grim specter of biological evolution, he is depressed by evidences of universal cruelty in all forms of life, which, as his uncle says, is a savage warfare carried on by microbes, plants, and animals. In such a world justice, liberty, and other ideals are illusions. Schopenhauer's interpretation, therefore, is especially convincing:

Schopenhauer, more austere, more honest in his thinking, pushes aside that branch [of the tree of life, which is called liberty, responsibility, right], and life appears as something obscure, and blind . . . a stream moved by a force X, which he calls will and which, from time to time, in the midst of organized matter, produces a secondary phenomenon, a cerebral phosphorescence, a reflection, which is the intelligence (512).

The tree of knowledge, that is, science in combination with reason — Andrés argues, without realizing the contradiction in his dependence upon undependable reason — thus lifts the veil of illusion and makes life seem meaningless and dull. Life is uninteresting because it holds no "future" for the individual, who exists only as a momentary flash of intelligence, an incidental excrescence of matter, and then disappears into nothingness. The fundamental conflict in Andrés is between a materialistic concept of the universe and a desire to believe in the importance of individuality as a dignified and undying reality. If the subjective values necessary to the second concept cannot be honored, life is indeed boring.

The big question for Andrés to answer, then, is what to do with his life, believing as he is compelled to believe that he has little significance in the universe when considered as an individual. There are, in the opinion of Iturrioz, only two possible solutions for a man who would maintain his peace of mind: either an abstention from life, and an indifferent contemplation of everything, or limited action within a small area. The second of these two solutions is a semiactive, or semipassive, stand which allows the individual to indulge his idealistic impulses, thus partially countering his boredom, without falling victim to the folly of opposing the general rule of a materialistic universe. Andrés, whose reading of Schopenhauer has inclined him decidedly toward inactivity, chooses a course of limited action, making a modest affirmation of individuality by carrying out the practice of medicine.

His first assignment is in a provincial town, where his moderately hopeful efforts to enter into life meet with disappointment. He finds little evidence of good will among the people and is especially impressed by the cold lack of sentiment, as seen, for example, in his degenerate landlord, who blatantly displays his superiority to all sentimentalism by deliberately allowing a cat to consume a helpless bird. The human race as observed in this backward provincial state is, as in the city, an animal species, stupid and soulless. With this impression uppermost in his mind, Andrés remains apart from the crowd. He continues to be lonely and bored as he moves on to other locations (other people whirl and bustle about, Gorky's hero had said, "but I'm bored": *Foma Gordyeeff*, p. 211) and he eventually returns to Madrid, resigned to an uninteresting existence and hoping to find a certain relief from boredom by the mere choice of another "experience." The brief conversation cited below is an eloquent expression of unenthusiastic conformity with one's lot and is typical of Baroja's compression of a comprehensive outlook upon life into a few seemingly trivial words of dialogue or a few rapid narrative fragments. When his uncle asks him what he is going to do Andrés replies halfheartedly:

"See if I can find somewhere to work."
"In Madrid?"
"Yes, in Madrid."
"Another experience?"
"That's it, another experience." (545)

In a narrative that records the aimless drifting of a person more or less resigned to a meaningless existence, the reader may find his major interest centering on small incidents and details along the way: a short train ride, a walk in the country, brief glances at curious human specimens. These seeming incidentals constitute a basic part of the composition, since their very small-ness looms large by contrast with the quiet monotony of life and thus magnifies the impression of emptiness. The author, however, does not expect this rather jolting fragmentariness to take the place of dramatic plot development, for he visualizes his "drama" as centering on the decision of his protagonist in the face of a destiny that promises nothing beyond the present moment.

After a period of tentative, unenthusiastic participation, An-drés makes one major effort to plunge decisively and optimisti-cally into the stream of life — to engage himself, as one would say about a Sartrian protagonist. He does so by marrying Lulú, who has long exercised a soothing influence on him. For a brief time he finds contentment in companionship with his wife and in simple social activity. The question of individual survival after death is still in the back of his mind, for he lets it be known that he does not pretend to be satisfied with the kind of conti-nuity promised by the arrival of an expected child. Still, he is able to go about his work with a certain enthusiasm, possessed almost with a spirit of adventure. The image of zestful living proves to be a mirage. Andrés' wife dies at the birth of a son, and he, once more overwhelmed by the ruthlessness of life, commits suicide. He has reached for the illusion of happiness and succumbs before the vision of a muddy life stream conjured up under the shadows of the tree of knowledge.

Like *Foma Gordyeeff*, *El árbol de la ciencia* is the account of a youth whose preoccupation with thoughts of the individual's destiny places him at the doorway of life, inspires him briefly with a mild heroism, and leaves him puzzled, uneasy, and finally defeated by the vision of a senseless world of matter. In Gorky more than in Baroja the protagonist occupies the role of a by-stander and is more completely disorganized and inactivated by his philosophical ruminations. Baroja shows his capacity for systematic reasoning and presents a clearly defined though un-exciting drama, adopting with artistic intent a soft melancholy mood that logically results from his reasoning. Gorky, intellec-tually more chaotic than the Spaniard, is nevertheless motivated by the same distressing thought of the individual's absorption and nullification in a cold, impersonal mass urge to live. Consequent to this unhappy thought, there is in both writers a heavy note of boredom and, further, an outspoken displeasure with the animal passivity of the masses. Foma's disappointment at the submissiveness of the Russian peasant, for example, is comparable to Andrés' disgust at having to admit, in reference to some of the pariahs of Spanish society, that "nature not only made the slave, but gave him the spirit of slavery" (556).

Although Baroja was admittedly fond of the Russian novelists, of Dostoevsky and Tolstoy in particular,[27] there is probably little point in looking for evidences of influence in relation to Gorky.[28] The important consideration is that the Spaniard and the Russian voice in similar narratives the predominantly passive reaction of an epoch, finding in somewhat similar settings of decadence and suffering the manifestation of a grim materialistic law of nature that holds no meaning for the individual. The cosmic pessimism of Baroja, however, in contrast to the more erratic and violent mood of Gorky, is softened by the lyrical wistfulness of an irrepressible idealism. Andrés, with all his dispiritedness, dares to believe in a transcendent reality that surpasses the testimony of the life sciences. It may be, he thinks, that the vital instinct needs the realm of fiction in which to reach its culmination. Thus Don Quijote is "a symbol of the affirmation of life. Don Quijote lives more than all the sane people that surround him, he lives more and with more intensity than the others" (510). A doctor friend of Andrés declares, after the latter's death, that there was something of a precursor in him, which is to say that his idealism was not in vain. The author thus shows his willingness to believe in the possibility of finding his way out of the shadowy gloom cast by the tree of knowledge, and makes a concession, after all, to intuition, from which his first contemplation of Kant had alienated him. It is a timid reaching for faith, heavily colored with a desire to escape into a

27. *Reportajes* in *Obras completas*, VII, 1120.
28. The points of contact between Baroja and Gorky have never been discussed in detail, I believe, though their names have been associated; cf. George Portnoff, *La Literatura rusa en España* (New York: Instituto de las Españas, 1932), pp. 212-18. Baroja wrote a brief and rather unsympathetic article on Gorky in 1904, noting especially the latter's anarchistic, Nietzschean amorality: *Obras completas* (1948), V, 37-39.

dreamworld where he would be free to enjoy without scientific questioning the exciting adventure of a truth enveloped, as in the days of old, "in clouds like the ancient gods when they appeared to mortals" (510).

Zalacaín el aventurero (1909)

The dreamworld aspect, which comes to view in *El árbol de la ciencia* with just enough countercharge to endow the tragedy of individuality with dignity if not with stalwart heroism, assumes a dominant position in *Zalacaín el aventurero*. Somber philosophical thought in this novel is to be detected largely by inference, but if we keep in mind the author's strong philosophical bent, as seen in *El árbol de la ciencia* and many other stories, its presence can be felt hovering over the whole like an invisible cloud. The somberness is couched in a decided lyricism that converts the story into a soft recollection and suggests above all else a philosophical concept of time. Like other writers of his day, Baroja is oppressed by thoughts of a natural process grinding its way through endlessly recurring cycles toward no apparent end or purpose. In addition to this nineteenth-century biological orientation, he also reflects a prominent trend in which naturalistic emphasis shifts from physiology and psychology to more abstract subjects. It is fitting, therefore, to preface our examination of *Zalacaín el aventurero* by a glance at certain contemporary views on the subject of time.

In the early years of the twentieth century, time was still generally considered a separate reality or "substance" in which nature unfolded endlessly in a straight line of continuity. Moreover, continuity was visualized as a mechanical succession of separate moments strung together like beads on a string.[29] To this notion of a mechanical division of temporality into independent particles, Bergson had reacted before 1900 with a great deal of originality, insisting upon fluidity as time's essential quality and hence looking upon moments as fleeting appearances

29. An article on space and time by P. Picca, summarized in *España Moderna*, No. 222 (1907), 186-90, presents in its absolutist and mechanistic concept of time what was probably the most general view of the day.

that impress themselves on the rational intellect as though they were real entities. This refutation of the mechanistic view of time constitutes one of Bergson's favorite themes, especially in his early works (*Essai sur les données immédiates de la conscience*, 1889; *Matière et mémoire*, 1896; *Evolution créatrice*, 1907); for he recognized that creative advance could take place in nature only as continuous transition and that this could not be true if time (and life) were divisible into separate moments or states which are contiguous but otherwise essentially disconnected. He was a leader, therefore, in the revolt against mechanism as he was in the championing of the intuitive approach to an understanding of life, "that real, concrete duration in which the past remains bound up with the present" and with which science and rationalistic method do not deal.[30]

Bergson, however, was far from the concept of a flexible manifold time, which has arisen in the wake of twentieth-century Relativity and which has at least encouraged thoughts of freedom from time's absolutism. On the contrary, he enhances its ominousness by vitalizing it, virtually equating it with an endlessly flowing stream of life, a kind of substantive allness that is ever moving in one direction. Moreover, nonintellectual impulse is of the very essence of the moving stream. In thus predicating a continuity of unconsciousness as the means by which time is dispossessed of its inexorable successiveness, Bergson actually joins forces with Schopenhauer. For Schopenhauer also "thrust upon philosophy the duty of squaring itself not with the atomistic, mechanical, physical naturalism of the eighteenth century, but with the organic, evolutionary, biological, and psychical naturalism of the nineteenth century." [31]

Literary artists accompanied, or followed, Bergson in his plunge into a fluid psychological time; but his alternative to a mechanical starting and stopping of life in separate blocks of duration could not satisfy unless the impression of an irreversible flow were overcome. Hence arose an effort to validate a notion of simultaneity that would counteract the image of a one-way series of cause and effect. Toward this end writers found some

30. *Creative Evolution*, trans. Arthur Mitchell (London: The Macmillan Co., 1919), p. 23.
31. William Caldwell, *Schopenhauer's System in Its Philosophical Significance*, p. 19.

satisfaction in an appeal to the phenomenon of memory (a subject on which Bergson himself offers ideas that stimulate the imagination). The necessity for a straight-line continuity could thus be made to disappear in a dreamlike reality where memory fuses past and present. The viewpoint can be observed in the following remarks of Baroja's Spanish contemporary, Azorín (José Martínez Ruiz), who near the end of a long career voices an idea that had always intensely preoccupied him: "Things present themselves now to consciousness (*el espíritu*) in the distance, in remembrance, not successively, but in dreams, simultaneous and present all of them." [32] Romantic poets of the preceding century had called upon the sensation of a recurrent experience out of the past as a means of escaping the bondage of time. In the early twentieth century essentially the same tendency reappears, exemplified at its fullest perhaps in the mammoth *Remembrance of Things Past* of Marcel Proust.[33]

In this quest after a simultaneity that would obliterate the distinction between past and present and still be experienced in nature rather than in an ideal world, the imagination is easily pulled into regressive flight toward a homogeneity that obliterates the distinction between one person and another. In a homogeneous, prerational state where there is no perception of differences, everything coexists.[34] With such an image in hand, the poet can free himself of the sense of time, but only at the expense of surrendering allegiance to reason, or self-consciousness, with which the sense of time is identified. Man remains submerged in nature and, as Jung declares, "as long as we are submerged in nature we are unconscious"; [35] and it profits us little when we step outside Bergson's one-way stream if we are to end up in the depths of an ocean. In either case individuality disappears with the obliteration of distinctions. Even Bergson's "creative" advance can justifiably be considered a restless and

32. Translated from "Como en un sueño," *El cincuentenario de "ABC,"* June 1, 1955, p. 1.
33. See Georges Poulet, "Timelessness and Romanticism," *Jour. of the Hist. of Ideas*, XV (1954), 3-22.
34. Cf. J.-M. Guyau, *La Genèse de l'idée de temps* (3rd ed.; Paris: F. Alcan, 1923), pp. 8-23.
35. C. G. Jung, *Modern Man in Search of a Soul*, trans. W. S. Dell and Cory F. Baynes (New York: Harcourt, Brace and Co., 1933), p. 110.

futile activity moving toward an eternal sameness.[36] The sameness looms ominously because of the ponderous weight of what
lies behind the present. Despite Bergson's emphasis on creativity,
one can hardly escape the heavy impression of a past that is ever
growing and swelling and pressing against the present. There is
enough, at least, in his discussion of time and memory to turn the
imagination to a stream that is ever flowing backward into an
eternity of the past. If time must flow, perhaps this is the only
direction that it can follow; that is, if it be regarded as the mark
of process and not as the order of succession.[37]

Within a short period following the publication of his *Evolution créatrice* in 1907, Bergson was widely known and discussed;
and since he was a very influential philosopher in the early
part of the century, especially in his antirationalistic bent, it is
only natural that we think of him when dealing with a novel of
that epoch that raises the question of human experience viewed
as duration. *Zalacaín el aventurero* by Pío Baroja is just such a
novel, and although one would be mistaken to confine it within
a close relationship to Bergsonian or any other philosophical
thought, it can be profitably appraised in the light of Bergson's
Matière et mémoire. The relationship is to be found in the observation of two aspects of time: one, exhibiting a multiplicity
of moments or occurrences as perceived in the world of ordinary
experience; the other, underscoring memory or spirit, the immaterial world which is removed from perception and action in
the direction of dream. In Baroja's novel the first aspect impresses itself in the narration of a rapid succession of loosely
connected happenings which constitute the bulk of the novel's
action and the second aspect looms suddenly and dramatically in
the conclusion. At first reading the story appears to be one that
would appeal primarily to children or to young men looking
ahead to an unplotted future. Writing in a distinctly nostalgic
mood, the author undoubtedly tries to recapture some of his
boyhood dreams, choosing as a setting for his story his native

36. Andrew P. Ushenko, *The Logic of Events* (Berkeley: University
of California Press, 1929), pp. 119-24.
37. Cf.: "But the direction of time in the duration of a process is exactly
the reverse" (of the duration from past to future), D. S. Mackay, "Succession and Duration," in *The Problem of Time* (Berkeley: University of
California Press, 1935), p. 186.

Basque region. But he also writes with reflective posture, incorporating in a tale of youthful adventures a subtle intellectual quality that elevates the sequence of happenings to a plane of spiritual longing.

The story begins in the ancient town of Urbía some thirty-five years before the turn of the century. Surrounded by an ancient stone wall, the town lies at the foot of a hill dominated by a somber feudal castle; and everywhere a mantle of oldness rests on the land. But the atmosphere of ruins, by which Baroja sometimes attacks the backwardness of his country, is in this case more than offset by a softening note of remembrance. Even the ordinary objects of the town's general store — packsaddles, halters, colored flasks, fishing poles, tin picture frames, dirty flyspecked engravings — are possessed of an air of enchantment as though coming from "a Pandora's box, from an unexplored world full of marvels" (168).[38]

Out of these shadows of the past there emerges the portrait of a boy who, like the author, is a rebel and, like the author's ideal, a free and adventurous spirit. Martín Zalacaín, born of humble peasant stock, lives with his widowed mother and a younger sister in a hut outside the ancient wall. An outsider scornful of his more socially proper contemporaries, he is the recognized leader of the country boys against the town dwellers and is generally victorious in combat. His extrasocial tendency is encouraged by his old uncle, Miguel de Tellagorri, with whom he and his sister live after his mother's death. Tellagorri, a fit companion and counselor for a hero of Baroja, is a man of mockish wit, anticonventional, antiaristocratic, and so anticlerical that even his dog avoids the church building except to look for a crust of bread now and then. Martín turns gladly to his uncle's primitive ways, hunting, fishing, and contemplating the beauties of nature. The even tempo of his existence is punctuated at intervals by small happenings that include an occasional friendly talk with Catalina Ohando, daughter of a noble family, and his fleeting acquaintance with another girl (Linda), who passes through town with a circus. In a manner that leaves an impression of leisureliness within a quick passage of time, the

38. Page references are to *Obras completas* (1946), I. Translations are my own.

author follows his protagonist through a miniature Dickensian world of marvels and launches him on a life journey whose unknown goal is a continuously beckoning but elusive and vague challenge. Untrammeled by convention and unenslaved by environment, Martín takes on the semblance of a hero and adventurer who will put life to test and in the process test his own destiny.

The test of heroism appears at first as a conflict with Carlos Ohando, brother of Catalina. When they are boys, Martín defeats Carlos in personal combat, and the latter's hatred increases as they grow to maturity, being especially intensified by the fact that his sister falls in love with his enemy. Though remaining in the background most of the time, Carlos stands like a symbol of fateful limitation upon the hero's freedom of action. The suggestion of this symbolic role appears in the early mention of how an ancestor of Martín's died at the treacherous hands of an Ohando, into whose family he had married. The symbolism is reiterated in the conclusion: for Carlos' hatred, outweighing the accompaniment of Catalina's love, is a major factor in determining the hero's earthly destination. It may justifiably be regarded, also, as the symbol of a broader limitation bearing upon the human spirit itself — something like the dead material weight (traditionalism, for example) of spent energy. As such, it is a powerful force, though visibly a mere circumstance in the life of one who moves continuously on, grasping for some kind of higher destiny but vaguely sensed. Love, hate, conflict are all engulfed in a narrative of restless and seemingly aimless movement, itself symbolical of the individual's fate.

The author calls the body of his narrative "Travels and Wanderings" (*Andanzas y correrías*); and the central thread of narrative action is, figuratively and in good part literally, a wandering journey, which is at once an unplanned venture and an unsatisfiable yearning. After reaching maturity, Martín carries contraband from France to supply the Carlist troops who have begun the last of the futile Carlist attempts (1872-1876) to seize the Spanish throne. He is not at all a sympathizer with the uprising; the author, in fact, delights in satirizing the Carlists, who in his mind represent the worst of traditionalism. Martín is merely following the advice his uncle had given on his deathbed to remain aloof from politics and profit commercially from the approaching conflict. The war becomes also an opportunity for adventure and amusement. We follow Martín, for example, in a rapid succession of events as he, in company with his brother-in-law, Bautista Urbide, travels through the mountains with a load of military supplies, comes to a town where he finds Catalina, learns that her mother plans to put her in a convent, is taken captive by a Carlist band led by a derelict priest ("El Cura"), and, pretending for the moment to be one of them, joins with them in song and story around the supper table. The fast-moving temporality of his existence is dotted in this way with experiences befitting a hero from out of the past.

Like a hero and adventurer of old, also, Martín is entangled in the admiration of more than one woman. Wounded while rescuing the beautiful Rosa Briones and her mother from "El Cura's" band, he is nursed back to health by the admiring young woman, in whose presence his love for Catalina appears to be something less than ardent. Nevertheless, he remains true to his first love, resumes his travels, discovers Catalina about a year later in a convent, kidnaps her by a ruse, only to become separated from her once more while passing through a town where he visits Rosa Briones — at the latter's request. Coming from his visit with Rosa and a group of friends, he is called to the home of another woman, who turns out to be Linda, the same person who as a small girl had let him into the circus when he had no money to buy a ticket. Like Ulysses entertained by Circe, Martín remains for some time under Linda's spell before resuming his adventurous journey.

Love and adventure, however, are scarcely more than incidents along the way. Both are subordinated to a constant looking-forward-to-something-else, which bears the stamp of reflective quietness if not of actual dispiritment, and hence converts heroics and excitement into a reverie. Martín's eventual marriage to Catalina is passed over hurriedly, receiving no more attention than one of the many stops at village inns. A year after his marriage he is still in restless movement, serving as guide to government troops, who are now pursuing the defeated Carlists. His life runs its course swiftly, smoothly, like "a wheel along an inclined plane" (193), not complicated by psychological conflicts, nor by a harsh struggle for survival amidst a cruel environment, nor even seriously disturbed by the hazards of his wanderings. Though rebellious against civilized society, he is fundamentally a small boy playing at war, and love, and adventure. As the author says of Martín and Bautista, "the two Basques . . . had in the bottom of their souls a dream guileless and heroic, childlike and primitive" (197).

With the sureness of a foreordained fate, the dream moves on to its end. In a small French town Martín and Catalina come upon the latter's brother Carlos among the defeated soldiers who have crossed the frontier. Still bitter with hatred, the brother brutally insults his sister when she advances toward him in greeting. Like a tiger Martín springs upon Carlos and drags him to the feet of his wife. At the same moment "el Cacho," friend and constant companion of Carlos, fires a shot into Martín's back. With his wife's hands at his lips, lying on the ground not far from the spot where Roland had met his end, the hero dies, treacherously wounded as his ancestor had been some five centuries before. The Ohando force thus asserts itself like an instrument of fate repeating its relentless annihilation. In two brief pages the author recounts the meeting with Carlos, the hero's death and burial, and Catalina's departure to live with her sister-in-law. In an equally brief space, attention is focused upon Zalacaín's resting place, a small cemetery in a quiet pastoral setting, where one summer afternoon many years later three diminutive old ladies, dressed in mourning, come to place roses on the hero's grave: "One of them was Linda; she went over to Zalacaín's grave and left on it a dark rose. Another was Señorita Briones, and she left a red rose. Catalina, who went every day to the cemetery, saw the two roses by the gravestone of her husband and respected them, and she placed next to them a white rose, and the three roses lasted for a long time on Zalacaín's grave" (257).

So ends the story of a restless unharnessed spirit moving swiftly through a few brief moments of existence known as life, calmly, almost nonchalantly answering an unknown destiny, yet living a dream of heroism and winning a prize — the prize of honored memory, at least. The decidedly lyrical note on which the story ends gives the novel a firm artistic consistency, producing the effect of a tale of fantasy. It also establishes a philosophical quality which strongly suggests that Zalacaín's dream is the author's dream of individual immortality faintly colored with hope.

The author's casual summation of personal experiences that apparently lead only to an empty beyond prompts us to ask whether or not the hero's restless activity can be regarded as anything but a futile substitute for hope of participating in an endless present. The word "action" is very prominent in criticism of Baroja and in his own vocabulary, but the meaning of the word as illustrated in his novels can almost be limited to mere "movement." If, as Andrés argues in *El árbol de la ciencia* (513), truth is attainable only within small, arbitrary limits, one is easily persuaded to accept the immediate circumstance as true and enjoyable even though certain to be quickly erased. On the other hand, if one tries to relate the circumstance to a universal truth, one becomes lost in unreality and may be inclined to regard grandiose ideas, such as individual immortality, as hardly worth the effort of sustained thought.[39] One may therefore decide to confine one's attention to small day-to-day experiences, free of the responsibility of relating them to a meaningful whole, content to discover what lies around the corner, and sometimes plainly seeking escape from boredom. So it is that the incidents in Zalacaín's life follow their own whimsical way, rising briefly in their separateness and being always replaced by other incidents equally transient and equally unnecessary to the creation of a sense of completion. The author's technique produces an effect of sharp contrast between disconnected particulars of the immediate world and a formless beyond that is always erasing them.

Action, then, as Baroja interprets it, is primarily the restless movement of one who longs for an unknowable something and yet scarcely ventures more than the satisfaction of curiosity with respect to things close at hand. Zalacaín, with all his restlessness, is really a bystander who watches his earthly destiny transpire in a rapid succession of casually related happenings,

---

39. "No hay que tener demasiada ambición," Venancio says, reflecting on such matters (in *La dama errante* [Madrid: E. Caro Raggio, 1920], p. 58).

and then faces suddenly an immensity that fuses all fleeting events in one vast stream of memory. As though playing a dual role, he is the illusory reality of successive moments and the vague constituent of an endless duration. It is in this connection that Bergson's *Matière et mémoire* comes to mind.

In this work Bergson takes what amounts to a dual view of his subject, making a distinction between time as it appears to the intellect in measurable fragments and as an unbroken flow, for which memory is the thread of continuity. Perception, identified with the body through its perceptive centers, corresponds with the material world, which from the necessities of action divides itself into multiple independent objects, and from the necessities of rational analysis divides itself into separate moments. Perception thus belongs primarily to the realm of matter but it is linked with an immaterial world by the memory image, which partakes of both its material, perceptive base and the realm of pure memory or spirit. The true office of perception is to prepare actions; and action, which belongs to the conscious, sensori-motor present, takes place essentially on the plane of materiality (322).[40] Memory, on the other hand, belongs to another plane and is the purer the more removed it is from action in the direction of dream. "When we pass from pure perception to memory," we are told, "we definitely abandon matter for spirit" (313). Thus we have, on the one hand, self-consciousness, spatialized time, and action; on the other, unconsciousness or the quiescent state of memory, unbroken continuity in the form of activated memory, and dream.

Now, Zalacaín's history can quite justifiably and pleasurably be viewed as materializing on a plane of action, that is, movement, and then fading into the realm of pure memory on the plane of dream. Linkage between the two planes in the form of a recollection partially perceptual and partially dreamlike is indicated by a nostalgic tone in reference to concrete places, by the youth's dreams of freedom and heroic deeds, and by the delicate evocation of heroic personality from the past — the allusion, for example, to Ulysses when Zalacaín is detained in the home of Linda and, again, at the time of Zalacaín's death, the

40. Page references are to *Matter and Memory*, trans. Nancy Margaret Paul and W. Scott Palmer (London: The Macmillan Co., 1911).

reference to the horn of Roland. The dreamlike quality overwhelms all else in the conclusion; but before this we witness —
on the plane of action — the steady rhythm of time marking off
the passage of life as perceived and rationalized by intellect. The
incidents, large and small, sprinkled along the hero's path and
held together by little more than chronological relatedness, are
like the ticking of a clock marking off minutes of a life span.
Chance happenings and passing acquaintances — listening to
songs and stories around a kitchen fireside, planting a flag on the
wall of an enemy city and being acclaimed a hero for the daring,
wandering along the streets of an ancient city in company with
a foreign newspaper correspondent — take their place alongside
love, marriage, and death and contribute with equal magnitude
to the impression of a moving chain of independent objects
forcefully speaking for the extended world of matter. These are
the blocks of time that conform to the natural inclination of intellect to specify a deterministic necessity of mechanical succession.[41] In Zalacaín's life they constitute a kaleidoscopic
panorama of things, from which the individual remains detached, knowing that his reality cannot be identified with them.
Yet the freedom from mechanism which Bergson offers can
hardly be enjoyed if it must merge with a vast sea of unconsciousness; and since Baroja does not willingly bow down to
the Great Unconscious, he chooses to emphasize the dream
aspect of Bergson's thesis.[42] This alteration is only slightly more
heartening, because the spirit world in which personal continuity
is assured is scarcely more than an abstraction bearing the name
of memory and holding appeal to a person's fancy but hardly
satisfying the rationalistic part of his intelligence.

Bergson does not intend his argument to end in fantasy, for

---

41. "Absolute necessity," Bergson asserts (p. 330), "would be represented by a perfect equivalence of the successive moments of duration,
each to each."

42. Baroja published an article in 1899 expressing his lack of sympathy
with the current tendency to exalt the unconscious: "El arte actual nace
de lo subconsciente ... Esa subconsciente es como la parte del Dios-Natu-
raleza que late en el universo entero unido en el misterio a la chispa del
Dios-Ideal de nuestra personalidad ... El arte camina hacia la inconsciencia, y la inconsciencia se llama también muerte." Quoted by Guillermo
Díaz-Plaja, *Modernismo frente a Noventa y Ocho* (Madrid: Espasa-Calpe,
1951), pp. 31-32. I have been unable to locate the article in the magazine
referred to by Díaz-Plaja: *La vida literaria*, May 18, 1899.

he bases it upon an analysis of perception and memory from the viewpoint of physiology and psychology and uses memory as the evidence of duration and not as the essence of an immortality that resides in the past. He is careful to declare that "memory does not consist in a regression from the present to the past, but, on the contrary, in a progress from the past to the present" (319). Yet it would be a natural consequence to find in the hands of an artist a change of emphasis which, instead of raising a continuously fresh vision of things to come, looks to a nebulous reality that consists precisely in regression to the past, and as such becomes ever fainter, like echoes from the horn of Roland. This kind of shift in perspective takes place in *Zalacaín el aventurero*, in which time — that is, time past — reigns supreme. The human individual flashes across the horizon, embracing the illusion of a forward-moving succession of live moments, and ends in a vale of memory that gradually recedes into the distance.

The suggestion of Bergson's conception of time and memory seems very strong in *Zalacaín el aventurero*,[43] but there is no need to interpret the novel exclusively in the light of Bergson's viewpoint. The ideas that found their way into Baroja's writings come from many sources. Especially to be remembered are two lines of thought known to be influential on Baroja's thinking in general: the Nietzschean call to positive action and the stronger, more hypnotic Schopenhauerian inducement toward anesthesia. Pertinent to our present discussion are some of Nietzsche's ardent assertions expressing the wish to raise the individual to glorious heights and to have man transcend himself. Consider the following:

What is great in man is that he is a bridge and not a goal.

I love the great despisers, because they are the great adorers, and arrows of longing for the other shore.

I love him who seeketh to create beyond himself, and thus succumbeth.[44]

43. As far as I know there is no specific external evidence that Baroja read Bergson, but the latter's *Matière et mémoire* was translated into Spanish in 1900 (Palau y Dulcet, *Manual del librero hispanoamericano* [Barcelona: A. Palau, 1949]) and certainly he had attracted enough attention by 1909 to be noticed by such a wide reader as Baroja.

44. *Thus Spake Zarathustra*, trans. Thomas Common (New York: Modern Library, n.d.), pp. 8, 9, 68. This work was translated into Spanish in

Nietzsche's superman is to a very large degree a protest against the all-powerful, solutive "Will to Live" of Schopenhauer, which is an unindividuated "striving forward in boundless space, without rest and without end." [45] Now, Zalacaín is an "arrow of longing for the other shore who seeketh to create beyond himself." He, too, is a protest against the Schopenhauerian Will that recognizes no individual will; but there is a marked difference in the tone of protest. Nietzsche tries to liberate himself from the thought of "willing to become non-willing," calling it "a fabulous song of madness," and declaring rebelliously that "Something higher than reconciliation must the Will will which is the Will to Power." [46] Baroja, on the other hand, is not possessed of Nietzsche's fiery determination to have the self lift itself by its own bootstraps. He merely wishes that it could be done, and in a melancholy, nostalgic mood drifts into a dreamworld where time flows endlessly. The quiet passivity of Schopenhauer thus asserts its dominance over Nietzsche. [47]

The transition that we have made from Bergson to Schopenhauer comes easily if we substitute for the latter's inexhaustible "will," which lies outside of time, Bergson's "real duration," which also lies outside of time (as the term is usually understood). In both cases, phenomena separately perceived are fleeting and superficial, like bubbles on the surface of a stream; the important consideration is the fact of fluidity and the general tendency of the total stream. For Schopenhauer, the highest goal of the individual is the surrender of all volition and the attainment of a state of mind that will permit the peaceful acceptance of what amounts to a passing away into empty nothingness. [48]

1905, and several other works of Nietzsche's were translated before that time (Palau y Dulcet). There is in *Zalacaín el aventurero* a suggestion of the Nietzschean theme of eternal recurrence, in reference to the hero's following a fateful path similar to that followed by his ancestor and other famous persons of the past; but this aspect should be considered secondary and auxiliary to the more prominent theme of time's fluidity.

45. Schopenhauer, *Selections*, ed. Parker, p. 92.

46. *Thus Spake Zarathustra*, p. 155.

47. The novel of Baroja which, as is generally recognized, most clearly recalls Nietzsche is *César o nada* (1910). But one should realize that in this novel Baroja is actually opposing Nietzsche's most assailable aspect (aggressive egoism); for the protagonist, presented as an unsympathetic person, attempts self-glorification in a Machiavellian way and is made to know (as though reminded by Schopenhauer) the futility of his ego.

48. Schopenhauer, *Selections*, p. 280.

For Bergson, one may say, the goal of individuality is the surrender of an intellectual concept of duration in favor of an intuitive union with the life force or creative impulse that lies deep in memory, which is to say, the unconscious. Potentially his outlook is much more invigorating than that of Schopenhauer, but for one (like Baroja) already under the latter's spell it did not uphold individuality strongly enough to bring liberation.[49] A shadow of Schopenhauerian passivity resting like a mantle on the Bergsonian juxtaposition of time and eternity could only increase the story's melancholy, dreamlike quality, helping to convert an epical impulse to heroic action into a lyric composition which in the conclusion is very nearly a wistful song.

Whereas Gorky allows the ideal of individuality to be demolished in the chaotic meaninglessness of materialistic forces, Baroja actually converts meaninglessness into unknowableness, which causes him to retreat into quiet reflection but does not tear him asunder. The Spaniard expends some of his unhappiness in social satire but he also takes refuge in a lyrical art which is much closer than Gorky's literary manner to the early twentieth-century inclination to use art as a form of anesthesia. The literary anesthesia contains, in Baroja's case at least, the faint hope of glimpsing a bearable truth about man's situation. Reading the unpretentious *Zalacaín el aventurero,* one is left with a haunting remembrance, as of a youth standing on the banks of the stream of time, yearning to venture from its unindividuated flow whence he came, resigned to the necessity for eventual fusion again, and yet hopeful that some moment of his temporality may have established its permanency. The story, therefore, is not altogether a dream. The author is protesting against death, but is so possessed of the idea of individuality as to wish its immortal nature into reality and thus, perhaps, to prove it.

49. One must remember, of course, that Bergson in some of his later works (*Les deux sources de la moralité et de la religion* [1932], for example) accords individualism an important role as the necessary instrument of creative advance; but even so, it is always in the service of the *élan vital.*

7

Creative Doubt

Miguel de Unamuno

MIGUEL DE UNAMUNO
1864-1936

WHAT APPEARS IN BAROJA as wistful reflection
surges forth in Miguel de Unamuno as a determined and creative
search. Calling a halt to passivity, the latter engages in a duel
with the notion of an impersonal, unknowable God and emerges
with an affirmation of the validity of human individuality. It is
in reality a compromise stand which allows God (as Idea) to be
actualized in human experience by way of individual determination. These two concepts — the world as idea and the integrative,
creative power of individual mind — are perhaps the most important facets of Unamuno's thought. In one respect (as idealist)
he is oriented toward the past, but as a result of his persistent
search for newness he allies himself more with the second generation of twentieth-century thinkers, in and out of Spain, than
with the generation of 1898, to which chronologically he belongs. He is included in the present survey, therefore, in an
intermediate position. More easily than any of his contemporaries he can be placed in a category by himself, but his ideas
have special relevancy in the epoch of Existentialism which in
its general significance extends to the present time.

Since Unamuno has expressed himself with sharp forthright-
ness in his numerous essays, we shall do well to draw on these in

an introductory approach to his novels. Maintaining the stand of poet and philosopher in unison, Unamuno stays within the boundaries of his chosen vantage ground, seldom concerning himself with science as such. He welcomes the scientist's search for truth and is consequently much more sympathetic with theoretical than with applied science.[1] His scientific orientation is clearly to the nineteenth century and pertains to such generalities as the laws of the conservation and degradation of energy and of evolution in the broad sense of progression from the simple to the complex. He seems to take these major scientific ideas for granted, without dismay over their philosophical implications, including them in an ageless perspective where man is required to ensure the predominance of the spiritual over the materialistic viewpoint (ST, 239-42). He does not, therefore, specifically admit being depressed by nineteenth-century materialism, but he is not free from the depression which the naturalistic attitude has imposed on European thought with particular intensity since the eighteenth century; and he is one of the most conspicuous spokesmen for the modern uneasiness that finds individual consciousness called upon to justify itself in a world view that holds the physical universe in the spotlight and relegates the human self to the background.

In facing his problem, Unamuno can find no satisfactory philosophical answer in any of the dualist or monist systems known to him. He declares that "The immortality of the soul is accounted for only by the dualist systems, which hold that human consciousness is substantially distinct and different from the other phenomenal manifestations" (ST, 85-86). But he does not believe that the soul is a substance that can be separated from the body. His unity of consciousness, his *yo*, is his entire body in all its living manifestations of thinking, wanting, feeling (ST, 89); and he summarily dismisses Cartesian dualism: "All efforts to substantivize consciousness, making it independent of extension — remember that Descartes placed thought and extension in

1. See *Verdad y vida* (1908), in *Obras completas* (Madrid: Afrodisio Aguado, 1950), III. References in parentheses hereafter will be to the Afrodisio Aguado edition (6 vols., 1950-1958), with the exception of *Del sentimiento trágico de la vida* (1912) — referred to as *ST* in parentheses — for which the text is the third edition (Madrid: Renacimiento, 1928). Translations are my own.

opposition to each other — are only sophistic subtleties to establish a basis for the rationality of faith in the immortality of the soul" (ST, 91). Rationally, therefore, Unamuno is forced to agree with "scientific psychology — the only rational kind" (as compared to "spiritualistic psychology") that the unity of consciousness is *fenoménica* and not substantial.[2] Reason thus leads him to monism, which presents the unhappy prospect of the self's obliteration in the All.

In this critical aspect of his thinking, Unamuno, of course, is identifying reason with rationalism and opposes to it his "feeling," which raises questions that "pure" reason cannot answer. Hence he presents a kind of Kantian conflict between analytical reason and subjectivity, and Kant naturally comes to mind when one thinks of influences.[3] In actual practice, however, Unamuno is arguing for a unified reason and in his own way contributes toward mending the breach between rationalistic and intuitive thought which assumed such great proportions in the nineteenth century. He is a partner with Bergson, Husserl, and others in exalting intuition (though he seldom calls it by this name) and in focusing attention on consciousness as the heart of the universe. But he retains enough of the rationalistic influence to produce a drama of conflict which propels him forward in an expanding horizon of understanding. His intellectual career is really a demonstration of creative synthesis rising out of a continuous contraposition of opposites. In this respect he gives us a performance — almost as though he were on the stage — of the Hegelian dialectic; and his indebtedness to Hegel is probably greater than he himself realized. But he could not follow Hegel all the way in the process of spiritual self-realization by way of struggle, because of the danger of losing his "self" in the Absolute.[4] In the threatening presence of an all-absorbing absolute

2. Cf. in this connection the assertion of William James that consciousness is a functioning and not a substantial entity separate from experience: "Does Consciousness Exist?" (1904) in *Essays in Radical Empiricism* (New York: Longmans, Green & Co., 1912).

3. Cf. Julián Marías, *Miguel de Unamuno* (Madrid: Espasa-Calpe, 1943), pp. 79-80; François Meyer, *L'Ontologie de Miguel de Unamuno* (Paris: Presses Universitaires de France, 1955), pp. 109-10.

4. José Ferrater Mora, *Unamuno: bosquejo de una filosofía* (Buenos Aires: Editorial Losada, 1944), pp. 57, 68-69, points out this important distinction between the dialectical process in Unamuno and Hegel. Possibly it is for this same distinction that Meyer barely mentions Hegel in his

Idea, he draws back, determined to establish his footing in the midst of the life conflict itself, which he feels must extend beyond the visual boundaries called birth and death. Reflecting on the uncertainties of this vast extension of life, he sometimes retreats from the heat of combat, as though falling under the spell of Spinoza's serene and impassive Deity, who offers little solace for the sense of personality while allowing for freedom from the bondage of nature's process. The retreat, however, is not a concession to the passivity imposed by doubt; it is, rather, a temporary repose in an endless quest.

Emphasizing *intrahistoria* (the presence of eternity in a temporal setting) rather than history as chronological succession, he envisages a timeless creative renewal that carries him along in a restless and "continuous flow of illusions, in perpetual renovation, beginning to live each day" (*Recuerdos de niñez y de mocedad:* I, 97). When he tries to identify his own consciousness with this perpetual activity he finds himself in a dreamworld, whose shadowy outline he tries desperately to make concrete. His world is decidedly a personal world, but he knows that the literal biological creation with hereditary and sociological determinants is not the "self" that he is searching for in his tireless effort to define the undefinable. His struggle to maintain belief in a real and living God is grounded in his struggle to unravel the mystery surrounding his selfhood. "Mystery pains me," he declares (*El secreto de la vida* [1906]: III, 721), and he insists on an intimate acquaintance with God in a living demonstration of his divine relationship, even though he has to interpret the incessant combat with mystery as a combat with God (*Mi religión* [1907]: III, 820-22). Whether or not he constructs a meaningful religious view out of his wrestling with the mystery of God is open to debate, but there can be little doubt of his desire to place his understanding of individuality on a vital and rational foundation.

If we use "existence" to mean "life" as we ordinarily think of it, the individuality with which Unamuno is preoccupied may be regarded as belonging to three stages that merge imperceptibly with each other: pre-existence, existence, and postexist-

---

study, though his exposition of Unamuno sounds at times like a Hegelian demonstration.

ence. In his poetic comprehension of individual continuity, he
sees in the consciousness of childhood some of the profundity
and simplicity that belong to the whole expanse of consciousness. It is a profundity, however, that has to be stimulated
through an embrace of "the life of the world ... and [the child]
on letting himself be carried along by the current of everyday
life, which flows noisily through his spirit, attains his highest
freedom in the bosom of the strictest necessity" (*Recuerdos de
niñez y mocedad:* I, 100). What is the higher freedom in whose
conquest individual consciousness is engaged? Freedom from
the painful sense of self, which rises with the existential stage and
then recedes to the quiet simplicity of childhood? If it is a return
to simplicity, which is dangerously close to homogeneity, what
of the creative results achieved in the life struggle? Can they be
erased from the individualized march of consciousness? These
are questions that constantly plague Unamuno and lead him
into poetry and allegory as a supplementary aid in his rational
efforts to answer them. Three of his novels in particular —
Niebla (1914), *Abel Sánchez* (1917), and *San Manuel Bueno
Mártir* (1931) — invite our attention to the three phases of
consciousness mentioned above and can appropriately be examined in sequence as forming a major unity. The first and last
stages of individuality with which they deal are necessarily in
the cloudy realm of ideas and are therefore open to the threat of
being lost in abstraction. No one is more conscious of this
threat than Unamuno, who tries earnestly to rescue himself from
the abstractness of his metaphysical approach to his subject.
The world is something of a dreamworld which stands always
like a challenge demanding its confirmation as reality. Unamuno
meets the challenge by pulling distant horizons toward the
place where he himself stands; that is, he tries to breathe life into
the two nebulous horizons of the individuality span by joining
them with the middle or existential section, where he feels the
throb of life. From an aesthetic viewpoint the stories suffer because, as a result of the author's unrelenting intellectual approach
to his subject, they are too obviously allegorical; but the richness
of the thought content saves them from being aesthetically bare.

Niebla (1914)

As *Niebla* begins, Augusto Pérez, the protagonist, seemingly having stepped bodily into life out of the misty realm of ideas, appears on a city street, where he sees and becomes interested in a young woman, Eugenia. Unamuno thus dispenses with all environmental preliminaries and, like a true existentialist, exhibits a disregard of the natural history of man. If man is God's idea, perhaps God's dream — as the author says in the prefatory *Historia de "Niebla"* (1935) — the relationship between the individual consciousness and the divine consciousness is direct and immediate and the important consideration is the concrete demonstration of the divine idea in its fullness. Augusto is a representation of love (his friend Victor on a later occasion calls him "one in love *ab initio*") and believes that he as a creative idea of God has caused Eugenia to rise out of the mist (*niebla*) which envelops existence and pre-existence: "Perhaps my love has preceded its object. More than this, it is this love which has raised and extracted its object from the mist of creation" (707).[5]

As Augusto steps into the world of concreteness, then, his first experience is an awareness of otherness, which will not only produce in him the sense of self but will involve him in a warfare for which he is not prepared. In keeping with the idea of love, which he is enacting, he reflects at first an ebullience and magnanimity befitting his role. Undaunted by Eugenia's scorn, he volunteers to pay off the mortgage on her family estate and even offers to find a job for Mauricio, the loafer with whom she is in love. However, realizing that "The dream of one alone is an illusion, an appearance; the dream of two is really the truth, reality" (749), he turns his attention to Rosario, his laundress, a young girl who appears willing to accept his love on any terms he may specify. Otherness now comes forth aggressively in the person of Eugenia, who changes her attitude and welcomes his attention, wishing only to take advantage of the generosity he had previously shown. Augusto senses that his independence is threatened and decides in self-defense to make a psychological

5. Page references for the novels are to Vol. II of the Afrodisio Aguado edition of the *Obras completas*.

study of women, using Eugenia, Rosario, and his cook as material for his research. But he is a mere apprentice in the contest between the self and the other and soon falls a victim to his adversary. Following the advice of his friend Victor, who tells him that matrimony is the only laboratory for a study of women, he proposes marriage to Eugenia and is so quickly accepted that he is somewhat stunned, feeling more "like a frog" than a psychologist. He is further shocked when his bride-to-be elopes with her lover, leaving for him the pliable Rosario, who meanwhile has been seduced by Mauricio.

In this humiliating situation Augusto thinks of committing suicide but is told by his creator, the author, that he is not free to do so because he is a mere entity of fiction, an idea in the author's mind. The concluding part of the story thus centers attention on the question of a creature's independent reality. Augusto, who has seen his own individuality materialize and in the process has given indications of getting out of hand, answers his creator by placing himself and his originator on an equal footing. Since the whole idea of creation is enveloped in *niebla*, he argues, the author and his characters are of equally questionable reality and therefore need each other for their confirmation. Moreover, the created one refuses to surrender his uniqueness. The author brings about Augusto's death, but the latter still asserts his identity, appearing in a dream and telling the author that his own particular kind of being, dream or fiction though it may be, can never be duplicated.

It is on the subject of uniqueness that Unamuno turns sharply from the Hegelian path which the story seems to follow for much of the way. He brings an idea into the world (specifically, the idea of love), personalizes it by placing it in a relationship with otherness, and allows the relationship to take on the appearance of warfare. Eugenia, in particular, illustrates the aggressive aspect of the relationship between the self and the other: when she sees that Augusto is on the point of disregarding her altogether, she resolutely declares, "There is another woman, no doubt about it; now indeed I am going to reconquer him" (786); and just as resolutely she carries out her plan of attack. It is quite evident that Unamuno is impressed, in this novel and throughout his writings, with the necessity for a unity between the one and the many as a requisite for the reality of any part of the whole. "What is the real world," he says through Augusto, "but the dream that we all dream, the dream we have in common?" (749) It is equally clear that he believes in the necessity for strife, and his contraposition of the self and the other is apparently his way of recognizing the inevitability of a situation in which both love (or union) and antithesis are continuous. But he rejects the thought that the individual self can be superseded in the synthesis emerging from the conflict. The doctor who attends Augusto at the time of his death asserts that one exists only for others; and since Augusto dies "through synthesis" of his constituent parts — head (intelligence), heart (sentiment), and stomach (biological life) — the doctor implies that one finds one's reality by passing *por síntesis* into something not individuated.

This is the view, of course, that Unamuno combats by investing the fictional character (creature) with independence and placing him in opposition to the author (creator), thus demonstrating the autonomous stature that an idea acquires once it is expressed by its author. As a representative of the idea of love, which is creative, Augusto exemplifies creative thought advancing to the point where it imposes itself on the creator and where it may possibly take the lead in creative activity. This interpretation is scarcely more than suggested in the novel, because Unamuno is intent most of all on the subject of *living* idea. Augusto muses, "An idea is always immortal.... We immortals do not live, and I do not live, I survive (*no vivo, sobrevivo*); I am idea! I am idea!" (856) Then, as though correcting his former doubt, he declares to the author after his death that "Though asleep and dreaming I still live" (864).

Unamuno clearly wants to escape entrapment in a world of abstraction and in the epilogue he leaves at least the suggestion of a way out of his difficulty. Augusto's dog, Orfeo, wonders whether his master may not be "in the pure Platonic world," which is also "the world of incarnate ideas" (866). He thinks of this after puzzling over the "here" and the "there": "It is as if there were another world for him. And of course if there is another world, this one is not." In other words, the world of abstract idea and the world of incarnate idea cannot have separate realities. The logical inference is that they must be one; and we shall find that in Unamuno's view the one world is *here*.

Abel Sánchez (1917)

In *Niebla* Unamuno places individualized idea in the position of defending its own reality after issuing from the divine Mind and even allows it to try to help God crystallize His ideas into living fact. Augusto Pérez, however, is hardly more than halfway incarnate. His successor, Joaquín Monegro, in *Abel Sánchez*, is a fully developed human being seen at the height of his passionate struggle with the question of his identity. Consequently, with much greater intensity than Augusto Pérez he rebels against the abstract Idea, though convinced at the same time that it is essential to his own being. As champion, and victim, of incarnate individuality he finds himself opposing a more abstract individual (Abel Sánchez), who can be thought of also as another view of his own personality.

The narrative runs its course simply as a contest between the two friends, Abel and Joaquín, the one exhibiting above all a cool aloofness from struggle, the other the fractious disposition of a person overwhelmed with fear and envy. Joaquín, who from childhood has resented Abel's self-sufficiency and has had to bow repeatedly before his quiet power, carries the torture of hate and envy into adult life, seeing Abel win without any apparent effort the love of Helena, whom he had hoped to marry, and watching his friend's fame as painter grow. The fact that Abel is an artist is undoubtedly symbolical, for he immortalizes ideas in his paintings, and his seemingly emotionless bearing harmonizes with the abstractness of an artistic ideal. Similarly, Helena represents the abstract idea of beauty. Joaquín, on the other hand, in the role of scientist and doctor stands for the hard, agonizing facts of life. The depiction of subtle selfishness in Abel and of a cold disdain in Helena underscores the author's sympathy with Joaquín and his hostility to the perspective of individuality as an idea that has duration without life. "You will immortalize her," Joaquín says, referring to Abel's portrait of Helena. "She will live as long as your paintings live. That is, she will not live! Because Helena does not live; she will endure. She will endure like marble, of which she is made" (886).

Joaquín nevertheless realizes that he needs the "other" and tries heroically to overcome the impulses of envy and hate. At times he experiences the spirit of magnanimity, once, for example, after curing Abel of an illness and again when he delivers a speech at a banquet celebrating the acclaim won by his friend's painting of Cain and Abel. On this occasion he openly declares the human need to rise out of a self-centered existence: "we see in our innermost selves only the mud of which we are made. It is in others that we see the best of ourselves and we love it" (916). Joaquín's heroic efforts, however, are always followed by a recurrence of anguished depression, and neither his marriage nor the birth of a daughter alleviates his suffering. Eventually he arranges for Abel's son to work in his office and brings about the latter's marriage with his daughter, hoping thus to achieve a certain unity with his rival, though still obsessed with the belief that he is a tragedy of contradictions.

Some of the questions that puzzle Joaquín are suggested by the Biblical story of Cain and Abel. Why did Cain's offering not meet with God's favor? If Cain was evil, why should he be punished for an evil that he did not originate? Unamuno's protagonist, like Byron's Cain (Joaquín borrowed Byron's *Cain* from Abel and read it while the latter was painting a picture of the Biblical story), is rebellious at a punishment seemingly undeserved and wonders why he is unavoidably bad. We thus find reference to the subject of original sin and the transmission of evil. But Unamuno is not greatly concerned with the guilt complex in his reflection on man's separation from God. He is concerned primarily with the question of "being" as measured in terms of the absolute and the temporal, and he visualizes the duality as a conflict between static and dynamic interpretation of idea. His Abel, we may say, is the favored child of God because in the capacity of artist he approaches the fullness of being. Hence the serene effortlessness ("sovereign egoism," Joaquín calls it) of his power. By contrast, Joaquín, a flesh-and-blood product of life, represents the lack of being which is a constant suffering because it is never fulfilled. Moreover, in his urge to attain the fullness of being he is threatened with extinction, since his very existence, which is the striving to satisfy a need, depends upon his not reaching his goal. The human individual, therefore, seems forced to suffer for his lack of "being" in payment for being alive, and seems doomed to the lifelessness of Idea if granted the status of "being."

This dilemma, of course, is typical of the existentialist position — forcefully presented by Jean-Paul Sartre, for example (see chapter 8) — and is portrayed by Unamuno as by other existentialists in a spirit of protest. For he will not be content with anything less than a reinterpretation of the God and man relationship which will permit the individual to be himself and yet be in possession of God's allness: "To be myself and to be all" (*ser yo y serlo todo*), as he says repeatedly in *Del sentimiento trágico de la vida.*[6] This attitude of all or nothing is equivalent to demanding divine completeness in life at this very moment. Joaquín expresses the ideal indirectly in his desire to be another and still live. The goal seems impossible of attainment, for "to be another is to cease being oneself, to cease being what one is" (950). Yet he feels that somehow his eternal, serene self (Abel) and his striving self (Joaquín) must be one, and he shows a willingness to meet the "other" halfway in an effort to achieve unity. The author co-operates with his hero by portraying in Abel the "humanizing" effects of the relationship between the two friends. Abel loses some of his static serenity and actually reveals his own sense of lack when he takes a certain vengeful delight in the fact that his and Joaquín's grandson likes him better than he does Joaquín. The latter, however, meets this show of humanness with a more violent kind when he accuses his rival of stealing his grandson's affection, and in a burst of anger grabs him by the throat. Abel, who has already shown symptoms of a serious illness, dies of a heart attack, and Joaquín continues to be burdened, until his death some years later, with an inability to understand the seemingly incurable duality in himself manifested by his need of the "other" and the irrepressible aggressiveness of his *yo.*

The conflict between the self as idea and as conscious action, between the self as fullness of being and as continuous striving,

6. Pp. 44, 52, for example. *Serse y serlo todo* is the phrase adopted by Meyer in his exposition of Unamuno's underlying motivation.

thus comes to an end without a satisfactory solution. But there is plainly a suggestion of solution through supplanting the two contrary viewpoints by a single and different one. While Joaquín puzzles over the objectives of medical science and art (chapter 35), his wife determines to save their grandson from both art and science "for life itself." Once more, as in *Niebla*, Unamuno is saying that the two worlds, the ideal and the vital, the hereafter-heretofore and the now, must be regarded as one. In short, the fullness of being must be within the grasp of the living. How is this oneness to be defined? Perhaps love holds the key to the answer. On his deathbed Joaquín asserts his belief that love for his wife would have saved him. But the indefiniteness of an answer haunts him, as it does Unamuno, who seeks desperately to pacify the analytical demands of his reflective self.

San Manuel Bueno Mártir (1931)

The period of *Del sentimiento trágico de la vida* and *Abel Sánchez* finds Unamuno at the height of his restless search for an alternative to a dualism that visualizes man at war with himself and a monistic idealism that relegates him to lifeless abstraction. As the years pass, success seems to recede further from his reach; and a mood of despair colors his outlook at times, particularly when personal circumstances, such as his exile in France (1924-1930), add to his unhappiness. Concession to the impossibility of finding a clear solution to his philosophical problem comes to view, not in desperation but quietly, in his last major work, *San Manuel Bueno Mártir* (1931), a prose poem whose predominantly melancholy tone reflects the quiet sadness of one who is constrained to look upon himself and all creation *sub specie aeternitatis*.

The story of the priest, Don Manuel Bueno, as related by Angela Carballino, who looks on him as a spiritual father, is based after the manner of a short story on a single motivating force: the priest's realization that his immortality probably does not include his so-called human personality or corporeal self. In perfect harmony with the prospects of a dreamlike eternity is the pastoral setting, a small village situated by a lake where, accord-

ing to legend, is buried a city whose cathedral bells still ring from
time to time. Don Manuel's deep-lying passion, his martyrdom,
is the obedience to the thought that his "self" must be selfless
in both time and eternity; and his life is a practical demonstration of charity toward others, in conformity with the eternal
principle of selflessness to which he submits. That he refuses to
disturb the simple faith of his flock by imposing on them his own
doubts concerning an ultimate resurrection of the human body
is an act of charity in itself. For he knows that the simple villagers would not understand the nature of his uncertainties and
feels that the particular form of their belief is of much less consequence than the fact that they believe. To his viewpoint he
wins Angela's brother Lázaro, recently returned from America,
who forsakes his anticlerical attitude, goes through the formality
of conversion, and becomes a disciple of Don Manuel.

The priest's sadness in contemplating an eternity which is perhaps emptied of the sense of person is accompanied by an outward contentment with life based on the belief that eternity is
very much a live reality. He demonstrates his faith in the principle of life by engaging in numerous activities of the villagers,
including both their work and their entertainments. He insists
that all be happy to live and not resigned to death as though it
were a gateway to heaven. In reply to an assertion by Angela's
mother, who says on her deathbed that she is going to see God,
Don Manuel declares, "God, my daughter, is here as in all places,
and you will see Him from here, from here. And all of us in Him,
and He in us" (1205). It is quite apparent that in arguing for an
unbroken continuity of life, the priest is trying to bolster his
belief in an "afterlife" for himself. His attitude is comparable to
Unamuno's constant practice of affirming something which he
thinks ought to be true in order to create a belief in the affirmation. The intellectual striving is not for this reason a mere acrobatic exercise. It is, instead, the determination to erect a new
confidence in the place where an old one has stood.

Don Manuel's passion is that of giving up the sense of a material personality in favor of a spiritual personality which he can
only vaguely understand but which he nevertheless tries confidently to interpret. "My life, Lázaro," he tells Angela's brother,

"is a kind of continuous suicide, a combat against suicide, which is the same thing" (1219). The thought of self-sacrifice strikes him with such force that when he sees his death approaching he feels like crying out, as Jesus did, "My God, my God, why hast thou forsaken me?" (1222) When he says to Angela, "pray for us ... and pray also for our Lord Jesus Christ" (1222), he is apparently drawing an analogy in which he associates himself with Jesus and compares his own problem of body and spirit with that of Jesus and Christ, the one representing the human, corporeal self abandoned to its earthly destiny and the other the Christ consciousness which "ascends," claiming its rightful unity with God. This last kind of individuality is the eternal self which coexists with the one Mind on a common ground of quintessential harmony. The same harmonious union (not fusion) embraces all nature — the lake which "dreams the sky," the shepherd girl singing on the mountainside, the old village Valverde de Lucerna, "feudal and medieval," all of which breathe a timelessness that is an attribute of "nature and not of history" (1218).

The vision of timeless substance, which becomes especially impressive in the concluding part of the story, reminds one of Spinoza, whose translation of the human personality into the infinite intellect of God also appears to us as a quiet refinement of particularity into a universal harmony; and it is quite probable that while writing *San Manuel Bueno Mártir* Unamuno feels a closer affinity with Spinoza than he had ever felt before and a greater inclination to join him in humble subordination of personal will before the cool sublimity of God. In a way he is giving in to the same tragic sorrow which he has declared the *Ethics* expresses.[7] Even so, he still insists on believing in the uninterrupted stream of individual life, and Don Manuel's synchronization of self with the communal activities of his village is as much a determination to affirm life as it is an acquiescence in the sacrifice of self to the whole. The major basis for his faith is the consideration that life is both uniquely and collectively manifested and that the self probably finds its highest realization in

7. In *Del sentimiento trágico de la vida* (p. 37) he says of Spinoza's *Ethics,* "decidme si no se oye allí ... el eco lúgubre de los salmos proféticos. Aquella no es la filosofía de la resignación, sino la de la desesperación."

the expression of love toward all people.[8] Through its bonds with all creation the human personality affirms its divinity by demonstrating it in the life which is here as well as hereafter. Looking back on the lives of Don Manuel and her brother, who had carried to his grave an outlook similar to the priest's, Angela declares, "One must live! And he taught me to live, to feel life, to submerge ourselves in the soul of the mountain, in the soul of the lake, in the soul of the people of the village, to lose ourselves in them [the souls] in order to remain in them" (1229). To remain *in them* and not in *self?* The story ends, in effect, with a question, leaving us on the dim borderline between reason and dream but leaving us also with a decided affirmation that something *remains* "beyond faith and beyond despair" (1232).

San Manuel Bueno Mártir, then, may be regarded as a yielding to poetic uncertainty rather than a surrender to the idea of nothingness after death. After insisting throughout his literary career that poetry and philosophy are one, Unamuno is at last obliged to take himself at his own word. The change is one of emphasis, not of belief, and is marked by a relaxation of the militant demand to *know*,[9] in favor of "saving uncertainty, our supreme consolation" (ST, 123). Significantly, Unamuno's last major work, and perhaps his greatest artistic accomplishment, is a poetic prose narrative in which uncertainty is both a consolation for the author and a source of aesthetic pleasure for the reader.

Against a background of indefiniteness, or *niebla*, the three novels which we have discussed should be linked together as an allegory of the self passing in review before the critical gaze of reason in unity with dream. The subject is given specific focus and concreteness in terms of individuality visualized as passing to and from the perspectives of time and timelessness. As regards philosophical-religious inferences, it is appropriate to ask whether Unamuno concedes that personality, after having ma-

8. Cf. *Ethics*, V, Proposition XX: "This love towards God cannot be stained by the emotion of envy or jealousy: contrariwise, it is the more fostered, in proportion as we conceive a greater number of men to be joined to God by the same bond of love" (trans. R. H. M. Elwes; London, 1898).
9. Typified by the following from *Mi religión* (1907): "No puedo transigir con aquello del Inconocible...Rechazo el eterno *ignorabimus*," III, 820.

terialized out of idea, is transformed again into an impersonal, unconscious "truth" or whether he insists to the very last on placing his now somewhat deflated ego in the company and service of a Divinity who he believes recognizes and depends upon his personal contribution.

The second of these possible viewpoints is the more justifiable. The belief, or "faith," which the viewpoint involves is of course quite different from belief that one's destiny rests wholly in the Creator's hands, to be disposed of according to His decision. It is far different also from belief in the dualism of body and soul and the ultimate resurrection of the former, which we can almost positively say Unamuno did not hold after giving up some of the religious teachings learned in his childhood. Despite his hyperbolical declamations, which sometimes (in *Del sentimiento trágico de la vida* especially) sound as though he wanted to see his body rise from the grave even in advance of his death, he does not believe in a mechanical arrangement whereby a supernatural Power first breathes life into clay, then separates the two realities of spirit and matter at death, and later reunites them. His intellectual task was to find a replacement for this kind of dualism, and we can be sure that he was moved not solely by desperation at the loss of his childhood faith but by a creative urge to build a philosophy that would be both emotionally satisfying and rationally believable.

In his striving to understand and express himself, Unamuno thinks of personality from two principal viewpoints. In a general way his stand is comparable to that of Spinoza, who counters Cartesian dualism by conceiving of a single reality having dual aspects. But he is much more an experimenter than Spinoza and focuses his gaze on the one reality from various positions of vantage. From one vantage point he sees the human being, in a usual or popular sense, as an agitated combination of intellect and emotions (not a mere physical organism) seeking a harmonious equilibrium. From the other major viewpoint he sees the individual as a potentiality, as a vitalized principle, a symbol come to life. This is an abstract but by no means empty conception, because it embraces not only the fullness of being inherent in Principle but also the achieving of Principle in a live situation.

Although Unamuno speaks of individuality and personality in

many places and occasionally makes distinctions in terms, he does not leave us a consistent exposition of terminology — possibly because he refuses to fall into the static rigidity of system. We are obliged, therefore, to gauge his ideas in a comprehensive sweep, and in doing so we are probably correct in emphasizing most of all his interpretation of one's self as the one whom one wants to be. Referring to the three selves defined by Oliver Wendell Holmes (in *The Autocrat of the Breakfast-Table*), Unamuno declares, "And I say that in addition to the self that exists as God sees him — if one is someone in God's view — and in addition to the self that is in the eyes of others, and the one that one believes himself to be, there is the one that he would like to be. And this last one, whom one wants to be, is in his inner depths the creative, the real self." (Prólogo, *Tres novelas ejemplares* [1920]: II, 982.) What Unamuno says in effect is that a man's real self is his own creative achieving of the individuality that he grants himself at the highest possible point of his capacity to think. Don Quijote's "I know who I am" becomes "I know whom I want to be" (*Vida de Don Quijote y Sancho* (1905): IV, 135); and since the ideal of God is always uppermost in Unamuno's mind, we may say that he conceives of personality, or individuality in a temporal setting, as a line of intercommunication which involves at once both the human and the divine stations for the actualization of either of them. It is an activity full of the anguish of striving [10] but not an impasse between two contrary views of personality. The *yo* which represents God's viewpoint is not a "pure" *yo* apart from the world of circumstance; [11] it is very much in the world, but it has to be comprehended as invisible functioning and not as dimensional substance.

Unamuno is trying to formulate a meaningful concept of the spiritual man, and his difficulty is that of almost anyone who tries to establish a concrete footing out of things unseen. The words that Jesus addresses to Nicodemus (John 3:8) expresses

10. Cf. Frank Sedwick, "Unamuno, the Third Self, and *Lucha*," *Studies in Philology*, LIV (1957), 467. I would agree with Sedwick in part, but not with his conclusion that there is a deadlock between two opposing selves.

11. As Julián Marías interprets Unamuno's beliefs: *Miguel de Unamuno*, 81-82.

the problem poetically: "The wind bloweth where it listeth, and thou hearest the sound thereof, but canst not tell whence it cometh, and whither it goeth: so is every one that is born of the Spirit." Because of the poverty of human language Unamuno circles his subject time and again, never able to say exactly what he wants to say and sometimes leaving the appearance of self-contradiction. But the fundamental truth which he intuits centers clearly enough on the conviction that the ideal personality is a present reality. It is not a static concept preserved in heaven as in a museum; nor is it a realization hoped for in some distant future, nor a dead illusion residing in a distant past. True, Unamuno projects himself toward eternity, but at the same time he brings eternity to himself by affirming that eternal selfhood is a present possibility to him who would bring it to life.[12] "You must look for living eternity," he tells Nicodemus, ". . . in the very bowels of the present . . . in God, for whom yesterday and tomorrow are always today" (*Nicodemo el fariseo* [1899]: IV, 21).

From this viewpoint, eternity is better understood as durability than as duration — a distinction, incidentally, which could be used to explain an essential difference between the Spaniard's and Bergson's viewpoints. The imperishable *intrahistoria* that Unamuno stresses always is a *quality* manifested within a framework of time (history) without being imprisoned by it. The moment that does not pass, the permanent momentaneity, "is inside or under the course of time, and not outside or on top of it";[13] and it holds within itself the whole, "the depth of the world."[14] Time and eternity, therefore, are co-operative rather than hostile to each other, but the former must be held in the perspective of an auxiliary contributing to the unity of the two.

12. For this reason it is well to regard with caution statements like the following: "Siguiendo una tradición española, busca el sentido de la inmortalidad en lo perecedero de la vida; en lo que ésta tiene de sueño y ficción": Luis Farre, "Unamuno, William James y Kierkegaard," *Cuadernos Hispanoamericanos*, No. 58 (1954), 73. Unamuno argues that immortality is to be found in life itself, not in something that takes place after life has passed.
13. "Cartas de Unamuno a Warner Fite . . . ," *Revista Hispánica Moderna*, XXII (1956), 90.
14. Cf. Carlos Blanco Aguinaga, quoting from *Paz en la guerra*: "Interioridad y exterioridad en Unamuno," *Nueva Revista de Filología Hispánica*, VII (1953), 688.

What Unamuno does, even as he reflects darkly on the prospects of his disappearance into a dead past, is to remove time from an absolute to a relative position, making of it an adjective instead of a noun. The stand is similar to that taken by other twentieth-century thinkers, both scientists and philosophers, who break away from the mechanistic and absolutist view of the universe, toward a more open viewpoint appropriate to the age of Relativity.

The new orientation necessarily faces the problem of finding a substitute for "substance," whether this be regarded as spiritual or material, and seems to demand that consciousness be considered a principle in action.[15] Of course, if it is no more than the principle of integrity at work, the question arises as to how it can attain a result that will persist and still retain the properties necessary to a consciousness of it. The question hovers over twentieth-century man like a cloud, and Unamuno is different from many others only in the fact that he talks about his problem more frequently and more loudly than most of them. Nevertheless, twentieth-century thought, including that of Unamuno, is not helpless in so far as the question of the persistence of uniqueness is concerned. In order to see how the Spaniard may be regarded in an area of forward thinking on the subject in this century, it is appropriate to examine briefly the view of a prominent scientist-philosopher, Alfred North Whitehead, who presents the concept of a continuous achievement in stages held together by an intrinsic pattern common to them and the totality to which they belong. Let us remind ourselves, as we have done before, that we are taking note of similar trends of thought rather than endeavoring to trace influences.

Whitehead's philosophy is based on the premise that any theory of science that discards materialism must start with "event" as the ultimate unit of natural occurrence.[16] He accordingly

---

15. William James, in his essay "Does Consciousness Exist?" is a notable example of one who faces the necessity for regarding consciousness not as a fixed entity but as a functioning in which the subjective and the objective attributes of experience are of one piece.

16. See *Science and the Modern World* (New York: The Macmillan Company, 1925), p. 151. See also Errol E. Harris, *Nature, Mind and Modern Science* (London: Allen & Unwin, 1954), pp. 418-36, for a concise and sympathetic discussion of Whitehead's philosophy. Whitehead uses the term "event" to mean "a part of the becomingness of nature, coloured

visualizes an organismic progression, of which each successive stage is an emergent structural unit that mirrors the enduring values common to the total process. The temporal aspect of evolution, which tends to impress on our minds the image of an inflexible one-direction movement in time, is made subordinate to purposive achievement in units of activity. An event (a human personality, let us say) has its own pattern of creativity and is limited in duration by the time system to which it belongs. In a sense, then, the event is terminated once and for all; but the completion of one phase carries also the stamp of a future event, which is another concrescent phase of the same intellectual intending. The whole world order is of the nature of thought process; for each concrescent unit has a "mental pole" that integrates it in a total process whose intrinsic pattern is manifested in a linkage of achieved events with events yet to be achieved. In a very general way, Whitehead's philosophy reminds us of Hegel's theory of spiritual evolution, but we should keep in mind one major distinction especially: the one-way journey to an eventual absorption of individuality in the Absolute, which is inherent in Hegel's theory, now gives way to a freer extension toward indefinite possibilities.

Whitehead, of course, was stimulated by the theory of Relativity, especially by the concept of the relativity of simultaneity, that is, the phenomenon of two or more acts being successive from one viewpoint and yet being simultaneous from another viewpoint. Einstein, in demonstrating that a law of nature (the speed of light) holds true exactly the same for different frames of reference in uniform rectilinear motion with relation to each other (the Special Theory) [17] and for different frames of reference in any state of motion whatever with relation to each other (the General Theory), makes it necessary to understand that each body of reference or system of co-ordinates has its

---

with all the hues of its contents," including duration: "the endurance of a block of marble is an event": *The Principle of Relativity* (Cambridge: The University Press, 1922), p. 21.

17. Einstein uses as an illustration a situation where an observer standing on an embankment sees two flashes of lightning simultaneously, whereas a passenger on a train moving parallel to the embankment sees the flash at the spot that he is approaching before he sees the one at the spot that he leaves behind: *Relativity. The Special and General Theory*, trans. Robert W. Lawson (New York: Crown Publishers, 1931).

own particular time. Hence, "unless we are told the reference body to which the statement of time refers, there is no meaning in a statement of the time of an event." [18] An event, therefore, has as many dates as there are time regions from which it is observed. As an illustration of the General Theory we can think of an occurrence, let us say a sunspot,[19] as being perceived by observers from different stations in the universe. The occurrence necessarily appears at different dates (because of having to take into account the constant speed of light, there is no such thing as instantaneous action at a distance; there is action at a distance with the velocity of light) [20] and thus becomes manifest continuously and with different aspects in the many space-time regions of the universe.

Now, it is easy to conceive of these varying manifestations as being simply a succession of images of the same thing, even though appearing under somewhat different aspects to the different viewers. If one were to think of the occurrence as a human personality's appearance in the universe, a similar division into variously observed dates would follow; so that the termination of an individual life span would complete an event that would then recede irretrievably into the past (as far as the individual is concerned), no matter how long it might wait before being observed in another time region. But the thought potential released by Relativity cannot be so lightly dismissed. There is, for example, the possibility that the continuing image might be an actual process manifesting change while passing through various time systems. The genuineness of the process would especially be easy to believe if the image's source were considered to be always generatively active. The diverse manifestations in space-time might then be explained as partial representatives, and partial only, of a nexus of persistent properties. A set of facts, though seemingly dead in the perspective of one time system, is convertible, by way of their intrinsic aspects, into an actual event in another time system.[21] The course of changing

18. *Ibid.*, p. 32.
19. The illustration is used by A. P. Ushenko, *The Philosophy of Relativity* (London: Allen & Unwin, 1937), pp. 18-19.
20. Einstein, *Relativity ...*, p. 57.
21. To grasp the possibility more concretely, consider an event as a combination of facts whose transformation into an act is independent of

perspectives, which belongs to a complex of multiple time, thus follows the path of an enduring pattern that maintains the particularity of an event in the very heart of process.

Any single philosophical extension of the theory of Relativity is probably less important than the freedom of thought that it inspires; and the important consideration for us, in the present discussion, is the fact that Unamuno fits easily into an area with someone like Whitehead. The fact that he uses poetic or mystical language in conveying his thoughts should not be allowed to obscure their similarity to ideas arising from a scientific starting point. Without any particular interest in Relativity or other branches of contemporary theoretical science, he envisages a world perspective compatible with the concept of a continuous creative activity (or life) "measured" in terms of achievement. He does not consciously make use of evolutionary theory, as Whitehead does, in bringing time and eternity together; but his assertion, repeated in one way or another many times, that "History, the only live part of it, is the eternal present, the fleeting moment which remains while passing, which passes while remaining" (Prólogo, *Cómo se hace una novela:* IV, 912), is consistent with the concept of individuality as an unbroken emanation of constant principle active within a continuum of contiguous durations, each of which constructs an event whose intrinsic quality is transferable to another duration.[22] His emphasis on action or achievement is unmistakable; for he frequently equates "being" with "doing" and even speaks of personality as the equivalent of "work" accomplished: "Person, in Latin, was the actor in tragedy or in comedy, the one who played a role. Personality is the work (*obra*) which is fulfilled in History" (*La agonía del cristianismo* [1925, 1931]: IV, 843).

Combine this equation of *obra* and personality with the equation of now and eternity, and we have a general idea of Unamuno's venture in twentieth-century liberation from the abso-

their becoming manifest to an observer. The event must consequently be assumed to have intrinsic properties that are not contingent upon observation in space and time. (Mine is a rather free handling of Ushenko's discussion of events in relation to multiple time systems: *The Philosophy of Relativity*, pp. 18-28.)

22. Cf. Whitehead, *Science and the Modern World*, pp. 157 ff; and William W. Hammerschmidt, *Whitehead's Philosophy of Time* (New York: King's Crown Press, 1947), p. 26.

lutes of time and substance. Although in our analytical mood we visualize time as a straight line of infinitely divisible parts, creativity, it can be assumed, involves a total process all at once; and if there are no unoccupied regions of time, the existence of one present or block of duration necessitates the existence of all of them together. Man's being may thus comprehend all of time in each of its "present" moments, as Bergson in one of his major insights imagines.[23] The "I" can meaningfully be conceived of as both a becoming and a being, with most weight on the latter. "I become what I am," we may say in the perspective of Relativity; and this assertion represents a decided shift of emphasis from the historical perspective of the nineteenth century, which says in effect, "I am what I become." It should not, therefore, seem strange to say with Unamuno and many others that man *is* existing from all eternity, or that he is not born and he does not die.

The real significance of Unamuno's preoccupation with the "man of flesh and bone" lies in his insistence on the presentness of man's essence in the life that is lived. The individual is the visible evidence of the invisible divine selfhood, and personality is the human act of personalizing the divine consciousness — *Conciencia del Universo*, Unamuno calls it — which depends on the individual to give it meaning for himself. We may, from this viewpoint, conceive of God as an achieved Personality who is also being achieved. This is quite different from saying that He is an emergent God who grows into being out of an unconscious mass, or that He is a mere creation of our imagination. It means, more certainly, that He is of the nature of thought, that He is consciously engaged in creation and is constantly disclosing what He can do. His power is not limited but it reaches out toward what is yet unknown, and the individual is asked to be a partner with Him in an expanding horizon of creation that is predictable only in its general direction. The individualization of God is in a sense the work of man, but only as the actualization of a possible that is already a reality.

23. Cf. Jorge Millas, *Idea de la individualidad* (Santiago: Universidad de Chile, 1943), p. 47, who stresses this viewpoint, acknowledging his indebtedness to Bergson, though extending the latter's ideas to stress the future: "sólo se crea aquello que extraemos del futuro" (p. 50).

Placing himself in partnership with a creative Mind, Unamuno boldly shoulders his responsibility, striving — all too strenuously — to play his part, apparently feeling that he must rescue God as well as himself from nothingness. His is unquestionably an unblushing egoistic stand, but it is not a selfish one. The center of the universe is in oneself, but one "cannot live if he does not decenter himself (se descentra)" (Vida de Don Quijote y Sancho: IV, 203). The company of others is indispensable in the process of self-creation. The novelist, for example, creates his novel in order to create himself, but this can be done only by including the reader at the same time: "Only when novelist and reader make themselves one do they save themselves from radical loneliness. When they become one they become actualized and by actualizing themselves they become eternal" (Cómo se hace una novela: IV, 985). We might be justified in remarking in this connection that misery seeks company, but we cannot afford to overlook the emphasis that Unamuno puts on the love of others. God, after all, is a God of love. At the same time, "He is the son of love in us," and in this relationship of mutual faith and love, man and God create each other (ST, 172, 195-96).

The fact that the relationship of mutual dependence entails an endless affirmation of creative faith is a major source of Unamuno's anxiety. For he is faced with the prospects of a continuous state of unrest suggested by the proposition that creation is an endless extension of the present toward a goal that always stays in front of the seeker, creating itself anew in proportion as it is possessed. Not only is the individual's responsibility never relaxed; it is weighted with the loneliness of one who, lifting himself above the nostalgic memory of a self localized in time and space, inquires of God about his destiny and hears only his own thoughts in reply. God's eternal silence and the belief in a deathless creative continuity accompany Unamuno and San Manuel Bueno Mártir to their graves.

Combining our excursion into Unamuno's essays with our view of the three novels discussed above, we see the latter as a journey of spiritual individuality taking place on a horizontal plane where the potential is actualized and projected forward toward another indeterminate potentiality. Basically, Unamuno relies on the argument that something cannot be created out of nothing or end in nothing, and the idea of individuality (pre-existence) with which he begins in *Niebla* is more than a misty abstraction because it is included with two other perspectives (existence and postexistence) at the same time. If one stage of existence is real, all three stages are real. In this phase of his thinking the *novelador-filósofo* is most confident; for he is an inveterate idealist. It is the question of distinction between the three stages that causes him the trouble. He is obviously disturbed, but he insists that his personal stamp must somehow remain on the principle of individuality that passes through the perspective of time. Even though the temporal phase may seem a destructive warfare, as in *Abel Sánchez*, it is really a testing ground where idea is proved by its contact with situation. It is also an area of growth. "You must live," Unamuno reminds Nicodemus, "gathering in the past, treasuring up in eternity your time, in growth and not in mere advance" (*Nicodemo el fariseo:* IV, 22). San Manuel Bueno occupies a more advanced stage of growth (through love, let us remember) than either of his predecessors and, despite the aura of sadness enveloping his farewell to his temporalization, may be said to catch the vision of a larger kind of selfhood. Personality thus can be seen to enrich individuality [24] and to persist in the latter as a special quality.

The destiny of San Manuel Bueno, then, can just as easily be regarded with hope as with despair. Without much question the author is saying that his hero loses his earthly dress never to regain it. But does he lose the birthright which, as in the case of Augusto Pérez, he has never been without? He is an activated idea of the Thinker-Creator, and can an idea of God be obliterated? (ST, 154) Consistent with Unamuno's arguments in fiction and essay, the personalized idea represented by his fictional characters cannot cease to be what it potentially is within an infinity that has neither beginning nor ending. The activity of individuality is an unfoldment in understanding along a course followed by a single principle. It is not a warfare between two different kinds of self, one of the flesh and one of the spirit, one

24. Unamuno uses the terms in this sense in *Del sentimiento trágico de la vida*, p. 174.

mortal and one immortal. The conflict and contradiction lie in the author's struggle to comprehend a single unbroken line of living individuality which he knows must be visualized above the horizons of birth and death.

Unamuno knows this not only through "feeling" but through that excruciating reflective reason which he openly opposes to feeling. His intellectual career is a vivid illustration of impulse under the guidance of rational deliberation, and it represents a much greater achievement of unity than he apparently was aware of. For his philosophical outlook was not an exaltation of extravagant mysticism or of irrationalism but of a complete reason, which numerous other thinkers of this century have sought to re-establish in a place of honor.

In his determination to find a meaning in life, Unamuno sometimes overplays his personal role in the man and God relationship. One can justifiably charge him with a certain recklessness, even exhibitionism, in his impassioned efforts to compensate for his lack of faith in traditional doctrines — both Catholic and Protestant.[25] Moreover, while claiming his right to divinity, he actually lowers the divine nature to his level by making it share in his suffering and the suffering of Spain, thus placing the tragic sense of life on God Himself. But it would be unjust to judge him by the darkest side of his outlook only. His was above all the creative doubt [26] which accompanies creative thinkers and hammers at the barriers to expanding thought, causing the impossible to give way to the possible. In this respect he belongs in the forefront of twentieth-century metaphysical thinking. Like existentialists in general, he expresses the anguish of trying to make something out of what the self has in its immediate

25. Antonio Sánchez-Barbudo is probably correct in pointing to the theatrical aspect of Unamuno's battle with doubt; but he surely exaggerates, especially in calling Unamuno an atheist, apparently assuming that the loss of one kind of faith is the same as a loss of all kinds. See: "El misterio de la personalidad en Unamuno," *Revista de la Universidad de Buenos Aires*, July-September, 1950, pp. 201-54; "La formación del pensamiento de Unamuno, una experiencia decisiva: la crisis de 1897," *Hispanic Review*, XVIII (1950), 218-43. Cf. Hernán Benítez, who promptly challenges Sánchez-Barbudo's stand: "Nuevo palique unamuniano (Introducción a doce cartas de Unamuno a González Trilla)," *Revista de la Universidad de Buenos Aires*, October-December, 1950, pp. 479-534.

26. An agonizing doubt which creates a singularly convincing faith, as Martin Nozick rightly argues: "Unamuno and his God," *South Atlantic Quarterly*, XLIX (1950), 332-44.

reach. Unlike some of them, however, he refuses to believe that existence and essence are incompatible, and he consequently spends his energy trying to construct a new affirmation instead of analyzing negativity. The comparison will become clearer in later references.

8

The Challenge of Absurdity

Jean-Paul Sartre   Ramón J. Sender

JEAN-PAUL SARTRE
1905-

THE NOVELISTIC ACTIVITY of greatest importance
in the second quarter of this century represents perhaps a climax
of reaction against strongly entrenched beliefs of the nineteenth
century. The depiction of a disoriented and rebellious ego seeking its authentic being outside a status quo conception of togetherness is probably to be explained in large part as a climactic
accumulation of resentment on the part of individual consciousness for having been pushed into a defensive position that seems
more and more difficult to defend. Political and economic conditions undoubtedly contributed to the general spirit of demor-
alization that became particularly noticeable in France and Spain
after 1940. But the ideas and attitudes that pervade the contemporary novel go much deeper than the political situation. If one
were called upon to contain the complexities of contemporary
thought within a simplified perspective, one would surely have
to place in a position of prominence thinkers' concentration on
the concept of *now* and their efforts to get at the heart of man's
significance by an examination of his individual existence on the
basis of itself alone. This viewpoint is fundamental in Existentialism, which — if it be regarded as an attitude and not as a
specific system of thought — is an intellectual posture of major

consequence; and anyone who discourses on literature of the past thirty years is obliged to consider some of the main features of the existentialist outlook.

A useful, possibly necessary, way to look at Existentialism is to regard it as a revolt against the historical viewpoint that dominated the nineteenth century. It is especially a refusal to seek an explanation of human existence in a causal chain of being, whether this be conceived of as a mechanistic juxtaposition of stages or as organic fluidity. Evolution in the spatiotemporal world is accepted as a matter of fact, but it is scorned as a source of knowledge concerning man's essential nature, even when it is translated into a spiritual evolutionism of Hegelian stripe. Hence we find a rejection of not only the old dualistic compartmentalization of the universe but also of the idealistic and naturalistic monisms of the nineteenth century. Human existence is visualized not as process but as situation, in which relationships are horizontal rather than vertical. As Sartre maintains in *L'Etre et le Néant*, the temporalization of consciousness is a flat movement, not a vertical progress toward a cause. Origin and destiny, therefore, cannot be dignified as meaningful background or purposeful direction.

This outlook can hardly be said to contribute to one's peace of mind. The act of cutting oneself off from any field of orientation apart from self most often results in a feeling of futility. It is something like trying to analyze an idea outside a frame of reference or trying to establish reason in a world where there is no ground to build on. At the same time it is an effort to underpin a "free" human consciousness with an unknown quantity, which by virtue of its mystery sometimes assumes an aspect of terror. The resultant pictures of the human situation left by artists produce an impression of disorientation and absurdity. It is an absurdity related in good part to the thought of standing on a mystifying emptiness, but it also reveals a persistent protest against the haunting vision of man's identity with a materialistic allness.

Because of this attitude of protest and a refusal to accept old interpretations, the existentialist presentation of the human situation must not be considered a one-sided gloomy view. Even though unable to dispel an anxiety of uncertainty and indefiniteness, existentialist man appears to be stationed on an open road, his destiny undetermined by preconceived rational ideas or natural laws. If the temporalization of consciousness is a flat movement, as Sartre says, we can think of man as standing at eye level with the being that represents his ultimate potentiality. The transition from one state of being to another, from potentiality to actuality, let us say, or from actuality to potentiality, takes place as coetaneous action. Existence and essence, then, may be regarded as coexistent and interdependent, in accord with the more optimistic and constructive aspects of Unamuno's thought. If the existentialist exhibits his frustration at not being able to bring existence and essence together, we still must realize that he is not a defeatist. He is actually looking absurdity in the face and daring to "be" in spite of the threat of nonbeing.[1] He is thereby implying not only the necessity but the possibility of overcoming the estrangement that exists between his self and the transcendent Self which he cannot forget. Existentialism can be fully appreciated only when its negative emphasis is extended to include its implied affirmation. The affirmative attitude (noticeably for some writers more than for others) lingers hesitantly and somewhat defiantly at a distance, waiting for new interpretations that can bring it into action. For reconciliation cannot be effected by way of surrender to certain traditional viewpoints. The gods that Nietzsche fought against cannot be resurrected, but a new understanding of God is called upon to assert itself, and existentialist man is reaching for the new understanding. He does so convinced that he must achieve his reconciliation with Being, his salvation from nothingness, within his own finite freedom. Meanwhile, his freedom weighs heavy on his shoulders, and the fictional expression of his puzzlement affords vivid pictures of the human consciousness left to fend for itself in a world that depends on it for its meaning.

The isolation and stark nudity of existential man have been portrayed with a near-stultifying deadliness in various novels of the decade 1940-1950 in particular. For purposes of a necessary simplification, the novelistic portrayal can be thought of as two

1. Paul Tillich forcefully makes this point in *The Courage to Be* (New Haven: Yale University Press, 1952), one of the most constructive and sympathetic interpretations of the existentialist position.

major postures (exemplified by Jean-Paul Sartre and Ramón J. Sender): one expressive of a dull throbbing discomfort arising from a meaningless existence cut off from Being and the other a sharper, more violent response to the mystery of the unknown ground of Being.

The early Sartre, to whom our attention will be directed in this discussion, appears to be tortured by the necessity for adjusting to a monistic view of the world (a new kind which he is unable to formulate) after reluctantly discarding the convenient solutions held out by dualism. Consequently, the motivations underlying his novels are not far different from those found in some of the works already discussed in the present study. Although he has little to say about "soul," the following quotation from Unamuno's *Del sentimiento trágico de la vida* is quite relevant to an understanding of his own situation: "Only the dualist systems allow for the immortality of the soul ... and reason is naturally monist." [2] But, whereas Unamuno fought with quixotic fervor against seemingly impassable barriers to his understanding and in some degree transcended them, Sartre maintains the posture of a stubborn but uncomfortable disengagement from meaning.

Sartre has undoubtedly been influenced by science in a general way, but he shows more aloofness from it than love for it. His unfriendly attitude pertains primarily to biology and is particularly noticeable — if we infer his attitude from his figures of speech — in his novels and his discussion of psychoanalysis. This aversion to biology is a logical accompaniment to his commonly known opposition to deterministic psychology. It is a hostility easily understood as a reaction to the continuing tendency to examine and explain man "from the ground up." If one must believe that intellectual life arises from a "purely physical point of departure" and follows an upward path "of sensation to metaphysical emotion," [3] or that human existence represents on the scale of being a point midway between body and soul,[4]

2. Translated from Spanish (3rd ed.), pp. 85-86.
3. A viewpoint (and no doubt a common one) taken by André Berge, "L'Esprit de la littérature moderne," *RDM*, LIII (1929), 184-85.
4. E. Bréhier (citing M. Pradines), "L'Etat présent de la philosophie," *Revue Philosophique de la France et de l'Etranger*, January-February, 1938, p. 18.

man is an unhappy mixture of two incompatible elements, whether viewed as a refined body or an adulterated spirit. When we consider the persistence of this kind of thinking, it is not surprising that a contemporary artist like Sartre evinces an aversion to matter as violently as Flaubert did a century ago. On the other hand, because of his admiration for a hard, clean substance — as compared to biological flux — Sartre shows a certain friendliness toward physics; though he is apparently adversely affected by physicists' inability to lay hold of a stable substance and their perplexity over the question of continuity in the transmission of energy. The porosity of matter and the emptiness of interphenomenal space, which modern physics has encouraged us to visualize, are suggestive of the fissures in the structure of reality which Sartre regards as fundamental in the analysis of human existence.

Like other existentialists, Sartre takes his stand on the unqualified actuality of his being present in the world. From this Cartesian-like premise he develops his analysis of being in *L'Etre et le Néant*, a major philosophical dissertation; and since an acquaintance with this work contributes to an understanding of the author's fictional compositions, we can afford to examine it briefly, looking for ideas that have special bearing on the novel presently to be discussed. Sartre is apparently motivated by the admirable conviction that if individual human consciousness has any validity it must be made to prove it without recourse to arguments about causality and origin. Accordingly, he declares himself free of all prejudices having to do with the genesis of the psyche. "Consciousness is consciousness through and through" (lvii),[5] he insists, and is full grown and completely on its own from the moment of its appearance. Thus in one bold sweep he disposes of evolutionism, determinism, and all kinds of creationism. It is a courageous beginning, but the complete isolation of human consciousness inevitably involves its champion in contradictions that overshadow his insight and impress his readers more with his opposition to old ideas than with his presentation of a new perspective.

The source of greatest contradiction in Sartre, and probably

5. Page references are to *Being and Nothingness*, trans. Hazel E. Barnes (New York: Philosophical Library, 1956).

his greatest weakness, is his aversion to the concept of creation; because it not only deprives him of a principle with which to reconstruct the historical world that he first destroys but leaves him unhappy with a flat-surface world that has no forward movement. By dissociating himself completely from any chain of being prior to his own existence he automatically places on himself full responsibility for self-creation as well as the necessity for creating meaning in the world. But self-creation is not what he wants. If we are to judge by the intensity of his preoccupation with the subject, his deep-lying desire is a stable *essence*, a tangible substance in effect, which he can move toward and eventually grasp without having to resort to the medium of creation. Such a concept becomes his unattainable ideal, which is described as an impossible union of the being-for-itself (*pour-soi*), or self-consciousness,[6] and the being-in-itself (*ensoi*), which possesses permanence but not consciousness.

The problem of establishing meaning thus assumes in Sartre's mind the appearance of a contest between two incompatible entities, one visualized as static (essence) and the other as fluid (existence); and though he is presumably a champion of the latter, he reveals a servitude to the former. The ideal state would be a union of the two, symbolized as a liquid solid, but in effect the liquid is allowed to become exclusively solid. The goal of existence is always to attain the concreteness of the in-itself, which is cast in "the bronze of being" (92), but attainment dissolves into nothingness before the overwhelming presence of the goal because the area of creative process is not recognized. "Value" resides always in that which is *lacked;* it cannot be found in the area of the *lacking* (93). In other words, the end sought after, like some distant, concrete heaven, is given all the glory; and the traveling toward the goal is given none.

This kind of reasoning is potentially of great constructive significance in that it demands the right to possess heaven or the fullness of being without the intermediate activity of "becoming." No one illustrates the affirmative side of this existentialist stand more vividly than Unamuno, for he openly and

---

6. Although Sartre makes some distinctions between certain aspects of consciousness, the term can be taken to mean simply individual human consciousness, exclusive of the subconscious.

boldly asserts his divine right. But he does so by bringing heaven down to earth, converting it into "activity." He undertakes the substitution of a process of being for a process of becoming. In the case of Sartre, who is much more firmly bound by traditional habits of thought than the Spaniard, the aim is to catch up with a reality that is separate from the seeker. The concept of becoming is replaced by the concept of mere passage through empty space, and the bridge between the seeker and his goal is necessarily a construction out of a void — in other words, an impossibility.

Sartre's obsession with a vision of rigid separateness in the structure of being thus closes the door to a possible conciliation between existence and essence by way of a relational field. To him the interphenomenal world enjoys its full significance as the negation of one phenomenon by another. Visualize with him, for example, two points A and B separated by a segment of distance. If the segment is apprehended as a full, concrete object, the two points are denied an objective status. "If, on the other hand, we direct our attention to the two points A and B ... the segment disappears as a full, concrete object; it is apprehended in terms of two points as the emptiness, the negativity which separates them" (20).[7] Sartre is thus unwilling to grant anything but the power of negation to the space that separates; it cannot be an area for construction.[8] To him passage is passage through and through; an idea in flight cannot share in the meaning of a neighboring idea.

7. Whether or not Sartre in this connection is influenced by theories dealing with the quantum is a matter of conjecture; but it seems clear that if he were to take a stand on the question of continuity and discontinuity he would align himself with those who emphasize the latter. He would allow for the localization of the quantum or for the distance it covers, but not for both in union. Quantum physics was of course widely discussed around 1930, when Sartre's basic philosophical outlook was taking form; for example, E. Techoueyres, "Le Continu et le discontinu en biologie," *Revue Philosophique*, Nos. 7-8 (1931), 97-107; Charles Fabry, "Ondes et projectiles. La guerre et la paix entre deux théories," *RDM*, XVI (1933), 181-90.

8. Contrast with Sartre's position that of Martin Buber, who is no more willing than the former to accept "the dogma of gradual process," yet stresses above all else "the sphere that lies *between beings* ... the kingdom that is hidden in our midst, the between us": *I and Thou* (1923), trans. Ronald Gregor Smith (New York: Charles Scribner's Sons, 1937), p. 119. Cf. further: "Spirit is not in the *I*, but between *I* and *Thou* ... Only in virtue of his power to enter into relation is he able to live in the spirit" (p. 39).

Thus, in a veritable apotheosis of the divisive force of analytical reason, the totality of being is broken into categories and the division artificially achieved is allowed to exclude the togetherness that preceded the separation. Relationship consequently becomes a mechanical sign which says simply that one thing is not another, and this simple negative sign solidifies into an impassable wall that cuts off all possibility of creative synthesis. "The cloud is not potential rain" (98); "the for-itself is not 'pregnant with the future'" (125); "between the past and the present there is an absolute heterogeneity" (119). An individual's activity, therefore, is given no chance of organizing itself into the durable coherence of a "continuous event."

This rigid fragmentariness, which is indicative of Sartre's strong orientation to the past, reduces essentially to a dualism based on the stark separation of the world into consciousness and what there is to be conscious of, the second category having practically the same significance as that of material objects. In his revolt against nineteenth-century thought, with its heavy biological coloring, Sartre looks toward the seventeenth century and, though unable to adapt seventeenth-century thought to his own age, is nevertheless swayed by it in his reflection on the human situation. Preoccupied with the idea of relationship between the individual and some kind of transcendent Being, he thinks of two major viewpoints found in post-Cartesian philosophy and is obliged to reject both of them, on emotional as well as rational grounds. The quintessence of personality common to the many and the One, which in Spinoza's thought seems inevitably to eliminate individual human personality, cannot appeal to Sartre at either its highest or its lowest level of interpretation: "If God is I and if he is the Other, then what guarantees my own existence? If creation is held to be continuous, I remain always suspended between a distinct existence and a pantheistic fusion with the Creator Being" (232). On the other hand, the notion of a Creator separated from the world is unacceptable, because "if Creation is an original act and if I am shut up against God, then nothing any longer guarantees my existence to God; he is now united to me only by a relation of exteriority, as the sculptor is related to the finished statue, and once again he can know me only through images" (232).

Since (primarily on rational grounds) he cannot accept the idea of a God apart who could confer permanence on human personality in a supernatural way, and since he rejects also (primarily on emotional grounds, because of an aversion to thoughts of pantheistic fusion) the concept of continuous creation, Sartre leaves self-consciousness floating in the void. After wresting freedom from the clutches of naturalism and supernaturalism, he can find nothing to do with it; for while discarding determinism he also discards the concept of organism, and his freedom is empty because it is deprived of the principle of creativeness. He is not only not determined; he simply *is*, without necessity and without aim. He is not really free, he is merely contingent; and even his brand of contingency is radical. For it includes two directional aspects, one looking back to the naked facticity of being in the world and the other looking forward to naked possibles, but there is no intermediate area of contingency compatible with the notion of probability. There is no allowance for the rhythmic pattern of regularity which in the macrocosmic world may be said to embrace and refine the irregularities of the microcosmic world.

The radical, all-or-nothing attitude that characterizes Sartre's analysis curtails his inventiveness. Yet, in all fairness, we must concede that his stubborn refusal to compromise is really a virtue. For underlying his depiction of the tantalizing interplay between being what one is not and not being what one is there is the positive conviction that existence and essence must be united in a way that bestows dignity on the individual human being. The "detotalized totality," the concept with which he concludes his analysis of Being and Nothingness and which he calls a "new notion of a phenomenon" (625), is a fracture impossible to mend. Yet the impossibility of mending it is an absurdity which, by the very nature of the reason that brought it about, has to be removed. The image of an ideal synthesis in which individuality possesses distinctness and permanence hangs over Sartre like a challenge awaiting the intelligence that can find a way to bring God into the world of human beings and in the act confirm the ideal of personality. It is this waiting for the impossible to happen that constitutes one of the most interesting and possibly one of the most significant aspects of Sartre's philosophical outlook. For it has affirmative implications much more stimulating than the author's harping on the necessity for accepting in "good faith" a freedom that has no orientation beyond its own self-endowment within a given situation. The affirmative significance, however, which we shall have occasion to consider later (chapter 9), is acquired indirectly, after an interplay of negations that set one thing against another in a contest which finally ends with no decision rendered.

The emotional overtones of this conflict become quite evident in Sartre's fictional compositions. In these he relaxes his intellectualism sufficiently to allow his spontaneous impulses a good margin of fanciful play. His novels are less deftly constructed than his plays but they can easily be appreciated as dramatic presentations of a philosophical problem that has assumed gigantic dimensions in this century — that of establishing some kind of tenable position in the face of the devastating thought that one's individual consciousness, suspended in the present moment and entirely independent of any prearranged destiny, is its lone justification and its lone defense in a cosmos apparently alien to it. Sartre's first novel, *La Nausée* (1938), is in some ways the most vividly expressive of the author's philosophical motivation. The series of three novels, however, which he groups under the title *Les Chemins de la liberté* (1945-1949),[9] is wider in scope if not richer in meaning. The first and probably the best of the series, *L'Age de raison*, is a logical choice for a special discussion, because it squarely plants the gnawing ontological question that preoccupies the author and traces its disturbing effects through a major, dramatic episode of the protagonist's life.

L'Age de raison (1945)

This novel may be considered a fictional treatment of the essential content of *L'Etre et le Néant*, depicting as it does an individual's vain efforts to attain self-completion in a synthesis of the stable *en-soi* and the fluid *pour-soi*. The attempt to weld together the detotalized totality has the dualistic appear-

9. Only fragments have appeared of the fourth volume that was originally planned.

ance of a contest in meaning between essence and existence, which reminds one of a contest between matter and mind. Sartre, of course, does not rationally give credence to a dualism of matter and mind; but his categories of in-itself and for-itself and the hybrid for-another, which stands between the two major categories a constant reminder of their incompatibility, are consistently endowed in their fictional form with attributes popularly associated with matter (inertia, opacity, etc.) and mind (mobility, lucidity, etc.). The irreducible plurality could, in fact, quite appropriately be called psychophysical parallelism, converted, under the effects of frustration, from peaceful to antagonistic separateness. For the two kinds of being, the stable in-itself and the fleeting for-itself, are inexplicable givens that exist side by side, impossible one without the other, yet never able to become unified into a single reality without the sacrifice of one of them. A monistic solution to the problem of consciousness, therefore, appears to be undesirable. Immobilized by reflection on the problem stands the protagonist of *L'Age de raison*, stunned but not quite overcome by his philosophical predicament.

The setting of the story is Paris in 1938. Echoes of the war in Spain and premonitions of war with Germany are in the air, but for the most part it is a quiet, dull time for the small group of acquaintances who comprise the principal characters in the novel. In the center of the group is Mathieu Delarue, thirty-four years of age, a professor of philosophy in the Lycée Buffon. Mathieu's metaphysical unrest forms the basis for the narrative development. His fundamental disturbance comes from pondering the status and destiny of individual human consciousness and includes, in addition to the antagonism of mind and matter, an auxiliary thread of emotion pertaining to the relationship between the One and the many.

The progress of the philosophical motivation brings to a point of special poignancy a debate of long standing that Mathieu has waged with himself on the subject of freedom. For a long time he has drifted, more or less without a goal in life, perfunctorily carrying out the duties of his job and maintaining with his mistress, Marcelle Duffet, a relationship which after seven years has become almost mechanical. In the course of this uneventful existence he is suddenly confronted with the fact of Marcelle's pregnancy and is thus obliged to take a decisive step, which is made especially difficult because of his confused interpretation of freedom. He has tried to remain free of social attachments and, as Marcelle has gradually come to realize while sinking into a dull kind of disillusionment, he has remained free of sentiment in his determination to possess freedom in the fullest possible meaning of the word. His desire to establish his own unfettered individuality on a plane above the literalness of personal relations he considers impossible of fulfillment if he is bound by marital ties. He therefore seeks to meet the exigencies of his immediate situation and avoid marriage with Marcelle by following the rather common practice of having an illegal operation performed; and he makes a further concession to his conventional self by insisting on an expert for the operation. This tentative solution of his practical difficulty necessitates some five thousand francs which he does not have.

Mathieu's aspiration to freedom from the routine version of existence symbolized by his relationship with Marcelle is basically a desire to transcend the usual historical and environmental interpretation of man's position, and as such it takes the form of longing for spontaneity and enthusiasm. It is an impulse timidly listened to, stifled for the most part by doubt, rather a longing for fervor than a fervent longing, but nonetheless a definite attempt to take winged flight from the earth. This aspiration has become associated in Mathieu's mind with the personality of a young Russian woman, Ivich Serguine. Ivich is a strange, uneasy, fractious wisp of a girl who is studying medicine in Paris and living in constant fear of failing her exams and having to return to the dull life of her provincial home. With her brother, Boris, she spends much of her time in the night club where the singing star is Lola Montero, her brother's lover, who is determined to hold him and her fleeting youthfulness as long as possible. Mathieu is continually in the company of the two young Russians. For him Ivich is entirely apart from the ordinary. She is perhaps a tragic bit of consciousness, he thinks, but one to whom he is attracted both in a carnal way and as a vaguely sensed ideal that draws him toward the highest kind of unleashed freedom. In the face of her irritable aloofness he is often apologetic, yet able to study her with detachment while weighing the question of his own reality.

The basic narrative situation, then, places the questioning, groping Mathieu Delarue between two relationships which may symbolically be regarded as lower and higher limits of existence. The protagonist, who oscillates between the two personalities, Marcelle and Ivich, would like to find in the latter the doorway to *being*, as compared to mere *existence*. His aspiration, however, is from the beginning of his recorded experience a faltering quest trammeled with disillusioning reflection upon a freedom that releases from one level, literal and material, without being able to reach a more ethereal level. His experience amounts to a mental odyssey in which he struggles free of a concrete, pantheistic monism and, while trying to avoid the temptations of dualism, is met by another kind of monism that leads only to abstractness.

At the earthy level of pantheistic fusion the author's attitude toward psychic "matter" finds outlet in vivid and sometimes sensational imagery pointing to the repulsiveness of a "foul dreadful flesh" that exercises a mesmeric hold on consciousness. Mathieu, while thinking about the fragility of consciousness and its inexplicable appearance in the world, cannot escape unpleasant thoughts of a human mind emerging from a viscous mass. The early stage of his unborn child suggests itself to him as "a little vitreous tide within her, slowly swelling into the semblance of an eye . . . opening out among all the muck inside her belly," acquiring life, yet with such a tenuous hold upon existence that a pinprick could convert it into "an opaque, dry membrane" (23).[10] Love, through which human life originates, is just a blind physiological act, "a gelatinous job done in a dark room, like photography" (24). And the resultant live object is "a bit of thinking flesh that screams and bleeds when it is killed," slightly more difficult to demolish than a fly (55). In the presence of a friend's small child Mathieu is almost spellbound by the little bulk of sentient matter: "the little creature had not long emerged from a womb, as indeed was plain: there he was, hesitant, minute, still displaying the unwholesome sheen of vomit; but behind

10. Page references are to *The Age of Reason*, trans. Eric Sutton (New York: A. A. Knopf, 1949).

the flickering humors that filled his eye-sockets lurked a greedy little consciousness.... 'And this thing thinks!' Mathieu reflected" (54-55). Under the spell of such thoughts the distinction between people and things seems very small. For example, in the Art Museum two women in a painting appear to change into objects, and the self-portrait of Gauguin looks like a "lush, limp, tropical fruit with pockets full of water" (92).

Visions of mental and material fusion such as these occupy much of the protagonist's thinking, especially in the early part of the story where the question of his responsibility to Marcelle is first raised. Sartre's aversion to the kind of fusion suggested by his vivid imagery is closely associated with his ideas on the relationship between the self and otherness. From his descriptions of viscous, sticky forms of matter we may assume that he expresses in *The Age of Reason* the same revulsion at the thought of the in-itself's being capable of possessing the for-itself as he does in his *Existential Psychoanalysis*, where he discourses on slime as a symbol of the "tendency of the indifferent in-itself, which represents pure solid, to fix the liquidity, to absorb the for-itself which ought to dissolve it." [11] "Slime is the revenge of the in-itself" for the appropriative act attempted by the for-itself and asserts its mesmeric, poisonous dominion even while yielding.[12] In other words, the relationship between self and otherness is visualized as a nauseating borderland of near-fusion where consciousness opposes while being dependent on matter. The unpleasant thought can very effectively be pictured by reference to the embryonic state of individuality as it emerges from the carnal womb.[13]

11. *Existential Psychoanalysis*, trans. Hazel E. Barnes (New York: Philosophical Library, 1953), p. 176. (Sartre's essay on psychoanalysis is also accessible in translation in Part III, chapter 2, of *Being and Nothingness*.)

12. *Ibid.*, p. 182.

13. Or, we may add, by description of a parasitic growth acquiring life and reality by way of bacteriological process. Cf. the following from *Nausea* (trans. Lloyd Alexander), pp. 170-71:

"But on the whole left side there is a little parasitic existence, which proliferates: a chancre...and the man tolerates, hardly noticing it, this tiny existence which swells his right side, which has borrowed his right arm and cheek to bring itself into being."

In descriptions like this, it may be argued, Sartre is simply portraying the nausea caused by the awareness of existence — of an existence that has no meaning; but it is an existence seen specifically as physical and psy-

When the author turns his back on this vision of emergent consciousness and thinks of the individual as an independent existent, he endows consciousness with both the quality of un-fenced mobility and the status of objective fact.[14] A dualistic pattern thus asserts itself in which subject and object compete for ascendancy. Any particular consciousness may find itself opposing all that it is not, including the person with which it is associated; and Sartre's technique of portraiture at times creates the impression of numerous detached consciousnesses swimming around in a sea of things. Two of the characters, Marcelle and Lola, who figure prominently in the network of acquaintances, are portrayed in a more or less traditionally realistic manner: both are primarily neglected lovers longing for affection and security. For the most part, however, the personages appear to be perplexed by their ability to think and sometimes try to ob-serve themselves apart from their bodies. This statement applies especially to Mathieu Delarue and to his friend Daniel Sereno, who, almost as reflective and self-analytical as Mathieu, is able to picture himself as a "disembodied vision" momentarily inde-pendent of its carnal home (111).

That the author is haunted by the shadow of dualism is further evidenced by the suggestion of a contest between good and evil in the personality of Daniel. In a realistic, psychological sense, Daniel's characterization is a study of hate developing out of self-disgust for being a homosexual and becoming gradually an apotheosis of guilt demanding self-punishment. At the same time his personality, in its enslavement to the senses, is a symbol of evil and assumes considerable importance in the narrative development, since his motivations of hate and guilt cause his refusal of a loan to Mathieu and eventually his proposal of marriage to Marcelle.

Mathieu himself is not conspicuously concerned about a con-test between good and evil, though his mood in the conclusion seemingly leads him to think, in the presence of Daniel, that Evil might just as logically as Good be placed on God's throne. His

---

chical fusion. The image of fusion can further be said to suggest the loss of consciousness in things or the degradation of consciousness to the level of things, either of which can easily be regarded as an absurdity.

14. Cf. *Existential Psychoanalysis*, p. 229: "the double property of the human being, who is at once a *facticity* and a *transcendence*."

(and the author's) fascination with dualism, however, is expressed in terms of mind and matter. Trying to avoid the paradox of two incompatible realities, he experiments in a monistic direction, aiming at the conscious attainment of "spiritual" transcendence. The success of the experiment necessitates the union of the self with the other at a level above the routine world which may be visualized as a compartmentalization of mind and matter. Typical of such a literal, conventional world, we may say, is the basement night club frequented by Mathieu and his friends, where the heavy atmosphere teems with objects animate and inanimate and a clumsy, naked girl dancer tries pitifully to please her audience. Such a world of mass reality is absurd when regarded as void of consciousness and equally absurd as the abode of consciousness. From it Mathieu turns toward Ivich Serguine, vaguely hoping to discover the ethereal union that forms his ideal of eternal subjectivity.

The striving in this direction is repeatedly thwarted by thoughts of the impossibile unity of plurality. On one occasion, while riding with Ivich in a taxi, he feels himself to be on the threshold of the ineffable, "suspended in the void, with an agonizing sense of freedom, and then, abruptly, he reached out his arm, took Ivich by the shoulders, and clasped her to him" (81). With this gesture love is brought into being as a material thing, and the possibility of entering into a mystic transcendence is shattered. There remains only the commonplace relationship between two separate persons of flesh and blood: "Five minutes ago this love didn't exist; there was between them a rare and precious feeling, without a name and not expressible in gestures. And he had, in fact, made a gesture . . . and this love had appeared before Mathieu, like some insistent and already commonplace entity," which offers no more desirable prospect than his carnal relationship with Marcelle (82-83). In a word, the ideal state that would combine the freedom and mobility of self-consciousness with the durability of objective otherness remains an impossibility. The would-be realization of the ideal results in materialized fragments of unity (and we should remember that this is a major preoccupation of the author in *Being and Nothingness*), thereby indicating that the abstract concept of unity cannot be lived except in one's vain imagination.

The impression of failure to catch hold of "being" beyond the level of mere existence, which is exemplified in the Mathieu-Ivich relationship, is reinforced by the author's fondness for imagery visualizing objects and ideas in a two-way process of change, passing from an abstraction to a particular object or reversing the direction. These images, incidentally, are much more suggestive of physics — or at least of hard physical objects — than they are of biology. Consider, for example, the episode in which Daniel makes a halfhearted attempt to destroy his cats. As the cats are carried in a basket toward their extinction in the river they are nothing but an abstraction: "For the moment the little cage contained nothing but a solid, undifferentiated fear: if he opened the basket, that fear would dissolve once more into *his* cats" (110). In this case the conversion of idea into object individuates and personalizes, while the reversal of the process results in mass abstraction equivalent to an unindividuated solid. The crystallization of individuality into objective form is further suggested by the following spontaneous utterance of Ivich: "This moment. It is quite round, it hangs in empty space like a little diamond; I am eternal" (253). Similarly, Mathieu is preoccupied with the idea of being impersonally eternalized in space and time and having no more consciousness than the light that "spanned the street and the roofs, serene and smooth and cold, like an eternal verity" (160). "It was a light that extinguished hope, that eternalized everything it touched." Therefore, "what's the use of continuing the struggle" if I am nevermore to have the experience of "*my* armchair, *my* furniture . . . *my* paperweight?" (161)

Although demoralized and confused by these thoughts of losing his identity in a grand Impersonality, viewed as either concrete mass or abstract idea, Mathieu stubbornly keeps himself disengaged, unhappily suspended in the flux of existence and yet unwilling to sacrifice a mobile and rational consciousness in favor of unthinking stability. Envious of anyone who has made a decisive commitment, he is tempted for a moment to follow his friend Brunet, who has joined the Communist party. But he knows that this step would be an escapist act, in reality a religious move in search of a substitute for God, to which one could renounce one's freedom. He therefore rejects this solution of his problem [15] and continues in the vacillation that sees him tossed to and fro between Marcelle and Ivich somewhat in keeping with his fluctuating hopes of obtaining money for the proposed operation.

The resultant indecision in Mathieu's behavior makes of the narrative action a struggle which draws the reader's attention now to the toughness of the protagonist's will in his quest of understanding and now to the demoralizing effect of failure to solve a difficulty that is both "practical" and philosophical. Denied a loan by Daniel, Mathieu turns in vain to his brother, a lawyer and champion of conventional viewpoints, who tries to enlist Mathieu in the established (*bourgeois*) order, which would be exemplified by his marriage to Marcelle. He has an opportunity to steal all the money he needs when he goes to Lola's room to recover some letters for his friend Boris, who in terror has fled from his lover's bed, mistaking her unconsciousness for death. Mathieu for the time being resists the temptation to steal and keeps on trying to borrow money. When he fails to obtain a quick loan from a government agency he slumps into passivity, then rouses himself, turns once more to Ivich, and again failing to find satisfying harmony in her company, rushes away impulsively, fully prepared to marry Marcelle.

In this climactic moment of his difficulty Mathieu is still straining against the destiny that finds self-consciousness absorbed in otherness, and his obsession with the subject results in what might be compared, in realistic terminology, to an hallucination. While walking along the street, he enters into the blurred borderland of near-fusion, that is, of the near-surrender of freedom, where the liquidity of consciousness is almost lost in the solidity of otherness: "The body turned to the right and plunged into a luminous haze at the far end of a noisome cleft, between iceblocks streaked by intermittent flashes. Dark masses

15. Sartre's increasing friendliness with Communism in the years following the appearance of *L'Age de raison* seems altogether inconsistent with the attitude manifest in his early philosophical and fictional compositions. One can suppose that his concern for the working class in its opposition to the bourgeoisie became a concrete activity more powerful in its attraction than abstract philosophical principle. But there is the possibility that his need for orientation led him toward the very action that he condemns in Mathieu's friend, Brunet.

creaked as they crawled past. At the level of the eyes swung a line of furry flowers. Between these flowers, in the depths of the crevasse, glided a transparency that contemplated itself in frozen fury" (344). From this borderland of annihilation Mathieu draws back defiantly. He takes five thousand francs from Lola's room (expecting, of course, to repay the "loan" sometime) and delivers the money to Marcelle, whose affectionate expectation, after having been led by Daniel to believe that Mathieu sincerely wanted to marry her, suddenly turns into bitter scorn.

The protagonist thus finds himself once more reversing direction in his groping quest, and his growing torment is that he cannot discover an orientation. For, in his zigzag course between the two poles of orientation represented by the two women, he is never able to forget that if he severs relations with one he is not for this reason any more at home with the other. When after leaving the money with Marcelle he returns to his apartment and finds Ivich there, he realizes conclusively that she is not the answer to his problem. He wishes that he were madly and irrevocably subject to her: his cruelty to Marcelle would then have some justification. But he has to admit, when Ivich at last appears willing to accept his love, that he knows not what he wants from her. All that he feels is futile and aimless anger. He is as much disgusted with himself as he is with Daniel, who in a culmination of self-hatred confesses to Mathieu that he is a homosexual and further martyrizes himself by determining to marry Marcelle. The hero's immediate difficulty is removed, and life goes on; Marcelle will be able to have her child; Daniel returns the five thousand francs to Lola. But the hero's gnawing metaphysical unrest remains unanswered and he still flounders in the discomfort of his philosophical problem.

Mathieu has complicated his problem all along by his dual interpretation of "existence." On the one hand, he equates existence with a free self-conscious mind unconfined by the mechanism of nature and, on the other hand, with fleeting biological life, which he likens to slimy vomit. He thus establishes in his thinking a pernicious order of opposites. If he were wholly free, in the monistic perspective that he tries to maintain, he should be free to embrace truth fully and immediately without being oppressed by visions of a cosmos divided against itself. Undoubtedly his confusion derives in part from his dualistic habit of visualizing the separateness and antagonism of mind and matter. Rationally, he does not accept dualism; emotionally, he cannot escape it, and he is angry at matter and objectified historical fact for possessing the durability that consciousness seemingly does not possess. The hero's predicament is further complicated by his unwillingness to let reflection give way to intuition. His behavior bears out what the author declares in *Being and Nothingness* (620) — that human reality's attempt to found itself through reflection results in "the radical separation of being and consciousness of being." The spontaneous, impulsive Ivich may be said to symbolize the intuitive aspect of being to which Mathieu cannot attain because of reason's constant, hammering insistence that one cannot be immortal and still be conscious of his immortality.

L'Age de raison, then, both psychologically and philosophically, amounts to the demonstration of an unsolved problem: the unity of self with the All, the one enduring Self. The principal character ponders two unsatisfying interpretations of identity: one at the biological level, warm, sticky, and repulsive, and the other at the level of cold impersonal idea, hard and lifeless. Repelled at both of these barriers, he maintains with stubborn resistance the right to make another choice and, by implication, the hope of finding an acceptable liberation from the concept of total freedom, that is, from the thought of a completely unattached existence. The hope seems rather faint, and the hero is numb after his torturous experience, but he does not come to a pitifully tragic end of total paralysis like Gorky's Foma Gordyeeff. Nor is he heroically tragic like Flaubert's Emma Bovary. The story is, after all, not a drama of defeat but one of refusal, and in a sense an unfinished story that could yet end in human triumph. Mathieu despondently reflects that "various tried rules of conduct had already discreetly offered him their services: disillusioned epicureanism, smiling tolerance, resignation, flat seriousness, stoicism — all the aids whereby a man may savor, minute by minute, like a connoisseur, the failure of a life" (397). But he does not accept failure and we can be sure that in his realization that he has reached "the age of reason" he faces the necessity of meeting the challenge to discover a new interpretation of the man-God ideal.[16]

One can say, of course, that Mathieu's realization that he has to shoulder his freedom by taking part in existence in company with other human beings comes in the sequels to L'Age de raison and hence constitutes a unifying theme when the series of novels is taken as a whole.[17] But the protagonist's real drama remains always an inability to find meaning in his freedom, and the creative suggestiveness of his (and the author's) attitude lies precisely in his indecision. Sartre does not try, as Unamuno does, to fight his way through the impasse that he constructs. But while drawing a picture of absurdity — by both rationalistic analysis and artistic portrayal — he lays down a challenge to overcome it; and by allowing his hero to assume the posture of one waiting for a breach in the barrier to understanding, he is secretly, perhaps unconsciously, holding the door open to an answer.[18]

RAMÓN J. SENDER
1902-

In his preface to Nathalie Sarraute's Portrait d'un inconnu (1947) Sartre speaks of the depiction (in that novel) of hostility between the inauthentic self of commonplace social living and the authentic self hidden behind the wall of inauthenticity and representing the opposition of particularity to gen-

16. Sartre himself says, speaking of his orientation toward the future as compared to Zola's deterministic emphasis on the past, that Mathieu "is still waiting for God, I mean for something outside to beckon to him. But he will only have the cause which he will have decided to be his own"; quoted from Les Lettres Françaises (Nov. 24, 1945) by Henri Peyre, The Contemporary French Novel (New York: Oxford University Press, 1955), p. 235.

17. R.-M. Abérès. Jean-Paul Sartre (Paris: Editions Universitaires, 1953), pp. 99 ff.

18. The notion that God is "celui qu'on attend," as presented by H. Passaic (Le Dieu de Sartre [Vichy: Arthaud, 1950]), is, it seems to me, an example of constructive thinking stimulated by Sartre's challenge.

erality: "But what is behind this wall? As it happens, there's nothing, or almost nothing. Vague attempts to flee something whose lurking presence we sense dimly. Authenticity, that is, the real connection with others, with oneself and with death, is suggested at every turn, although remaining invisible.... Nathalie Sarraute's books are filled with these impressions of terror ...sometimes these commonplaces break down and a frightful protoplasmic nudity becomes apparent." [19] Thus it is that the effort to get at the heart of human reality without making use of conventional interpretations — Nathalie Sarraute's novel is a striking example — results in the substitution of a fearsome unknown for traditional foundations of existence.

The mysterious "presence" that lurks behind commonplace existence has had a special attraction for Ramón J. Sender, who, though transplanted to American soil,[20] remains one of the leading contemporary Spanish novelists. Years before Existentialism had become a recognized movement in France Sender was experimenting in the novel with the notion that the heart of human reality is concealed in a nonrational and phantomlike quality (*Orden público* [1931] and *Siete domingos rojos* [1932], for example) which, despite its elusiveness, is a force immediately at hand. Bolder — and less organized — than the French in his expression of ideas, and less dedicated to novelistic technique as a goal in itself, he evinces a lusty primitivism whose existentialist affinity is an aspect rather than a systematic trend of thought. His writings therefore should not be viewed within the strict interpretation of Existentialism, which is possible in Sartre's case.

In some of Sender's novels the "protoplasmic nudity" of individual existence reveals his attraction to the pantheistic cult of the unconscious which has carried over from the nineteenth century and has acquired reinforcement from Freudian psychology. We must remember that before 1930 the psychoana-

19. *Portrait of a Man Unknown*, trans. Maria Jolas (New York, 1958), pp. xi, xiii. Copyright 1958 George Braziller, Inc. Reprinted with permission of the publisher.
20. Sender is one of the many literary artists and intellectuals who found refuge in the Americas following the Spanish civil war (1936-1939). After residing for a while in Mexico, he came to the United States and, for several years now, has been a professor at the University of New Mexico. He is still engaged in creative writing.

lytic theories of Freud had joined with Bergson's influence; and if these two personalities did not actually dominate thought in the 1920's, as some maintained,[21] there is little doubt that thoughts of the unconscious exerted "a powerful force of attraction, not only over sickly constitutions, but also over healthy and sure-minded persons as well." [22] The picture of man that is extracted from the unconscious by Freudian psychoanalysis is, however, a vision more liable to frighten than to give comfort; for the primordial affiliation uncovered is enough to make us conclude that "if we are to be judged by our unconscious wishful impulses, we ourselves are, like primeval man, a gang of murderers." [23] The inner recesses of man's psychic experience, in which he has sought refuge from distress, thus become a world of terrifying adventure rather than an escape. In the words of C. G. Jung, Freudian psychology "points no way that leads beyond the inexorable cycle of biological events." [24] So it is that "science has destroyed even the refuge of the inner life. What was once a sheltering haven has become a place of terror." [25]

One must grant at least the suggestion of Freudian influence in the kind of mystical savagery found depicted by a number of novelists of Sender's generation, but in so far as scientific background is concerned we should probably attribute more importance to physics. This influence is to be noted particularly in the sharp representation of a weirdly abstract world. It may be that a majority of thinkers discount the difference between the old and the new physics as regards philosophical implications, but there is no denying that the physics of this century has weakened man's faith in the strictly logical, though by no means undermining the "reasonable." [26] Moreover, the most reputable and influential of philosopher-scientists remind us of

21. For example: Mariano Ibérico Rodríguez, "Bergson y Freud," *Revista de Filosofía, Cultura, Ciencias, Educación* (Buenos Aires), No. 1 (1927), p. 375.
22. Translated from C. G. Jung, "El problema psíquico del hombre moderno," *Revista de Occidente*, CVII (1932), 227.
23. Sigmund Freud, "Our Attitude towards Death" (1915), *The Complete Works of Sigmund Freud* (London: Hogarth Press, 1957), XIV, 297.
24. *Modern Man in Search of a Soul*, trans. W. S. Dell and Cory F. Baynes (New York: Harcourt, Brace and Co., 1933), p. 139.
25. *Ibid.*, p. 236.
26. Cf. Jules Sageret, "La Physique nouvelle implique-t-elle une crise philosophique?," *Revue Philosophique*, Nos. 1-2 (1936), 170-96.

the disturbing thoughts aroused by the world of shadows identified with the porosity, the empty void, of the atom; [27] and as regards the now rather commonplace idea that the world in which we live is a four-dimensional space-time continuum, one finds testimony by eminent observers that the notion easily arouses in the popular imagination a mysterious shuddering "not unlike that awakened by thoughts of the occult." [28]

It is only to be expected, then, that literary artists would allow fearsome shadows to people the dramas in which they visualize the individual's struggle to comprehend his place in the whole. While trying to justify the personal element, they have sought, like Kierkegaard a century before, to restore feeling to the cosmos and have risen in passionate reaction not only against rationalism but against the abstractness of science as well. The concept of divinity has been emotionalized, and in harmony with certain aspects of psychoanalysis and modern physics, if not actually influenced by them, it is frequently charged with a good portion of dreadful mysteriousness.

It seems appropriate to cite *The Idea of the Holy* (*Das Heilige*, 1917) by Rudolph Otto as a representative work emphasizing the mysterious nonrational aspect of divinity. Otto does not seek to exclude the rational from the idea of God; he affirms, rather, that he wishes to balance the rational element with feeling and at the same time to steer clear of the morbid. But his instinctual approach to religion definitely stresses the unearthliness of the divine, and the *mysterium tremendum* surrounding the religious experience, as he visualizes it, does not "even at its highest level . . . belie its pedigree or kindred" of demonic dread, which with the primeval man was the feeling of "something uncanny, or weird." [29] The absolute unapproachability and overpoweringness of the divine make of the true religious experience a mystic surrender of the rational self in exaltation of a power that is wholly nonrational.[30] There is no support for reflective understanding and the sense of personality

27. Cf. A. S. Eddington, *The Nature of the Physical World* (1928) (New York and Cambridge: The Macmillan Co., 1930), p. 1.
28. Albert Einstein, *Relativity. The Special and General Theory*, p. 65.
29. *The Idea of the Holy*, trans. John W. Harvey (London: Oxford University Press, 1931), pp. 15-17.
30. *Ibid.*, pp. 20-22.

in the *mysterium tremendum*. The emotion that is usually associated with the sense of self can, however, be expended in worship of a God of passion and excitement.

Sender himself often leaves us with the impression that he is trying to fathom the *mysterium tremendum* of an inscrutable Deity. Unquestionably he considers it his literary responsibility to demonstrate the "primordial vision," as Jung puts it,[31] that leads the poet to pry into the mystery and chaos, the land of demons and gods that lies beyond the ordered world of reason. Moreover, he appears willing to fulfill his poetic mission instinctively, but his reflective self compels him at the same time to rebel at the thought of losing his "freedom" in a vicious circle that leads inevitably to the realm of death, where a person supposedly realizes himself in his own ruination.[32] Hence the subject of mortality is one of his major preoccupations.

From the time of his first novel, *Imán* (1929), Sender has been deeply disturbed by social and political injustice and particularly interested in the inconspicuous and seemingly insignificant members of society. The element of social protest is most noticeable in his early works, but even in these he shows a decided tendency toward steering his questioning into abstract realms. The grimness or the absurdity of a given social or political situation is, in his novelistic treatment, the starting point for philosophical musing. Since the end of the Spanish civil war his metaphysical inclination has been especially pronounced. The aspects of contemporary philosophical outlook found in Sender's writings are varied and suggestive enough to justify discussion of two of his novels in the present study. One of these, *The Sphere* (*La esfera*), though hardly representative of the novelist at his best, is of special interest because of its depiction of a fiercely passionate reaction to the concept of a mysterious, unknowable God. At the same time it contains, in incidental position, certain suggestively constructive ideas. The other novel, *El lugar del hombre*, is more likely to stimulate the reader's thinking about the question of "freedom" in a nonrational universe.

31. See the chapter "Psychology and Literature" in *Modern Man in Search of a Soul*.
32. See Ramón J. Sender, *Unamuno, Valle-Inclán, Baroja y Santayana* (Mexico: Ediciones de Andrea, 1955), p. 42.

The Sphere (1949)

The Sphere, which represents a wholehearted attempt to voice metaphysical inspiration by way of pure intuition, deals with the subject of death and immortality in the framework of an allegorical and fantastic tale. Appearing first under the title *Proverbio de la muerte* in 1939, it was revised and published as *La esfera* in 1947.[33] In the English translation, appearing in 1949, speculative passages were added at the heading of each chapter, which enhance the atmosphere of extravagant fancy already characterizing the narrative style and technique.[34] Simply put, the basic question is: Does one's self-consciousness have meaning as a separate reflective entity, or is it significant only as identified with a vast undying and unthinking "world spirit"? Unwilling to accept the idea that death is a substantial aspect of reality, the author seeks to identify himself with generic manhood (*hombría*), which he proclaims a partner with God in God's eternal struggle against nothingness. He thus tries to avoid what he calls "the error of Kierkegaard and perhaps of Christianity," the error of presupposing "an independent person — differentiated enough to imagine itself free — that can do nothing with its freedom" (125).[35]

An elaboration on this viewpoint and an effort to uphold it come from the central character, Federico Saila, whose "notes" at the beginning of each chapter supplement the commentary interspersed in the narrative account. Saila is in reality the author assuming the role of experimenter. The concept which he has visualized is a spherical universe in which all activity, utilized in God's struggle against nothingness, is a constant passing from being to not-being and a constant renewal of affirmation against

33. In his prologue to *Proverbio de la muerte,* Sender declares that he is expressing in this book something that cannot be expressed in the framework of everyday life: that "I am immortal" and that my immortality is not "a product of differentiation nor of individualization."

34. As the repeated revisions of the novel would indicate, the author attaches a great deal of importance to it. He has expressed his intention of modifying it from time to time in future editions. See Charles L. King, "Sender's Spherical Philosophy," *PMLA,* LXIX (1954), 993, note 3.

35. Page references are to *The Sphere,* trans. F. Giovanelli (New York: Hellman, Williams and Co., 1949).

negation. Each thing or each person, though headed always toward its not-self, does not end there; it simply moves on to "a successive stage of its own presentness" (14). The process is not a forward movement toward some future goal, in an evolutionary or Hegelian sense; it is simply a continuous passing "to another part of that same present in which we are all confined" (15). This eternal present, it is argued, is conceivable only as an enormous precinct in which all paths, curved just as they are on the earth and in space, turn ever toward the direction whence they come.

The image of curved space and time, suggested no doubt by mathematical physics, is heavily weighted with a physicalistic explanation of reflective consciousness, which necessarily occupies an important place in the proposed examination of the problem of individuality. The nature of mind allows an individual experience to assume the path of a trajectory aspiration "to self-affirmation, in full transcendence, in passage across its temporal not-self" (14) into another of its successive stages. But the flight of the trajectory is inevitably curved, and all things borne by the thirst to transcend return inevitably to their origins (15). The implication here, to be confirmed by the narrative development, is that man's eagerness to live transcendently, to possess an ideal reality of some kind, is an individual manifestation destined to be swallowed up in the total mass energy. The potentially stimulating notion of a continuous present, in which the self is always expressing itself, is thus turned ominously toward the notion of return to and absorption in the All. The prospects for individual contentment appear from the outset to point toward a rather grim sacrifice of self in favor of God's survival.

A strange, mysterious God of suffering and tragedy does indeed reside in Sender's spherical universe, imprisoned in His own fatality and enjoying at best a precarious existence. The conclusion of the novel underscores the grimness of the mystery. In the early part of the narrative, however, the protagonist is fascinated by thoughts of what may lie beyond the grasp of our rational understanding; and he hopes, by way of a special, ganglionic approach, not only to peek behind the veil of mystery but to pacify his urge for individual immortality. His experimentation, which is initiated as a gay adventure and ends in stunned bewilderment, constitutes the story.

Federico Saila has been placed by circumstances in a situation conducive to pessimistic musing. Having fled from Spain to France in the closing days of the Spanish civil war, he feels a strong resentment against the world, particularly against the French for not having come to the aid of the Spanish Republic, and is disillusioned with life in general. In this despondent mood he has taken passage on a ship to America, expecting to commit suicide on the way. While pondering the void left by the war he falls into whimsical speculation on the subject of reality, with particular reference to his own reality. Is he more than his person and the name that corresponds to it? Does he have a meaningful relationship to the Great Mystery that lies beyond the reach of his reflective self? His suicide could be the gateway to an interesting discovery, but there is the possibility that his will to suicide may not genuinely bespeak his profoundest relationship. Furthermore, he is fascinated by his freedom to play with life and death and wants to enjoy a speculative game before giving himself up, perhaps irrevocably, to a cessation of existence. He therefore decides to postpone his suicide while he tests a hypothesis in an effort to grasp his authentic relationship to the Whole, of which his personal, individuated form is probably only an insignificant particle.

Saila's hypothesis calls for an instinctive attunement with a broad generic reality. Avoiding — theoretically — a rationalistic approach, he appeals to his ganglia, the nerve centers of his being, which presumably are free of the errors of intellectualized and conventionalized existence. He takes the position that the brain is unreliable because from it is born one's idea of himself, the person, which ends in a corpse, "the crystallization of the differentia" (65). The ganglia, on the other hand, fuse us with common substance, perhaps with immortal humanity. Through them the path to reality leads from mind, as traditionally viewed, to objects. An atavistic quest is thus initiated in which Saila imaginatively returns to his material origin, placing himself alongside the lowest forms of life; and the images transmitted by his ganglionic wisdom, in which "he saw all his anguishes distilled and the essence of all joys" (36), assume the form of the elemental geometries of the insects, appearing as masses of color, sounds, lines, volume. More than one hundred years earlier Schopenhauer had declared that "the ganglion system, i.e., the subjective nervous system," which in the lower forms of life is predominant over the objective or cerebral system, was merely the physiological process by which instinct, while serving the species, performed an illusionistic role as regards the individual.[36] Whether or not Saila can surmount the pessimism of the Schopenhauerian view, in which the individual is absorbed in a kind of pantheistic mass substance, is the main question to be answered in defining the story of *The Sphere*.

Saila begins the test of his theory with an enthusiasm characteristic of a new adventure. Even though he is constantly reflecting, he creates for himself an illusion of complete relaxation, imagining himself free of the responsibility of thinking with his rational capacity. In this relaxation there is a noticeable element of social rebelliousness, a certain will to "return to nature" and defy the limitations imposed by despotic tradition. But the pleasure derived from ridiculing some of the social specimens on board the ship (the Catholic priest, for example, and Mr. Cash, the big-bellied merchant) is incidental to the pleasure derived from an imaginary synchronization with the primal world spirit. Assuming no other responsibility than that of following his spontaneous nature, content to let Truth seek him out, he spends much of his time lounging on the deck, an amused spectator of what goes on around him.

Among Saila's fellow passengers is a married couple destined to provide the major complications in the mystic experiment. The woman calls herself Hilde, but Saila knows that she is his former lover Christel, with whom he had lived years before in Riga and Vienna. He had first met her in the company of a friend of his; and being strongly attracted to each other, they had watched his friend drown in the Dvina River with scarcely more than a halfhearted attempt to save him. Hilde and her German husband, Jacob Lanz, whom Saila calls Hornytoad, are in the service of the Hermaphro, presumably a bisexual being symbolizing the suprahuman Hitler. On the boat also is a young

36. "Supplements" to *The World as Will and Idea*, in Schopenhauer, *Selections*, ed. Parker, pp. 346-47.

Jewish woman, Eve, who has in her possession some important papers relating to prisoners in a German concentration camp. Saila talks with everyone in a bantering and sometimes impertinent way, boldly making love to Eve, leading a voluble American to become interested in Hilde, and watching Hornytoad's venomous jealousy.

Saila's test of his theory thus appears to be a gay and daring game, but it is a game of grim possibilities, played in the very heart of God's fatality. The whole spherical totality is not only a mystery but a horrible mystery, from which man is probably protected by the very inability of his mind to comprehend all. Violence, chance, love seem to be the fundamental elements involved in God's contest with nothingness, and these elements permeate the major portion of the action recorded in the novel. Something of the terribleness of God's will is glimpsed by a strange person known as the Jebusite, the ship's stoker, who claims to receive messages from "Him." One message has revealed to him that on this voyage his ship will meet a white three-masted vessel, which will be a signal for him to place himself and all the passengers at the mercy of the Supreme Will by throwing all navigation instruments overboard and cutting the ship's propeller shaft. He is so loyal to his mission that he kills the chief engineer, who opposes him, keeping the deed secret for a while by burning the victim's body in a furnace. Saila can easily sympathize with the Jebusite, for he too is trying to imagine himself "on the border of everything" and is entirely receptive to the idea that God's fatality involves suffering and bloodshed. Nor is he perturbed by the prospect of drifting aimlessly at sea, because he believes that chance must play an essential role in man's destiny. Accordingly, he wonders whether it is not an important manifestation of Reality that Christel by chance should once more cross his path, thereby inviting a renewal of their love. Christel, for her part, enacts a fatalistic role by contriving to have Saila kill her husband. The turbulent mixture of fatalistic reality approaches a boiling point as a white, ghostlike vessel comes into view and the Jebusite prepares to carry out his intention of putting the ship completely at the mercy of the sea.

In all the excitement that follows the appearance of the ghost ship Saila is at the height of his mystic experiment, fully engaged in his game of life and death. Now he feels that he is beginning to comprehend his identity as a hero of the fatal and is pleased with the thought that he has more significance than that of a mere name on a passenger list. Willing to believe that "everything in life is ruled by magic and mystery" (130), he is perfectly content to leave all to chance, in contrast to the majority of the passengers, who as slaves of human orderliness wish to establish contact with New York. Under the spell of inspired spontaneity, also, he gives himself up to full sensual enjoyment with Eve, thus co-operating with the animal and mineral atavism that points to his essential being. Perhaps in this way, he reasons, he is obeying an unconscious intentionality toward reintegration into the oneness of man-woman that once had been.

With his interest fixed on spontaneous obedience to the basic motor impulses in life, Saila tries not to be concerned with the subject of morality. The question of individual responsibility is allowed to appear incidental to the dominant thought of cosmic indifference to the individual. Saila maintains that God knows not the morality that we are accustomed to because such morality is negative and He is aware only of positive action (191). Noticeable here is the author's social rebelliousness with respect to the deadening effects of conventionalism, but the primary viewpoint remains philosophical. Saila argues that God is indifferent to crime, which must be considered merely as a difficulty or a facility of continuing in the blind service of one's destiny (194). When he is accused by Christel of her husband's murder and defends himself before an improvised court he speaks from "God's viewpoint," declaring that crime is a "sanguinary accident framed in the perfection of God's reality" (195). Nevertheless, he cannot escape his conscience. Repeatedly he has remembered with a mild twinge of guilt the part that he had played in the death of his painter friend on the occasion of his first acquaintance with Christel. He had not killed his friend; he had merely failed to exert himself in trying to save him. The author seems deliberately to have depicted this halfway situation of guilt in order, as a part of his experiment, to give Saila a chance to free himself from conscience, that is, from the intellectualized and conventionalized part of his being as compared to his cosmic self, which is ruled by magic and mystery. Saila is placed in a similar situation when he shoots Hornytoad, for he realizes, with some feeling of guilt, that he might not have had to kill his enemy.

This resurgence of the reflective, socially conditioned self forms a growing counterweight to the spirit of ebullient experimentation and reveals a serious dissatisfaction with the heavily materialistic pantheism which Saila has sought to embrace. In quest of an alternative, Saila turns toward the realm of abstract or ideal union — turns from the subconscious to the supraconscious, we may say — associating the ideal with woman and showing nostalgia for his childhood religious faith. Accordingly, he looks to Christel, who now becomes for him a possible avenue of spiritual integration with the All, just as Eve had served as a possible atavistic union with a physicalistic oneness. After his death sentence has been pronounced, Christel remains alone with him while the other passengers disperse, some of them preparing for his execution and all of them excited and frightened by the storm that is bearing down upon the ship. For a few tense moments the two former lovers talk in friendly earnestness. Discarding the flippancy of his earlier attitude, Saila tells Christel that it is the role of woman to provide an ideal for man, thus enabling him to integrate his life as an individual,[37] and that she is the one who activates his own innate capacity for faith in a divine Idea. Responsive to this idealistic potentiality, she is moved by the thought that love in its humble plenitude lifts one into the area of miraculous communication with the Unknown, and fervently wishes that she could erase the frightful years that have passed since she and Saila first loved each other.

In the role of woman, however, Christel can produce only an imagined reality, which beckons to man but affords no solid ground for belief in the individual's ultimate significance. The pursuit of the ideal is only a fleeting solace for individuation in its path toward nullification in the totality of God's activity. Christel (a counterfeit of the Christ idea, one might say) has, in fact, unconsciously been carrying out her fatalistic mission as an instrument of the Supreme Will, playing the part of a siren and

37. This same idea forms the basis for the author's *El rey y la reina* (Mexico: Editorial Jackson, 1948).

leading men sometimes, as in the case of her husband, to their destruction. Symbolically, she is the illusion for which each man grasps in quest of his meaning; as a particular woman she has no reality. Saila assumes that Christel is a mere abstraction and in his determination to transcend the throes of individuation, he thinks that he can disregard her as a person of flesh and blood. After all, in the final analysis of human reality, there is neither male nor female, but only generic manhood.

Although talking himself in this way into a pseudo detachment from earthiness, Saila is no more content than he was with his instinctive approach to life's meaning. Trapped by his reflective consciousness, like Mathieu Delarue in *The Age of Reason,* he is repelled both on the plane of pantheistic fusion (the subconscious) and on the plane of abstract idea (the supraconscious), and in the end is stunned by the thought of having to choose between two alternatives that are equally undesirable because they both lead to the nothingness of self. Standing on the beach with a group of survivors from the shipwreck, he watches in a kind of hypnosis as two sailors seize the Jebusite, tie a rope around his neck, and lead him away to certain execution. When the Jebusite's foot becomes caught in a sandhole, one of the sailors pulls steadily on the rope, strangling him. Others of the group now turn toward Saila with menacing looks. Professor However urges him to flee toward the forest, but he hesitates, murmuring "I can't escape." The question that now puzzles him is: Shall he accept his fate stoically as the Jebusite did and stand ready for his execution in full obedience to a mysterious God of suffering or shall he refrain yet a while from complete surrender of his personal reality? Finally, he turns and walks toward the forest, joining Christel, who has withdrawn from the others because of not wanting to witness his execution. "Let's go, Federico," she says. He answers, "Let's walk northward." To her query "Why?" he replies, "I don't know." The hostile group from the beach follows them stubbornly. The narrative thus closes with a pronounced impression of stuporous disillusionment following an episode of buoyant experimentation with an earthy pantheism and a milder attempt to embrace an idealistic orientation.

The Sphere is an extravagant, but still an authentic, example of the modern artist's effort to rescue personality from the implications inherent in the concept of a supreme Impersonality. More specifically, it is a record of unhappiness arising from an inability to deify conscious knowledge. The author approaches the concept of a God who necessarily follows a path of adventure in continuous creativity — as contrasted, for example, with an Idea already formulated in static perfection. But he allows himself to degrade the potentiality of the concept by making God an unconscious mass, more or less equivalent to physical energy. "God doesn't know He is God," Saila says (225). "If He knew, then He would be only one more sterile experience." His natural laws speak for Him implacably (179). His sustenance comes from the energy expended in the anguish, glory, and death of countless individuals (254); [38] and only the aggregate energy survives in the cyclical movement of the struggle against nothingness. It is as though the author, frustrated by his inability to know God consciously, were determined to make Him an unbearable Idea.[39]

One is inclined to say that Sender in *The Sphere* has offered little more than Schopenhauer's pessimistic vision of man's place. Indeed, he seems to have clothed in fantastic dress the same basic conflict that motivated the German philosopher. For Schopenhauer, too, visualized the inexorable disappearance of illusory individuality in a cold, unthinking life force; and he, too, deified tragedy and suffering, declaring that "unless suffering is the direct and immediate object of life our existence must entirely fail of its aim." [40] Nevertheless, there is an important distinction. Schopenhauer's view is an irrevocable conclusion following a firmly wrought line of reasoning, and the conclusion leads to a determined passivity. Sender exercises an artist's license to leave suspended the solution to his problem and

38. This idea is fundamental also in *El verdugo afable* (Santiago, Chile: Nascimento, 1952).

39. It is true, as Charles L. King observes (*op. cit.*, p. 999), that Sender has assumed a "collectivist" attitude supporting the idea of undifferentiated manhood; but the important point is that he cannot be happy with such a view.

40. *Studies in Pessimism*, trans. T. Bailey Saunders (London: Allen and Unwin, 1923), p. 11.

thus clings to the hope attendant upon an answer that may yet allow for the reality of selfhood.

From the viewpoint of artistic composition, it must be said, the novelist has overstepped his license to abstain from strict rational demonstration, and the reader consequently feels that the general impression of bewilderment has been allowed to get out of hand. Apparently partaking of ideas from many quarters,[41] the author fails to reduce them to a firm consistency. Moreover, the phantasmagorial nature of the narrative detracts from its interest as a work of art. Yet the novel must be considered an earnest expression of contemporary man's effort to adjust to an ancient monistic view of the universe by reinterpreting it. Sender glimpses certain hopeful directions for speculative thought, even though he does not develop them: the concept of an eternal present, the unlimited potential of a continuous divine creativity, the totally positive mien of a divine animus that cannot validate evil or the negative aspects of experience.[42] Despite the story's predominant impression of doom, these ideas keep the way open to a confidently affirmative monism.

El lugar del hombre (1939)

In its manifestation of a strong emotional struggle with an unwelcome brand of mysticism *The Sphere* represents a major aspect of Sender's literary personality. *El lugar del hombre* is representative of another prominent aspect indicative of a moderately hopeful rationalism. Although the novelist always adheres to the belief that reality must be apprehended intuitively, in *El lugar del hombre* he relies on reason to lead him into the region where only intuition can continue. The two approaches to understanding, reason and intuition, thus appear in harmony

41. The many speculative passages in the novel bring to mind especially Rudolph Otto, Heidegger, Schopenhauer, and — more remotely — the *Bhagavad-Gita*.

42. In this connection, cf. the following from *El verdugo afable* (pp. 326-27): "Todos estamos expuestos a cada paso a caer en el mal, es decir, en la negación de las cosas que nos conducen a Dios. Porque el mal en sí mismo no existe sino como negación de ser. Ser malo no es lo contrario de ser bueno, sino lo contrario de ser."

with each other rather than in conflict, as is the case in *The Sphere*.

Motivated by thoughts of man's relative position in the universe,[43] Sender begins at rock bottom in the examination of his subject by subtracting a person's presence from the world of human relations and then observing the consequences of both his absence and his reappearance. It is an existentialist approach in that it proposes to deal with human reality entirely within the precincts of a person's mere "being here." The philosophical perspective embraces a number of questions bearing on the natural order and its relation to the social order: Is the cosmic system, including both nature and society, a logical, mechanically formal order of events; or is it inherently revolutionary and unpredictable? If the second possibility is true, is man's position altogether contingent, that is, entirely subject to chance happenings; or does it inevitably adapt itself to a pattern of probability that stabilizes and makes reliable certain general directions? What, finally, can be said of human values, including the sense of individuality? The author's purpose is to present the questions in a specific context and let the answers follow by implication; for this novel, like *The Sphere*, is primarily an experimentation.

The first narrative step is that of awakening chance (*despertar la casualidad*) by bringing into society a "monster" who is known to inhabit the wilds not far from a town in northern Spain, where the story has its setting. As a hunt is organized for the strange inhabitant of the wilderness, the narrator's superstitious grandfather makes reverential comment on the role of chance in human affairs, and the town's richest and most influential citizen, Don Jacinto, takes efficient command of the expedition. Don Jacinto is a champion of order, as understood in terms of established social and political rule, and considers it his duty to reclaim for civilization what is probably a human being

43. The title of Sender's novel, though designating a very common modern theme, could have been suggested by certain specific works. A chapter of Max Scheler's *El puesto del hombre en el cosmos* appeared in the *Revista de Occidente*, No. LXXIII (1929); and the work was later published in book form by the same magazine. Also, an article by A. S. Eddington, "El lugar del hombre en el universo," appeared in the *Revista de Occidente*, No. LXXV (1929). Sender, however, does not seem to have drawn on these works for specific ideas.

somehow strayed from society. The author takes great delight in satirizing Don Jacinto and places in opposition to him a political rival, the liberal and rather primitive Don Manuel. Social satire thus appears early in the story and sets the tone for what soon becomes an embarrassing disturbance of a logical, orderly sequence of events. Surveyed at first largely from a social viewpoint, the disturbance eventually acquires philosophical significance.

The "monster" proves to be Sabino García, a laborer who had disappeared fifteen years before and had been officially declared dead — murdered, according to the court's decision, by the two laborers with whom he was last seen. Sabino is the lowliest of human beings. Despised by everyone except his mother, married to an unfaithful wife, and ashamed of his status in society, he had withdrawn from the human world as an easy way out of an unhappy situation. A nobody though he may be, his return plays havoc with the neatly ordered course of affairs. His very personality had been definitively disposed of: "To the government, this man has no entity. He does not exist" (60).[44] His reappearance, therefore, is almost like a crime, because it contradicts all the logical decisions of society and raises various inconveniences, one of which is his insistence on reacquiring his wife Adela, now married to another man. The town government, nevertheless, under the control of Don Jacinto, faces its task of readjustment bravely, placing Sabino temporarily in the home of his mother and turning its attention to the two men who had been punished for his "murder."

The author's social-political indignation, no doubt a residue of the Spanish civil war, appears at its height as he drops back to recount events at the time of Sabino's disappearance. Juan and Vicente, the two laborers accused of murder, lived in the town of Castelnovo, stronghold of the leftist opposition that always voted against Don Jacinto. In the latter's opinion, Sabino was murdered by two men debased by liberal ideas. The law-enforcement officers, acting in conformity with this attitude, subjected Juan and Vicente to the cruelest of brutality until, in the stupor of exhaustion, they confessed their crime and were

44. Page references are to *A Man's Place*, trans. Oliver La Farge (New York: Duell, Sloan, and Pearce, 1940).

sentenced to life imprisonment. The logical decisions thus demonstrated by organized society are an indication, presumably, of what can be expected of a God conceived in the image of the established order. To such a divinity Sabino's mother appealed, hoping for her son's return and praying to a Christ crucified whose suffering "was like a terrifying blasphemy against the divinity that abandons men" (114). The author's depiction of man's futile "rational" guidance thus turns toward reflection on the cosmic order in its entirety, even though in the middle section of the novel it is heavily charged with social and political emotions. A seemingly inconsequential event, the disappearance of a person who meant nothing to the community, has by its mere actuality made the ideal of cosmic orderliness look like a farcical dream. "A crime no one committed has led to real crimes" (228), Juan muses after his release from prison, hopelessly unhappy despite Don Jacinto's efforts to make amends. More unfortunate than Vicente, he realizes that he cannot resume normal relations with his wife, whose love had been appropriated long before by another man. He feels a certain resentment against Sabino, but he is more confused than angry and believes that no one is really to blame for the distorted course of events.

When a single happening leads to an expanding network of consequences such as those depicted in *El lugar del hombre*, one may be inclined to think of the universal order as an irrational mechanism. The impression of mechanistic arrangement is given further support when one considers that, in the case of Juan and Vicente at least, the course of events cannot be reshuffled to bring about correction of the mischief wrought. Actually, stronger emphasis falls on the confusion in the relationship of all things, and hence on an antimechanistic kind of irrationality. Members of the town government, representatives of a concept of orderliness, could cope with the problem of restoring a young stork to its nest in the church tower, but were stupefied by the situation growing out of Sabino's reappearance. Enveloping this greater problem, "there was an overtone that fluctuated between idiocy and madness. The whole thing could be stupidity. But it could all equally well be madness and fear. Although no one formulated this thought, everyone felt it in an uncomfortable, vague way" (219). In the background the "witch" Ana Launer invokes divine justice while reciting her verses about Sabino's murder. A relatively harmless duel between Don Manuel and Don Jacinto further contributes a farcical note to the general atmosphere of absurdity.

One observes in the novel, then, certain rather terrifying aspects of the human situation similar to those presented in *The Sphere*. But the conclusion of *El lugar del hombre* leaves us with a comparatively optimistic impression. It is true that Sabino's disappearance and reappearance bring tragedy. Juan, feeling completely superfluous in the world, dies of tuberculosis, and Sabino's mother drowns herself, realizing that her son is more interested in his former wife than in her. Yet Sabino, who after all is the focal point of the story, undergoes a veritable regeneration. The attention showered on him has given him confidence in his own importance and a consequent firmness of character heretofore lacking. His sureness of self easily regains his wife's affiliation, her former depreciative attitude now changing to admiration and humble submission. His self-possession and magnanimity definitely include a sense of propriety and order, for he insists on Adela's peaceful separation from her current husband before he resumes marital relations with her. Further, he enjoys the respectable position of guard for the Irrigation Syndicate — thanks to the town government. His companions, still somewhat perplexed by recent events, look upon him as a kind of hero; and all because he had done "the least a man can do. I went away" (280). So it is that chance or, more exactly, an individual acting in co-operation with chance plays a game on society by first upsetting its staid sense of order and then resuming the orderly rhythm of the whole; the individual at the same time profiting from the venture and demonstrating the significance of his mere presence.

The completed narrative development thus suggests two main lines of thought, one bearing on the role of chance in the total scheme of things and the other bearing on the question of the individual's significance. Chance proves decidedly to be a disturbing factor but by no means one-sidedly wanton and destructive. It is not an autonomous factor intruding on the world of man from the outside. It is inextricably bound up with sys-

tems of time and causality and has reality only in the relation of
one system to another. Suppose we regard chance as a coincidence of two events in different causal systems.[45] We may say
then that Sabino's decision to withdraw from society, an event
within his own causal system, has the effect of a sudden chance
happening when related to the social system, which demands
an explanation for his disappearance. Similarly, his reappearance
is the coincidence of two lines of causality and creates a disturbance in both individual and collective orders. From the combination of the individual and the collective, however, new orders
result (in the life of Sabino and the town), which conform to a
pattern of causal sequence. Chance thus disappears with the
resumption of repetitive rhythm. The aggregate of events is
always subject to an invasion by the element of chance and it
can always be expected to resume a pattern of orderly sequence.
One is prompted to cite by analogy a common interpretation
of the quantum theory which holds that "the world of physics
has retained its causal consistency." [46]

It is appropriate to point out this analogy with physics in the
case of *El lugar del hombre*, because Sender is clearly interested
in the question of causality and freedom in the natural order of
things. Though he obviously derives pleasure from social satire,
it is his intention to examine man's place from a philosophical
rather than a social or psychological vantage point; and his preoccupation with the word "natural" is evidence that natural
philosophy is paramount in his thinking. Now, the nature of
material things, as commonly viewed in the interpretation of
quantum physics, is embedded in a combination of indeter-
minacy and causality, of freedom and conformity with a regular
pattern. If an individual's activity be compared to that of an
electron, for example, we may say that he is free in the sense that
he can violate logical predictability and mechanical control, but
he is not free of belonging with a unit larger than himself. In his
freedom he is an instrument of revolution within a total system
that by its very nature demands both revolution and order. The
inversion of order, therefore, is just as "natural" as the mainte-

45. As J. Delevsky states in "Le Hasard dans la nature et dans l'histoire,"
Revue Philosophique, Nos. 7-8 (1935), 80-83.
46. H. Margenau, "Methodology of Modern Physics," *Philosophy of
Science*, II (1935), 50.

nance of order. As the author of *El lugar del hombre* says, "Logic breaks down and we laugh or grow angry.... [but] when the whole natural order turns up side down, and does it naturally moreover, neither laughter nor anger will serve" (10). The implication is that an illogical sequence of events is just as natural as a logical predictable sequence. The total order of things thus operates not as blind chance but as a process that inherently contains an element of unpredictability.

When, therefore, the author depicts the travesty of man's administration of justice in the very shadow of a God who ignores the human situation he is attacking the kind of traditionalism that visualizes man's share of divinity as a mechanically stabilized perfection. In such a divine order there is no place for revolution and consequently no justification for the innovation that comes from activity of the individual. But the individual, Sender would argue, is the indispensable revolutionary factor which mirrors the cosmic principle of unpredictable variation and newness. The vantage ground where the novelist stands consists of little more than the circumstances of a man's relationship to a whole. The situation, however, virtually speaks for itself. Sabino's experience not only contradicts the notion that his person is superfluous, it also demonstrates that his person inevitably acquires a value that transcends the mere fact of his being present. Personal values arise just as surely as relationships between things. Sender, like Sartre, thus demonstrates that the individual cannot possibly escape the consequences of his "being here"; and, moreover, that by virtue of his presence in the world he carries the meaning of the universe on his shoulders. Individuality, in principle at least, stands validated.

Perhaps the novelist did not propose that philosophical implications be carried far beyond a basic starting point. His style itself places people and things in a simple perspective consonant with the intention of staying close to the naked foundation of the problem of man's position. But is it not permissible to extend our inferences a bit further and see in the individual, as presented in this novel, an approach to the question of divine personality? In a sense the individual is in the service of the All and is being "used" — as Sender darkly imagines in some of his other novels — in God's struggle against nothingness (which we may visualize as absolute homogeneity). Yet his activity is capable of constructing its own meaning by way of integration. This potentiality of integration, together with the unerasable effect of a person's being present in the world, opens the way to validation of the ideal of personality. Such an ideal is perhaps less absurd than its absence. In *The Sphere* an attempt is made to overcome absurdity by meeting it on its own terms; in a word, by engaging in it. In *El lugar del hombre* a reply is made to absurdity by illustrating the inevitability of its opposite.

9

The Ideal of Personality

IF THE FOREGOING ANALYSES of novels are reliable, the problem of validating an ideal of personality is one of the favorite subjects and one of the greatest challenges facing the modern literary mind. In what measure, the literary artist is repeatedly asking himself, can individuation be expected to assert and maintain itself in the cosmic order? The question is inseparable from the conception of Divinity, for man's ideas about himself appear always to reflect the image that he attributes to a divine Being. Modern man has found his faith in personality challenged if not actually destroyed, and it is probably accurate to say that he has given himself, or his notion of personality, the same treatment that he has accorded the concept of God and has suffered because of placing limitation upon the latter. In other words, the individual "self," which he must consider a conscious unity of multiple components and which he would like to consider a substantial and durable integration, may be said to possess the qualities granted an Ideal Self and to be limited in the same way that the Ideal is limited. The history that we have traced of man's preoccupation with his own private significance is something like a long drawn-out debate with himself on the question of what shall be included in the Godhead. Lurking at the base of the individual's troubled reflection is the suspicion that God is not personality and hence not capable of bestowing personal attention upon man.

In the world of Dickens and Pereda the ideal of personality

was undisturbed. Apart from the works of these authors, however, the novels covered in our survey, when visualized in one comprehensive sweep, present the story of a fractured personality that has been variously and severely truncated in the shift from a dualistic to a unitary view of the world. The necessity for compressing all things into one — mind and matter, soul and body, God and nature — has resulted in nullifying or crowding out some of the components of an ideal integration instead of unifying them within a perspective that transcends dualism. Under the unmistakable influence of modern science the two major human propensities, the mystical and the rationalistic, have been channeled through a central position, as through a prism of glass, and have shown serious refraction as a result. With tremors of uncomfortable containment, the literary imagination has followed thought, speaking for both the mystical and the rational urgencies, coming by one route to the unpleasant vision of an Unconscious God who *absorbs all* and by the other to a pure Impersonality that *excludes all*.

The mystic stream of consciousness, which appears in one of its most vigorous and most terrifying forms in the novels of Zola, followed in the nineteenth century the pantheistic direction, squeezing all intellect and all feeling into one unconscious whole called life. In this pantheistic fusion God is a churning sum of energy whose totality remains always the same while manifesting itself repetitiously in countless transient forms and cyclical movements, from simple to complex, from birth to death. In such a world perspective the individual is but a fragment rising from the mass like a droplet of water rising from a fountain and always returning to its source. If he seeks immortality, it must be by way of amalgamation and loss of self within the whole. On a social or a political plane the philosophical attitude may appear as an effort to find identity and security in the community or the party. But in literature it appears generally as a profounder kind of mysticism that glimpses the union of self with a Life Force unconscious and absolute in its nullification of individual personality. The view is forcefully described in the following reference to nineteenth-century pantheism:

There is no reason for the being of a conscious personality on the hypothesis of an Absolute which is itself unconscious; and effort to develop this personality in the line of the higher, intellectual, moral, spiritual life is merely to violate the law of its being, eventually to court disaster and pain in the process of final absorption within the unconscious. Individuality and freedom are the haunting shadows and the mockery of such a life.[1]

Whether one regards the union as taking place in pure matter or in pure spirit makes little difference in so far as individual immortality is concerned. In either case the distinction between self-consciousness and consciousness is quickly blurred, the one fading into the other and then into nothingness; and the sense of personality can hardly find more satisfaction with the idea of total absorption in Spirit than with the idea of a complete return unto dust. The Western mind finds it difficult to embrace the vision of a Nirvana-like immortality, however persuasively it may be presented. Consider, for example, the modernized Oriental philosophy of Aurobindau,[2] which corresponds in some respects to contemporary Western demands for a free and creative human personality but finds no eternal home for its individual manifestation. Drawing on the testimony of the ancient Vedantic seers, Aurobindau argues that the One makes ample allowance for the many; and he virtually regards the individual and the Transcendent as mutually dependent in an active terrestrial life. Yet the eventual destination of the individual is something like fusion with the divine, after a refinement of consciousness made possible by multiple reincarnations. One therefore is left with an impression of continuous cyclical movement within a closed universe, whose terrestrial phase reflects as its central motive a spiritual evolution within matter, the divine reality being concealed at the outset in inconscient material form.[3] Assuming that Divinity multiplies itself into many forms, it transforms them into itself again; and this constant passage is for the Western mind a passage into nothingness. Twentieth-

1. John Veitch, *Dualism and Monism* (Edinburgh and London, 1895), p. 195.
2. Sri Aurobindau, *The Life Divine* (Pondichéry: Sri Aurobindau Press, 1955).
3. *Ibid.*, p. 983.

century existentialists have registered their dissatisfaction with this idea, rejecting the "pure being" of Hegelian theory as well as materialistic pantheism, and have perhaps forced a climax in the trend toward resignation to the concept of a God who, by the very necessity of His homogeneous totality, is an end to which all particularity returns and in which it is merged.

In so far as man's rational endeavor has steered clear of mysticism it has passed through the prism of science with a resultant refraction that leaves imagination in bondage to "positive" knowledge. Even if science cannot in actual practice be separated from speculative theory, there is surely little doubt that the positivistic attitude, which gained such prominence in the nineteenth century, pushed the subjective aspect of intellectuality into an inferior position from which it is only now recovering. The critical, skeptical heritage of Kantian thought when filtered through positivism severely narrowed man's perspective by undermining the Kantian emphasis on subjectivity. With rationalism brought under control of mechanistic science in a unitary system of being, self-consciousness was in effect asked to regard itself as mechanical process and thereby automatically to eliminate itself. "Soul" and the subjective values associated with the term were pushed aside in favor of an impersonal Law which, though operating "intelligently," reflects only that emotionless aspect of intelligence observable in the formal manifestation of an abstract rule. Under the heavy shadow of this emphasis on the impersonal functioning of laws, the sense of person has sought with a feeling of desperate loneliness and frustration the embrace of a Supreme Person.

The poet, who is the spokesman for the personal as well as the suprapersonal viewpoint, has thus found himself pulled toward two extreme and equally unsatisfactory destinies, the one submerging his feelings and his intellect in nature and the other virtually excluding them from it. Persuaded that he must hold a concept of God and nature as a unity of some kind, he has allowed himself at times to picture the One as a monster who swallows all and at times as an impersonal and indifferent One who recognizes neither love nor the subjective aspects of reason. The ideal Individuality, deprived of the attributes most prized by man, leaves the human individuality unable to validate itself as an integrated whole. The resultant loss of orientation leaves man contemplating himself as though he were a gratuitous bit of consciousness, existing without necessity, without reason, irrationally. One can find in the contemporary novel vivid reminders of the "fall" and the accompanying anxiety of guilt, but the major problem calls for a restoration of reason to a place of honor in man's thinking — a complete reason that would integrate the ideals that have drifted apart.

From our survey of the modern novel, three major motives stand out like so many demands waiting for fulfillment. They appear most specifically in the three French novels that have been discussed. Flaubert, protesting vehemently against the exclusion of subjectivity from the Godhead, centers his attention on the subject of love. Zola, while plunging into the midstream of life and seizing hold of its primitive nakedness, exalts — unhappily — a God of sheer biological creativeness. Sartre, like Flaubert, registers a determined protest against the exclusion of subjectivity but does so on the grounds of reason. For him the repugnancy of unintelligent matter is as strong as the repugnancy of unfeeling matter was for Flaubert. With a characteristically French concentration on one theme at a time, these novelists have made separate attributes stand out as though each were God in its own right. In the case of Zola the creative life force is not something striven for so much as it is an overwhelming power. But in the case of Flaubert and Sartre the attributes of love and reason are singly exalted (that is, striven for) out of a desperate desire to incorporate them in the Ideal.

In the Spanish novel one does not as a rule find as much concentration on single threads of thought as in the French. There is more likely to be a variety of ideas pointing to a broad, if sometimes loosely unified, intellectual view. Among modern Spanish novelists, Galdós and Unamuno give us the philosophical perspectives of greatest breadth, and in each there is a firmer integration of ideas appropriate to an ideal of personality than in any of the other novelists included in our study. Participating in the dynamics of an evolutionary view of mankind, Galdós portrays the natural man climbing toward the level of his divinity or fullness of being by strength-giving labor. Unamuno, in conformity with his twentieth-century suprahistorical view, strips his stories of realistic collateral material and presents the existential man who, though not opposed to nature, is not dependent on it; for he assumes that man always stands on the level of his divinity and needs only to believe in and understand his position.

It is in this aspect of his thinking that Unamuno may be considered a leader in the twentieth century. His novels and essays are a standing invitation to new constructions of thought. They therefore strongly suggest an inquiry into neighboring ideas which together with them may point to new interpretations of individual man. Even a writer as negative in attitude as Sartre similarly leads us to ask what new understanding lies almost within his grasp. We are thus obliged to think of the novels of such writers as these as expressions of thought in fermentation which directs our imagination toward answers much more encouraging than the mood in which the questions are clothed. It is proper, then, that we consider whether or not their ideas go beyond the usual human complaints against a tragic destiny. Does the viewpoint, for example, that man individually must accept the responsibility of determining his meaning lead further than a mere recognition of the necessity? Does it permit "self-determination" to hold the ideal within its own reality? Can Mathieu Delarue's refusal (*L'Age de raison*) to be closed in by old solutions be considered as the expectancy of one who waits on a road open to indefinite but hopeful possibilities? Affirmative answers to these questions can be supported if first we think of new viewpoints in the form of demands that are implicit in the novels, and, further, if we keep the contemporary novel in perspective with the general intellectual ideas that form its background. The relationship between literature and other fields of thought is not always clearly detected when we ourselves are a part of the contemporary scene; but we can be sure that there is a relationship, and it is worthwhile to look for it.

In general terms, the demand found in the literature of which such novelists as Sartre and Unamuno are representative, and supported by ideas current in nonliterary fields, may be stated as follows: The individual must be the expression of a principle of ideal integrity *now*, in the life that he *lives*, not hereafter and not in a remote imaginary realm of abstract idea. For he

already *is;* he is not an organization into something but the enactment of something. The viewpoint here stated is not contradictory to an evolutionary perspective, but it requires that
evolution be kept subordinate to the principle of completeness
which it reflects. The demand, in short, states that the individual
must on his own initiative incorporate ideality in life itself and
still be willing to find it always in front of him.

What ideas, we may now ask, are there in twentieth-century
thought aside from literature that can lend support to belief in
the "ideal" stated above? As a general area of orientation, it is
well to think of the concept of wholeness, which is meaningful
in both philosophy and science because it invites us to visualize
any given phenomenon for what it is in its entirety at one time
and not merely as the fragment of either a process or a static
totality. It is within this perspective of wholeness that we can
appreciate the strong inclination in this century to challenge
the notion of unknowability and unattainability, and thus to in-
fuse meaning into the real and the ideal by bringing them together in life itself. The influence of Edmund Husserl's Phenomenology [4] in this respect is undoubtedly great; for his argument
proposes that the human ego claim its rightful home with a
Transcendental Consciousness which is accessible by way of
intuitive apprehension. His Transcendental Consciousness may
appear in its absolute purity to be an abstraction, but the concept
is used primarily to establish the principle that the basis of all
possible meaning and reality is consciousness itself. If the ideal
is impenetrable to formalistic intellection by itself alone, it is
approachable through the purifiable consciousness inherent in
the human ego, which of course is not to be identified with
naturalistic psychology. While thus appearing to lean too far
to one side in his antinaturalistic revolt, Husserl is actually arguing for the utilization of a complete reason, which — if we
borrow Karl Jasper's words — "creates the mental space where
everything can be caught, acquire language and hence validity
as a being in its own right." [5] He does so by a reversal of view-

4. As set forth particularly in *Ideen zu einer reinen Phänomenologi-
schen Philosophie* (Halle: Niemeyer, 1928). First appeared in 1913.
5. *Reason and Anti-Reason in Our Time* (New Haven: Yale University
Press, 1952), p. 58. Cf. the following statement of A. S. Eddington (*The
Nature of the Physical World*, p. 91): "The view here advocated is tanta-

point which in effect calls for a beginning with the ideal itself: "The science of pure possibilities must everywhere precede the science of real facts, and give it the guidance of its concrete logic." [6]

This desire to restore life and spontaneity to reason, which of course is exemplified in Unamuno,[7] finds a further notable exponent in José Ortega y Gasset, in whose philosophy of "vital reason" life is made the crystallizing agent of all meaning. Although criticizing Husserl for what he considered an extreme subjectivism, Ortega agreed with him in opposing a formalistic intellectualism that would base meaning upon pure objectivity or would seek to derive meaning from a conflict between subject and object. Reason, all-inclusive, is equated with life, which is a construction out of the total context of subject and surrounding historical circumstances. Reality thus is not a rationalistic construct but a lived and therefore constantly changing essence which involves intelligence in "preintellectual" necessities. It is better understood as action than as abstract thought, and its oneness does not permit an antagonism of parts, some rational and some instinctive, some real and some ideal.[8]

The demand that human life shall be its own justification, and that man must therefore claim his "being" by living it, is surely one of the most wholesome aspects of thought in the general area of Existentialism. It needs only to come to an understanding with history, or process, in order to assert itself creatively with

mount to an admission that consciousness, looking out through a private door, can learn by direct insight an underlying character of the world which physical measurements do not betray."

6. *Ideas: General Introduction to Pure Phenomenology*, trans. W. R. Boyce Gibson (New York: The Macmillan Co., 1931), p. 13.

7. I am referring not to the one-sided analytical reason that Unamuno opposed but to the "reason with feeling in it" that he generally called "feeling" only. The Spaniard's essential ideas, it must be remembered, are of an earlier date than those of Husserl. For suggestions as to the similarity between Unamuno and Husserl, see W. D. Johnson, "Vida y ser en el pensamiento de Unamuno," *Cuadernos de la Cátedra Miguel de Unamuno*, VI (1955), 18-23.

8. For the present subject matter consult *Anejo a mi folleto 'Kant'* (1929), in *Obras completas* (Madrid: Revista de Occidente, 1951), IV, 48-59; and *En torno a Galileo* (1933), in *Obras completas* (Madrid, 1952), V, pp. 11-164. It may be useful to think of Ortega as a "vital realist" and of Unamuno as a "vital idealist," but in any case they both stress the all-importance of life and, despite their personal differences, had much in common intellectually. Cf. S. Serrano Poncela, *El pensamiento de Unamuno* (Mexico: Fondo de Cultura Económica, 1953), p. 53. .

regard to the subject of flux and substance. Possibly the theory of Relativity opens a way for this conciliation. For does it not afford man the opportunity, as we have previously observed, of reshaping his thought so as to find himself equally at home in time and eternity? The General Theory, especially, impresses on us the necessity of keeping in mind a pliable complex of multiple time systems which bind themselves together with constant principle. (The speed of light, for example, remains the same for different frames of reference, whatever be their state of motion with respect to each other.) We are thus allowed to think of a particular time region as a mobile present that reaches out in all directions without losing its orientation in a unified whole. From any one of these time regions a particular consciousness can look out — not forward or back — on all eternity. It is appropriate in our day, then, to think of a kind of evolution that reaches out in all directions without sacrificing the present to either the past or the future. As Einstein explains, Newton's theory requires a picture of the stellar universe as being an island in infinite space, having less group density in its outer limits, and "destined to become gradually but systematically impoverished." [9] But with the development of non-Euclidian geometry we are enabled to believe that the world sphere, a surface of constant curvature, is at the same time finite and unbounded.[10] We can think of this as a "free" universe, and with this idea in hand one can feel the limitless possibilities of destiny, which in the realm of human consciousness could be an expansion of understanding and in the realm of a transcendental consciousness could be an extension of creation. The universe, we may believe, is free to extend itself indefinitely, in accord with constant principles; it is not doomed to exhaust itself in futile repetitive movement within a closed circle.

The freedom given to thought to expand in speculative theory, which has been furthered by mathematical physics, induces one to believe that the process of becoming is perhaps best understood as a process of being, in which the ideal, or unattained, is constantly merging with the real. If thought be considered a legitimate basis of reality and the nature of the thought

9. Einstein, *Relativity* . . . , p. 126.
10. *Ibid.*, p. 132.

process be understood as an unfoldment toward newness in harmony with unchanging principle, the grasping for something out of reach necessarily includes attainment in the process of advance.[11] Assume that the ideal is the integration and complete-ness appropriate to the particular occasion — Ortega y Gasset's "I and my circumstance," for example, or Whitehead's concres-cent stage along the path of an enduring pattern — the attain-ment is constant; only the expanding remains unaccomplished. The ideal, in short, is not something far removed in an imaginary heaven. It is not even the symbol of an absolute value. It is reality itself, which is always flexible and growing, "relative" therefore and yet within the reach of our consciousness. Ortega states concisely the significance of the new relativism when he says, "For the old relativism, our knowledge is relative, because what we aspire to know (spatio-temporal reality) is absolute and we do not attain it. For the physics of Einstein, our knowl-edge is absolute; reality is relative." [12]

The uniting of the knower with what is to be known, far from leading to the absorption of the ego in otherness, allows for its dignification by association with a larger reality. The self is constantly reaching beyond itself but it does not lose its identity because the "I" is always at the center of the process of enlarge-ment. From this viewpoint, the twentieth-century emphasis on subjectivity amounts to the exchange of an "It" God for an "I" God, and the interpretation of a divine "I am that I am" visualizes the coexistence of man and Deity in a relationship of mutuality where man faces the responsibility of individualizing Principle or God.

The reality that is waiting always to be individualized hovers over man like an invitation, but also like a warning against an overemphasis on the sense of person. Spinoza comes to view again as a sobering reminder that the concept of God must rise above the anthropomorphic level; and his insistence on con-ceiving of a "God beyond God" still is relevant for an age that

11. Cf. in this connection a viewpoint expressed by present-day scien-tist-philosophers to the effect that we are required to think of the knower and the known as being united in the process of knowing. See Henry Margenau, "Perspectives of Science: The Task of the Coming Philos-ophy," *The Key Reporter* (of Phi Beta Kappa), XXV, No. 1 (1959), 8.

12. *El sentido histórico de la teoría de Einstein* (1923), in *Obras com-pletas* (Madrid: Revista de Occidente, 1950), III, 232.

remains committed to the embracement of impersonal principle.[13] As a consequence of this broader vision of Deity or, to
put it another way, of conceiving of God in His image and not
in our own, the ideal of personality becomes an ideal of individuality from which the ordinary sense of person (the biological and environmental product localized in a temporal setting)
is excluded. Unamuno's quiet "recessional," *San Manuel Bueno
Mártir*, may be viewed in this light. In a strictly literal sense,
one can say that "mere individual personality is unreal. It is
only in so far as God is manifested in us that we partake of
reality." [14]

The exclusiveness of the ideal to which the individual must
look dignifies humanity when the twentieth-century respect
for subjectivity combines with the ideal and rescues it from
being frozen in a region apart from the self. The dignification
comes through the recognition of man's responsibility to use
the integrative "I" principle to bestow on himself the respect
that divinity grants him. Personality becomes a process of being
itself in an eternal present of coexistence with its Self, that is,
with the ground of Being which holds its possibility. It may be
viewed as an aspiration "to self-affirmation, in full transcendence, in passage across its temporal not-self," as Sender reflects
(*The Sphere*, p. 14), without developing the idea. In existentialist language, one "exists" one's being; and true existentialist
psychology should probably be understood to affirm that "being
toward," the intending, is the very heart of personal integrity.
"Self-transcendency, then, is not a speculation of metaphysi-
cians; it is itself the first fact that the true psychological empiri-
calness can make out." [15]

This psychology of personality, which can hardly fail to re-

13. It has in fact been maintained that Spinoza anticipated to a remarkable degree the world view held by twentieth-century philosopher-scientists, such as Eddington, Jeans, and Whitehead, who seek in one broad
sweep to unify science and religion: De Witt H. Parker, "The Philoso-
pher-Saint: Spinoza," *American Scholar*, II (1933), 43-57.
14. J. S. Haldane, *The Sciences and Philosophy* (London: Hodder and
Stoughton, 1929), p. 295.
15. Ulrich Sonnemann, "Existential Analysis: An Introduction to Its
Theory and Practice," *Cross Currents*, V (1955), 263. Sonnemann continues (p. 265): "The psychotherapist, it is true, must open his eyes to the
overpowering reality of the divine, of the spirit in man, to that in man
which is constantly searching for meaning."

mind us of Unamuno,[16] contrasts sharply with the more common kind that stresses adaptability and sees the individual as a formation out of heredity and environment. We probably should grant that naturalistic psychology has done a service to mankind by maintaining that mind and body are one, because the necessity for replacing the ideals thus undermined forces us to find new interpretations of man's essential nature. The new orientation perceivable in contemporary thought turns us away from an understanding of the self as being a concrete entity, whether of matter or of mind, or a combination of the two. It points, rather, to personality as an enactment of principle, a continuously active principle, from whose never-ending creativeness arises the anxiety accompanying an unfinished task. A century ago Jean Reynaud (*Terre et Ciel,* 1854) spoke of the mutual dependence of God and man, thinking primarily of man's journey toward perfection in accord with a principle of perfectibility pre-established in the bosom of creation. In our day the journey must be visualized not as a graded movement toward a fixed goal but as an undetermined advance into newness. The lead of the advance falls squarely on the shoulders of individual spontaneity, which — as Bergson asserts in one of the happiest phases of his exposition of creative evolution (*The Two Sources of Morality and Religion*) — springs free of the tendency, on the part of collective mind, toward fossilization.

Elevated to partnership with an Intelligence engaged in endless creation, the individual is called upon to assume a posture of waiting, as though desiring and yet not quite expecting categorical answers to questions about reality, truth, immortality. The answers, by no means assumed to be impossible of discovery, are perhaps just as continuously unfolding as the continuous merging of the real and the ideal, in which the latter is always taking the role of the former. The following assertion of Pío Baroja in 1918, even though colored with melancholy doubt, wistfully expresses an insight far beyond the limitations of a positivistic age: "What does it matter whether things [that

16. It also recalls the thought of William James bearing on the validity of aspiration as an essential of reality. Cf. "Faith based on desire is certainly a lawful and possibly indispensable thing" ("The Will to Believe," *Selected Papers on Philosophy* [New York: E. P. Dutton and Co., 1917]), p. 107.

is, all things, including values and ideals] are real or not if they function as though they were real?" [17] For someone more closely attuned to the age of Relativity than Baroja the same assertion could be made with a great deal more confidence. Certainly, contemporary artists have access to ideas pertaining to the notions of presentness and freedom that were not open to Flaubert, who was chilled by the vision of a Being remote and unapproachable, or to Zola, who was awed by the vision of an all-absorbing Earth Spirit. Spinoza's God can in the twentieth century be brought into terrestrial experience without becoming an undifferentiated mass.

Existentialism in some respects may be, as Ruggiero declares,[18] a sickness of negative introspection, a kind of pathological self-pity. But it is surely more just to say, with Paul Tillich,[19] that Existentialism is an ally of Christianity, because in its preoccupation with man's estrangement it leads us to rediscover the Christian interpretation of human existence. The intellectual stimulation provided by some of the existentialist novelists is of major significance because they are maintaining in effect that the ills and contradictions of the timeless human situation represent not a tragedy to be accepted but an absurdity to be rejected. Among the notions mirrored in a framework of absurdity are the suppositions that infinite Mind can be contained in a finite body or can even cognize a corporeal sense of person; that the ground of Being is an unconscious, unthinking mass substance; that it is a frozen abstraction never attainable through conscious experience; that it is an impassive, unknowable Sphinx.

Is it not possible, then, that even the most skeptical of contemporary writers are close to embracing a concept of God which, contrary to the forbidding symbols suggested above, is both reasonable and livable? Sartre — the early Sartre, at least — is probably closer to this position than most of his critics suspect. He attacks belief in a Creator separate from nature as well as belief in a pantheistic Being, thus contributing to liberation from two major views that have dominated European thought, some-

17. *Las horas solitarias* (2nd ed.; Madrid: R. Caro Raggio, 1920), p. 290.
18. Guido de Ruggiero, *Existentialism. Disintegration of Man's Soul* (New York: Social Science Publishers, 1948).
19. *Systematic Theology* (Chicago: University of Chicago Press, 1957), II, 27.

times tyrannously, since the time of Descartes. His destructive analysis, unhappily, proves to be a handicap, most noticeable in his struggle with the problem of a unified plurality, where he becomes entrapped in a narrow view of uniqueness that undermines his conception of individuality by depriving it of the attributes of love and creativeness. He recognizes the desirability of regarding individual man as a compound idea, a synthesis of mutually dependent parts; for the question of the one and the many, the self and the other, is perhaps his most puzzling problem. His preoccupation with a "detotalized totality" is an indirect admission not only that the problem is important but that its solution is not hopeless. The impact of the idea is suggested by saying that the disintegration of a personality proves the reality of its integration.

Sartre, of course, maintains that the integration or synthesis is impossible, but he does so primarily under the spell of his opposition to the concept of a God apart from the world; for he declares that if the integration were possible it would have to be a human reality, and not some remote Transcendence. Such a declaration does not deny God; it merely denies that He is some unexperienced, indivisible "substance" and that He has meaning outside of human existence. It is, in effect, a demand that God shall be a unified plurality and that He shall be humanly active. Unfortunately, it is a demand that Sartre does not follow up. Removing divinity from a distant heaven and from amalgamation with matter, he leaves it suspended in a no man's land. He thus assumes a halfhearted attitude in what could be a positive stand. It is as though in his role of human being he had claimed the right of divinity without laying hold of the power that a divine nature is supposed to possess. In short, he maneuvers himself into the presence of God and then fails to take advantage of his position.

From a somewhat similar position, Unamuno advances further and more boldly than Sartre. Questioning the reality of God, he reaches out and helps God re-establish Himself, inviting Him into a co-operative adventure in creation. True, he allows the magnitude of his personal responsibility to weaken God's role, for he tends to forget that the Being and power to which he aspires is already with him, and he consequently allows restless striving to overshadow the effortless fullness of being that beckons to him, demanding confirmation in human experience. This is the typically modern position, which finds man recognizing the necessity for assuming responsibility for his divinity while lacking full confidence in the Divinity that necessarily underlies his self-dignification. Lack of faith and an exaggeration of the importance of the human ego seem in the present age to go hand in hand. There is, nevertheless, a great insight in Unamuno's virtual declaration that the impossible is possible; for he is actually subscribing to belief in a continuous merging of reality and ideality, of existence and essence.

It is not unreasonable to say that Sartre also, despite his apparent belief to the contrary, indirectly supports a similar affirmative outlook. His "Ideal Synthesis" is impossible, he declares; but it is a reality, because the lack of it is the very foundation of consciousness (*Being and Nothingness*, p. 91). Hence it might be called an impossible possible; and Sartre does not close the door completely on a solution, for he refuses to renounce his reliance on self-conscious intelligence. He works against the full efficacy of intelligence because he adheres to the notion that what is to be known must always be different from the knowing and the knower, and he consequently fails to validate that aspect of creative thinking which requires knowing to be in continuous possession of what is to come. But he asserts that "knowledge puts us in the presence of the absolute, and there is a truth of knowledge" (218). Moreover, he maintains, without going as far as Husserl, that knowledge is intuitive and that deduction and discursive argument are only instruments leading to intuition (172). The puzzle of the human situation, in brief, is left squarely in the lap of integrated intelligence, which includes intuition as basic and deliberative intellect as auxiliary.

There is justification for thinking comparatively of two artist-philosophers as far apart in viewpoints as Sartre and Unamuno appear to be. The first is openly skeptical of any "inspiration" from a power greater than man and the second openly aligns himself with such a power. Yet, in both cases, there is an understanding of man's place which says in effect that man must take the initiative in individualizing the integration (of life, intelligence, love, let us say) which is God. The ideal of personality, in short, is a possibility that is already a reality waiting always to be actualized. This conception of a human-divine association is far different from that of an ultimate beatific union equivalent to a quiet nothingness of personality or from that of a natural-supernatural relationship in which an omnipotent One polices and rewards natural imperfection. It upholds a relationship in which God and the individual are together continuously engaged in an adventure having an element of indefiniteness about it because of its creativeness. Individuality, we may imagine, is engaged in possessing the completeness, including the immortality, of an ideal individuality by first expecting it and then confirming the expectation in the present moment.

The very difficulty of holding confidently to such a viewpoint makes it seem at times a futile posture. Intrepid as Unamuno was, he showed a faintness of heart. Certainly Sartre has not been able to remove the heaviness of doubt from the ideal inherent in his troubled quest of God. But in his opposition to the surrender of "self" to nullification in a totality of being he has enthroned an ideal-in-suspense. He has in fact, by way of rational analysis, frozen the union of the real and the ideal in a static relationship that needs only to be set in motion. The goal that he seeks is not a mere figment of the imagination; for, even though it is impossible of attainment, it is waiting to be attained. Mathieu Delarue waits for a reality, not for an illusion. Possibly all he needs in order to instill with zest the responsibility of choosing a course of action is to modify his thinking so as to go forward *with* God rather than *to* Him. This is another way of saying that God is both an achieved and an achieving.

The foregoing commentary on the philosophic aspects of the contemporary novel is undoubtedly an oversimplification of a complex subject, both because of the limited number of works on which it is based and the difficulty of seeing issues clearly when one is in their midst. But radical simplification is perhaps a necessary step in arriving at what is fundamental. If the analysis of motives presented in this study has been correct, the novel of the mid-twentieth century is far from being the expression of a decadent age. It appears, instead, to be a serious groping for orientation in a new world while at the same time evincing both the dissatisfaction with and the reluctance to abandon an old world. The nineteenth-century novel reflects man's effort to shift from a dualistic to a unitary world view colored predominantly by the theory of biological evolution. The novel of our day inherits the same problem and acquires the added burden of accommodating itself to the implications of Relativity and other theories of mathematical physics. In trying to understand the novelists' somewhat confused depiction of man's place, of one thing we can be sure: the idea of God and of man's relationship to Him is as vital an issue as it has ever been. The paramount consideration is not the denial of God but the denial of certain kinds of God. If the artist resorts to the depiction of absurdity, we must realize that it is sometimes difficult to believe in a God of love and intelligence who creates only good without first imagining the enormous absurdity of an unconscious, irrational Being (or principle of being) who validates evil and suffering by exalting, or even by recognizing, them.

The modern revolt against certain forbidding conceptions of a divine Being — and a consequent distrust of human values involved in these conceptions — appears to have been extended into a prolonged, destructive revolution that feeds on itself. There is unquestionably a deep insight in the existentialist preoccupation with the notion of nothingness; for it warns us that being, like meaning, is potentially full of holes and has to be constantly affirmed in order to avoid the emptiness of its porosity. This insight, certainly, has sometimes been obscured by a magnification of its negative aspects. But some of those who have shared in the rebellious spirit of this century know full well that the revolution must, to use the words of Albert Camus, renounce its nihilistic principle in order to recapture the creativeness of revolt, which can be made effective by embracing the principle that "instead of killing and dying to produce the being that we are not, we have to live and make live in order to create what we are." [20] The contemporary emphasis on man's presentness in the world thus assumes the affirmative viewpoint that the nihilation of nothingness comes not from fighting against nothingness but from reaching for something. Underlying this wholesome attitude there is a faith in individuality that allows

20. Translated from *L'Homme révolté* (Paris: Gallimard, 1951), p. 309.

for man's confirmation of his divine essence — which is precisely the ideal sought by most of the novelists whom we have discussed. It is a faith, however, that appears to linger hesitantly at a distance, waiting for him who is bold enough to accept its challenge.

Index